平凡的團隊

不平凡的使命

Ordinary Team

Extraordinary Mission

飛翅展教宣台灣

Taiwan Mission Taking Off

宣教系列

台灣宣教展翅飛 Taiwan Mission Taking Off

作者群Authors/台灣宣教各路英勇將士 Warriors of Taiwan Missions
總編輯Chief Editor/ 楊遠薰 Carole Hsu
執行副編輯 Vice Executive Editor/黃文秀 Wenly Hsieh
美術設計Art Design/廖安怡/台灣宣教基金會Sharon Liao/Taiwan Mission Foundation
出版Publication/台灣宣教基金會(美國) Taiwan Mission Foundation, Inc. (TMF), USA
P. O. Box 605035, Bayside, New York 11360-5035, U.S.A.
發行人Publisher/楊宜宜牧師Rev. Eileen YiYi Chang, 台灣宣教基金會會長, TMF President

  電話Telephone：   718-526-0078
  電子信箱Email Address： Eileen@Taiwanmission.org
  網址Website：   Taiwanmissionfoundation.org

亞洲總經銷Distributor in Asia/天恩出版社 Grace Publishing House, Taipei, Taiwan

  地址Address：   10455台灣台北市中山區松江路23號10F, Taiwan
  電話Telephone：   02-2515-3551
  傳真Fax：   02-2503-5978
  電子信箱Email：   grace@graceph.com
  郵政劃撥：   10162377天恩出版社

北美經銷處Distributor in North America/基督使者協會Ambassadors for Christ Inc.

  地址：   21 Ambassador Drive, Paradise, PA, 17562 U.S.A.
  電子信箱：   afc@afcinc.org
  網址：   http://www.afcinc.org
  訂書免費電話：   1-800-624-3504

出版日期/ 二〇一三年四月初版 2000本　April 2013 First Edition
     二〇一四年五月二版 3000本　May 2014 Second Edition

ISBN：978-1-882324-71-2

台灣印刷Printed in Taiwan

・版權所有 請勿翻印・ All Rights Reserved・Copyright 2014 © Taiwan Mission Foundation

目錄 Table of Contents

第一篇 序篇 I. Preface

序 1. 台灣宣教起程 / Douglas W. Fombell 博士 1
Taiwan Mission Taking Off / Dr. Douglas W. Fombelle

序 2. 今日宣教 / E. Johnson Rethinasamy 博士/牧師 7
Missions Today / Rev. Dr. E. Johnson Rethinasamy

序 3. 《台灣宣教展翅飛》序言 / 關榮根牧師 10
A Foreword to: Taiwan Mission Taking Off / Pastor Henry Kwan

序 4. 願台灣宣教展翅飛 / 楊宜宜牧師 14
A Wish: Taiwan Mission Taking Off / Rev. Eileen YiYi Chang

特邀稿 (A Special Invited Article)

序 5. 台灣宣教史的回顧與展望 / 鄭仰恩牧師/博士 22
The Review and Outlook of Christian Mission in Taiwan
/ Dr. Yang-En Cheng

第二篇 台灣宣教篇 II. Missions In Taiwan

1. 台灣宣教之門大開 / 張玉明牧師/博士 45
Taiwan Mission: the Door is Wide Open / Rev. Dr. Joseph Chang

2. 回台宣教 / 林華山醫師與劉碧珠 52
Taiwan Mission / Dr. Howshan and Mrs. Eunice Lin

3. 宣教的態度與抉擇 / 蔡國山牧師 58
The Attitude and Choices about Taiwan Mission / Rev. Kuo-Shan Tsai

4. 台灣外勞長宣 / 陳玉春宣教師 64
Foreign Labor Long-term Mission / Missionary Rita Chen

5. 尚待耕耘的台灣客家教會 / 曾政忠牧師 70
Ongoing Work for Hakka Mission in Taiwan /
Rev. John Cheng-Chung Tseng

6. 來自台灣客家的呼聲 / 蔡希晉 80
Call for Prayer from the Hakka People / Hsi Chin Tsai

7. 台灣客家短宣 / 周志忠 87
Journey of Taiwan Hakka Mission / George Chou

8. 更生團契的事奉 / 黃明鎮牧師 92
    Christian Born Anew Fellowship / Rev. Ming Cheng Huang
9. 監獄宣道的感想 / 黃清源 97
    Reflections on Prison Ministry / Chinyuan Huang
10. 她們是我們的姊妹 / 楊玖之 102
    They are Our Sisters / Sarah C. Wang
11. 更新！發光！ / 潘暉晉 107
    Renewed! Shine! / Jate Pan
12. 台灣音樂短宣 / 葉俊明牧師 112
    Short-term Music Mission in Taiwan / Rev. James Yeh
13. 讚美之泉 / 謝秉哲 117
    Stream of Praise / Eric Hsieh
14. 「香柏樹」音樂宣道 / 吳英俊 123
    Cedar Music Ministries / Bach Ying Chun Wu
15. 長宣在屏東 / 黃輝銘 128
    Long-term Mission in Ping-Tung / Hwe-Ming Huang
16. 壯圍中宣的回顧 / 黃政俊和黃碧輝 132
    Reflection on Mission in Zhuang-Wei / CC and Faye Huang
17. 鹿港短宣 / 陳明敏 136
    Lu-Kang Mission / Michael Ming-Min Chen
18. 探親成為短宣 / 周神耀牧師 141
    Family Visit Can Be a Short-Term Mission / Rev. Philip Chou
19. 快樂的福音志工 / 謝吟雪 146
    The Happy Volunteer for the Gospel / Linda Y. Hsieh
20. 護理之家的宣教 / 李碧珣 150
    Mission of the Nursing Home / Yana Lee
21. 育幼院的春天 / 高天星 155
    Spring in the Children's Home / Caroline Kao
22. 紐約長島豐盛生命教會與台灣宣教 / 高林麗蒂 160
    Long Island Abundant Life Church and Taiwan Mission / Lydia Kao
23. 紐約晨星教會短宣 / Pastor David Miller 164
    Morning Star New York – 2009 Missions Trip / Pastor David Miller
24. 台灣之友 - 舒曼徹(Chuck)叔叔 / 林青瑤 169
    Friend of Taiwan - Uncle Schumann / Cindy Lin Dillard
25. 鄉福宣教分享 / 舒曼徹 174
    Village Gospel Mission Experience / Chuck Schumann

第三篇 III. 台美青年回台短宣篇 Short-term ABT Taiwan Mission Teams

1. 籌訓「美語營」短宣隊 / 莊澤豐牧師 184
   How to Recruit and Train a Short-term Mission Team /
   Pastor Tse-Feng Chuang
2. 聖達教會台東短宣隊 / 王桂美牧師 189
   Hacienda Heights Summer Short-term Mission Team /
   Pastor Kwe-Mei Wang
3. 一個ABT的台灣宣教之旅 / 汪思涵 194
   My Summer Missions Trip to Taiwan / Su Han Wang
4. 改變生命的經歷 / 杜立欣 199
   A Life-changing Experience / Li-hsin Tu
5. 台灣短宣記 / 陳以理 204
   Short-term Mission in Taiwan / Daniel Chen
6. 上帝的差傳 / 曹仲恆傳道 208
   God's Mission / Minister Samson Tso
7. 我的台灣宣教 / 羅秀慧 213
   My Mission in Taiwan / Jessica Chan
8. 我的第一次宣教 / 馮傑利 219
   The First Mission Trip / Jerry Feng
9. 台中宣教經驗 / 黃孝一 224
   Taichung Mission Experience / James Huang
10. 豐原小學短宣記 / 陳家林 229
    Fong Yuan Elementary School / Jojo Chen
11. 我的見證 / 劉開尹 235
    My Testimony / Benjamin Liu
12. 「我愛台灣」宣教之旅 / 吳宏恩 239
    "I Love Taiwan" Mission Trip / Michael Wu
13. 2009年的台灣短宣 / 楊詩恩 245
    My 2009 Mission Trip / Stephanie Yang
14. 台灣短宣日誌 / 郭詩娜 250
    My Mission Trip in Taiwan / Johanna Go
15. 「我愛台灣」短宣訓練營 / 鄭清妍 256
    "I Love Taiwan" Short-term Mission Training Camp / Ching-yen Cheng
16. 短宣 - 我們仍在學習中 / 陳耀生牧師 263
    Short-term Mission - We are Still Learning / Pastor Mark Chen
17. 遇挫愈堅強 / 陳昭容 267
    Finding Strength in Trial / Terry Su
18. 復興台灣正是現在 / 彭榮仁牧師 273
    Time for Gospel Revival in Taiwan / Pastor David Peng

第四篇　IV. 海外宣教篇　Taiwan Missions Overseas

1. 巴西六家族的故事 / 莊守平口述　劉慈媛整理 278
   Six Pioneer Families in Brazil / Chuang Shou Phing / Liou Tsyr Yuan
2. 分享阿根廷短宣的經歷 / 卓邦宏牧師 290
   Sharing My Personal Short-term Mission Experience in Argentina /
   Rev. Philip Cho
3. 織就一張愛的網 - 哥斯達黎加短宣 / 蕭幸美傳道 295
   A Tapestry of Love - Costa Rica Mission Trip / Minister Hsin-Mei Weng
4. 美國台灣人社區的醫療傳道 / 楊士宏醫師 301
   Medical Mission in the Taiwanese Communities in America /
   Dr. Shug-Hong Young
5. 勝癌會 / 林順明牧師 306
   Triumph Over Cancers / Rev. Paul Lin
6. 生命的見證 / 林澄江 311
   A Testimony of Life / Chen Chien Hsu
7. 長島台灣教會暑期兒童營 / 賴弘專博士與楊靜欣 316
   Long Island Taiwanese Church Summer Camp-Discover the Wonderful
   Love of God/ Dr. Hung-Chuan & Daphne Lai
8. 讓愛走動 / 高如珊 323
   Passing on His Love / Kimberly Kao
9. 兩個海外台灣留學生團契 / 李昱平牧師 329
   Two Overseas Taiwan Student Fellowships
    / Pastor Fred Lee
10. 辛城台灣長老教會的留學生事工 / 郭正義 336
    Overseas Taiwan Student Ministry / Cheng-Yih Kuo
11. 溫馨的橋水查經班 / 楊遠薰 341
    The Bridgewater Bible Study Class / Carole Yang
12. 十字架的道路 / 陳義達 348
    The Way of the Cross / Daniel Gi-Tat Tan
13. 我的生命獻給 / 陳隆 354
    I Offer My Life to You / Long Chen
14. 「台灣宣教基金會」緣起 / 楊宜宜牧師/會長 361
    Origin of the Taiwan Mission Foundation(TMF) / Rev. Eileen Yi-Yi Chang

　　　　　　　附錄 Appendix

台灣宣教基金會六年照片集錦 372
Six Years Photo Collection of Taiwan Mission Foundation

第一篇 序篇
I. Preface

台灣宣教起程
Taiwan Mission Taking Off

I. 序篇 - 台灣宣教起程

Douglas W. Fombelle 博士
美國賓州伯特利神學院美東分院院長

我很榮幸能為這本書寫序。這是一本台灣宣教的編年史，記載著過去五十年來上帝把福音傳給台灣人民的歷史見證。呼召基督徒參與宣教是迄今不移的事工。每一個世代都有愛主且願意跟隨祂的基督徒，因受前輩們宣揚福音的事蹟感動而被呼召出來，向世人宣講上帝的恩典與良善。

約翰福音第八章31至32節記載：「耶穌對信祂的猶太人說，你們若常常遵守我的道，就是我的門徒；你們必曉得真理，真理必叫你們得以自由。」這些話著實鼓勵我們，也挑戰我們。我們透過真理並自耶穌獲得信心。耶穌說到真實，我們也因跟從祂這位真理之主，而獲得自由。當今世界很多訊息已被裁剪或編造過而不全然真實。我們因著和祂的關係而闢建了一條道路得以真正認識祂，知道祂就是我們和世界的救主。因著認識耶穌也使我們敢大膽向世界宣告：「祂就是真理」。

首先，耶穌帶給我們靈性的更新與平安，讓我們在充滿誘惑的環境裡得以領受主的祝福，承認耶穌是個人的救主。當主的靈充滿心中，我們感到自由、喜樂與新生。然而接著，許多教會見證到這種蒙恩很快地轉為挑戰。因為跟隨主的人不久念及身邊的愛人、親人或同胞依然生活在屬靈的黑暗中，便感到負荷。當他們想到世人依舊遠離耶穌的真理，便隱然心痛，因此開始思索如何使「耶穌成為全人類的救主」。

耶穌在其時開始擴大他們心中的理念，使滿懷宣教使命的基督徒想像世間男女因聽到真理而得到心靈解放、愛主的喜樂如潮水般洋溢整個社區該何其美好，因而認定此刻該是採取行動、出外宣揚耶穌真理的時候了。他們於是開始尋求向人宣揚耶穌的辦法，而在最後終於成為宣教運動的領袖。

宣揚福音需付出代價。這代價就是穿越街巷，到鄰舍解釋在基督裡的喜樂。耶穌說：「愛你的鄰人」，就是提醒你得用時間、精神與鄰居相處，其代價看來也還合理。只是當耶穌的靈引導基督徒走向遙遠陌生的地方去宣教時，其代價就相當可觀。每個人都會捫心自問：我願意去嗎？我將停留多久？居住在何處？如何生活？我是否在靈命上準備好去向那些拒絕認識耶穌與福音的人宣講真理？我是否要接受呼召去傳講基督的真理？我是否要順從耶穌？

當耶穌擴大宣教領袖的心胸時，向別人傳福音便不再是預算與支出，而是強烈的使命與呼召。台灣宣教運動已到達若不向台灣人民傳福音，其代價恐將遠遠超過募款與差派挑戰的階段。因此在此時，策劃與禱告應該轉變為差傳與支持。

在主的恩典裡，我祈禱這本書能觸動您的心弦，進而出外宣教與奉獻。我也祈求收割的主，讓書中的見證與宣教的先驅能點燃大家的想像力，相信耶穌是萬有的主宰！

Douglas W. Fombelle 博士
Dr. Douglas W. Fombelle

Part 1: Preface

Taiwan Mission Taking Off

Dr. Douglas W. Fombelle
Dean of Bethel Seminary of the East in Pennsylvania

It is a great honor to write a preface to this volume which chronicles some of the historic movements of God over the past 50 years to bring the Good News of Jesus to the people of Taiwan. The call to Christian missions is always a task for today. We who love and follow Jesus are called to tell our contemporaries about the grace and goodness of God. However, every generation stands on the shoulders of those who were previously moved by the Spirit of God to go and tell others the truth of Jesus. Their stories stir our hearts so that we desire to tell the story to our generation.

Jesus's words in John's Gospel to some "who believed Him" are both encouraging and challenging. "If you hold to my teaching, you are really my disciples. Then, you will know the truth and, the truth will set you free." (John 8:31-32) These words encourage us as Christ-followers. We gain confidence from Jesus through this truth. Jesus speaks with integrity. He invites us to follow Him, the One who is Truth, and we become free. In the world in which we live, much of the information we receive has been edited or given a particular spin and is not altogether truthful. A personal relationship with Jesus opens to us the pathway to truly know and understand Jesus, who is "salvation for us and for the world." Knowing Jesus gives us the confidence to proclaim Him as the Truth to the world!

At first these moments of insight from Jesus bring us such spiritual refreshment and peace that we are tempted to simply rest in our blessings and merely confess, "Jesus is my personal Savior." The joy of the Lord flows into our hearts

and we want to hold on to those moments of joyful freedom and renewal. The church has often witnessed that moment when the initial blessing moves forward and becomes a challenge. At some point followers of Jesus begin to think of others. We become burdened by the thought of loved ones, family members, or countrymen who still walk in spiritual darkness, separated from the truth in Jesus. When our hearts are gripped by this, we are moved to think more broadly than ourselves, "Jesus is Lord of all people, everywhere."

The realization begins as a nagging ache in our hearts when we remember those who are still walking in darkness. Jesus begins to enlarge these convictions in the hearts of some who eventually become the leaders of mission movements. These leaders are able to visualize what could happen if the truth about Jesus was proclaimed in the heart language of a people. They see the joy of the Lord flooding into communities, and can envision what will happen in the lives of men and women who hear the truth and are set free by Jesus. These mission leaders resolve to take action. Someone must go and tell others about Jesus; I must find a way to tell people about Jesus!

Missional convictions have real costs. It is one matter to cross the street and try to explain the joy of the Lord to your next door neighbor. Jesus' words, "Love your neighbor," come to us in that moment, and the time and effort it takes us to engage our close neighbors seems to be a reasonable cost. When the Spirit of Jesus directs us to neighbors or countrymen far away, the costs have to be counted differently. Will I go? How long will I stay? Where will I stay? How will I live there? Am I spiritually prepared to tell others who may resist my invitation to meet Jesus, and may not realize that the Gospel is good news? Am I called by God to go and prepared to proclaim Jesus' truth? Am I ready to obey Jesus?

As Jesus enlarges the hearts of missional leaders, the expense of telling others becomes not just a budget or cost, but a compelling vision and call. The

Taiwan Mission Movement has come to that moment. The cost of not proclaiming the truth about Jesus to the people of Taiwan is far greater than the challenge of raising the funds and deploying those who will proclaim the truth to the people of Taiwan in new and fresh ways. The day of planning and praying has become the day of sending and supporting.

I pray that this volume will stir your heart to go or to give. I pray that the Lord of the harvest will touch your heart by these accounts of faithful witness and testimonies. I pray that the fire of God's call on the hearts of these pioneers and leaders will spark your imagination to believe that Jesus is the Lord of all!

Douglas W. Fombelle 博士 和他的妻子
Dr. Douglas W. Fombelle and his wife

今日宣教
Missions Today

Rev. E. Johnson Rethinasamy博士
紐約白石鎮以馬內利路德教會主任牧師
美國路德會亞洲宣教都市宣教策略督導
Rev. Dr. E. Johnson Rethinasamy
Lead Pastor of Immanuel Lutheran Church in New York - Missouri Synod
Asian Mission - Urban Strategist

今日宣教

Rev. E. Johnson Rethinasamy 博士
紐約白石鎮以馬內利路德教會主任牧師
美國路德會亞洲宣教都市宣教策略督導

身為紐約市白石鎮以馬內利路德教會主任牧師，我為台灣宣教基金會能勇敢向台灣及散居美國的台灣人見證上帝救贖之大愛表示由衷感佩。

在我們的世代，神正興起無數本土領導人以自己的文化來分享耶穌基督的福音。在過去許多宣教意涵中，福音殖民化與宣教被劃上等號，然而隨著如「台灣宣教基金會」這般具有本土意識領導人的機構不斷增長，終能強而有力地戳破這種視「宣教為福音殖民化」的迷思。由一個有本土意識的領導人全力自由運作，使福音更有效地普及整個社區族群，是相當獨特的方式。

台灣的宣教在十九世紀中期，由西方改革宗的傳教士開始。最近一篇關於台灣宣教事工的文章指出:「現在應是設計一種創新福音植入法的時候，因它能使勞工階層的人，也都能接觸到耶穌基督的福音信息」(註)引起我的注意。 我非常同意這篇文章的觀點。(註：請參考「今日基督教」網站http://www.christianitytoday.com/ct/2006/may/32.45.html?start=1)

願主繼續擴大「台灣宣教基金會」和其領導團隊的視野，特別是楊宜宜會長，使他們成為千千萬萬在紐約、東亞直到地極的台灣人民的祝福。

作者 Rev. E. Johnson Rethinasamy 牧師博士與夫人
Author Rev. Dr. and Mrs. Johnson Rethinasamy

Missions Today

Rev. Dr. E. Johnson Rethinasamy
Lead Pastor of Immanuel Lutheran Church in New York - Missouri Synod
Asian Mission - Urban Strategist

As a senior pastor of Immanuel Lutheran Church in Whitestone, New York, I appreciate Taiwan Mission Foundation's bold witness in proclaiming the redeeming love of God among the people of Taiwanese diaspora in the United States and in Taiwan.

I think, in our times, God is raising hundreds of indigenous leaders to share the Gospel of Jesus in their own cultural context. In many of our mission contexts, colonization and Christian missions are viewed synonymously. But, the advent of many organizations like the Taiwan Mission Foundation with an indigenous leadership could powerfully decode this myth in the midst of academicians and various culture brokers in all strata of our society. Empowering an indigenous leader empowers the whole community at large in a unique way.

Missionary endeavors in the Taiwan region started in the mid-nineteenth century mostly by reformed missionaries. One article I was reading recently about mission and ministry in the Taiwan region drew my attention. It states that it is time now to boldly make innovative inroads to spread the Gospel message of Jesus in a way that it will be accessible for the working class community in Taiwan. I agree with that article. See the link: (http://www.christianitytoday.com/ct/2006/may/32.45.html?start=1)

May the Lord continue to enlarge the horizon of Taiwan Mission Foundation and its leadership team, especially Eileen Chang, to be a blessing to hundreds and hundreds of Taiwanese people in greater New York, in East Asia and to the ends of the earth!

《台灣宣教展翅飛》序言
A Foreword to:
Taiwan Mission Taking Off

關榮根牧師
紐約法拉盛第一浸信會主任牧師
Rev. Henry W. Kwan
Lead Pastor of First Baptist Church of Flushing in New York

《台灣宣教展翅飛》序言

關榮根牧師
紐約法拉盛第一浸信會主任牧師

我出生在香港，就讀美國德州休士頓大學二年級時認識主。我第一次訪問台灣，是在八十年代初期，剛從德州達拉斯神學院畢業不久。隨後因為各種宣教事工，我又到台灣數次，每次都對台灣基督徒的殷勤與熱情感到印象深刻。雖然台灣基督徒的人口比率比其他亞洲國家的少，但聖經的經文明白指示，神渴望台灣百姓能夠認識祂並成為祂的門徒。我相信參與宣教大使命是每位信徒應有的責任。多年來，我企盼主在北美地區培育一位屬靈的僕人來喚醒台灣的教會。

大約2004年，我認識了楊宜宜姐妹。她當時是紐約伯特利神學院的學生，後來她在修讀教牧博士學位時，成了我的學生。宜宜出生在台灣，年輕時即到美國，對宣教一直有著強烈的使命感並對事工忠心。我相信她是神回應我的禱告，一個在北美洲帶領台灣宣教的僕人。爾後，她獲得不少台灣牧師與基督徒的支持，於2007年在紐約成立「台灣宣教基金會」。

「台灣宣教基金會」在過去幾年從事了不少在台灣與海外台灣人社區的宣教事工，詳情都可從其通訊中得知。這本《台灣宣教展翅飛》不僅是對上帝感恩的象徵，也是作為對上帝帶領與祝福「台灣宣教基金會」的見證。願大家在讀這本書時，心被激勵，重新點燃為主事奉的熱情。

「所以，我親愛的弟兄們，你們務要堅固，不可搖動，常常竭力多做主工，因為知道你們的勞苦，在主裡面不是徒然的。」（哥林多前書15:58）

Taiwan Mission Taking Off

Rev. Henry W. Kwan
Lead Pastor of First Baptist Church of Flushing in New York

I was born in Hong Kong and came to know the Lord during my sophomore year at the University Of Houston, Texas. Soon after graduating from Dallas Theological Seminary in Texas, I visited Taiwan in the early 1980s for the first time. Since then, I have visited Taiwan on many occasions to serve in various ministry projects. During my visits, I have been impressed by the hospitality and passion of my fellow believers. Though the proportion of believers in Taiwan was less than that of many other countries in Asia, God's desire for the people of Taiwan to come to know Him and become His disciples is clearly commanded in Scripture.

I believe it is the conscious responsibility of all believers to play a role in this great venture. For many years, I have been asking God to raise up a servant from North America who can create an awakening spirit in the churches in Taiwan. About 2004, I came to know Sister Eileen Chang while she was a student at Bethel Seminary of the East, New York Center. Later, I also served as her on-site supervisor in her Doctor of Ministry studies.

Eileen was born in Taiwan and came to the United States at an early age. I observed her passion for ministry and I witnessed her faithfulness on numerous occasions. I believe she is the answer to my prayers that God raise up a servant from North America to lead a mission movement back to Taiwan. Since then, with the support of many Taiwanese pastors and believers, the Taiwan Mission Foundation (TMF) was founded in New York in 2007.

For the past few years, TMF has successfully conducted various ministry projects in Taiwan as well as for Taiwanese residing overseas. Details of this

Preface 3 : Taiwan Mission Taking Off   **13**

ministry can be found in the newsletters published by the Foundation. This book, <<Taiwan Mission Taking Off>>, is both a token of our thanksgiving to God's leading and a witness to God's blessings through the ministry of TMF.
By reading this book, may our hearts be stirred and our spirits rekindled for His work and His service, "Therefore, my dear brothers, stand firm. Let nothing move you. Always give yourselves fully to the work of the Lord, because you know that your labor in the Lord is not in vain (1 Cor. 15:58)."

05/05/12關榮根牧師於台灣宣教基金會5周年慶證道
05/05/12 Rev. Henry W. Kwan made encouraging remarks at TMF 5th Anniversary Celebration banquet

願　台灣宣教展翅飛

A Wish: Taiwan Mission Taking Off

楊宜宜牧師
台灣宣教基金會創始人及會長 - 紐約
Rev. Eileen YiYi Chang
Founder and President of Taiwan Mission Foundation in New York

願　台灣宣教展翅飛

楊宜宜牧師
台灣宣教基金會創始人及會長－紐約

台灣基督徒人數的比例一個半世紀以來一直未能突破百分之三左右。一些海外的台灣基督徒沮喪地自我評斷「台灣教會問題重重」，甚至自責「台灣基督徒不熱心、不傳福音」。

1998年，「世界華福中心」和「大使命中心」聯合出版《二十一世紀華人事工新策略》一書，關切中國宣教的問題及突破之道。書中開頭的宣言提到：「攔阻教會履行大使命最大的阻力，不是外來的，乃是教會內部的紛爭、矛盾與分裂」。余勵山牧師關於普世差傳的挑戰一文也說：「二十一世紀的初期肯定是個偉大的差傳時段，世界各國正整裝待發，特別是第三世界的教會。…為什麼大部份華人教會仍然裹足不前？」再看十九至二十世紀經歷英國威爾斯「大復興」的約瑟克普牧師(1872-1933)在他一篇「教會復興與傳福音」講章中的信息。他說：「今天的教會，傳福音的使命被濃雲暗霧遮蔽…可憐的是，今天教會把傳福音的使命認為是教會額外的工作。」可見宣教不力、福音少傳並非台灣教會及基督徒的單一現象。

當心理學的「舒適區理論」流行在十九至二十世紀之際，基督教界據此省思基督徒是否同樣走不開舒適的教會座椅而影響了宣教的果效。華爾街日報記者羅伯強生也寫了一篇文章「一個難題：教會座椅應該是舒適區嗎？」因為隨著經濟起飛生活豐裕，美國教會在教堂硬木座椅舖上了軟墊。當西方教會為「舒適與宣教」的議題討論得沸沸揚揚之際，不受舒適問題煩擾的第三世界反而悄悄地掀起了宣教的波濤，以非洲為最。如今中國基督徒比例也已達到百分之十。

身為平信徒五十年才讀神學的我，一直不肯也不願相信我們的台灣基督徒是懶散怠惰的。那些經過受洗查經聽道的基督徒必都知道他們應該傳福音，也知道那是他們的主耶穌諄諄託付的。他們也多少聽過證道說：「羊是由羊生的，不是牧者生的。」久不傳福音的基督徒必鬱積了不少的苦悶與罪惡感。到底什麼原因導致羊群走不出去生不出羊呢？具有積極個性主動出去分享見證、傳福音、生小羊的信徒或宣教師畢竟是少數。經過二十餘年的懇切禱告用心觀察與

思考，我深深感到「缺乏宣教管道」是一個重要原因。紛爭的教會、舒適的座椅及豐盈的物質生活，多少會影響基督徒的熱心及事奉品質，但是「缺乏管道」才是關鍵性問題。「沒有管道」即便有心也走不出去。羊需要有路可走即便是羊腸小徑；羊的個性也需要引導。建立多種管道幫助羊群隻隻得以輕易走上宣教之路是台灣宣教的當務之急。

上帝按祂的時間表適時把我呼召出來。祂讓我在人生晚期同時遇到一群貴人，並因他們的鼓勵而設立了「台灣宣教基金會」，其中特別要感念那位邀請我，並帶著我環島觀摩全台灣各宣教區的恩師張玉明牧師。上帝也把宣教管道一個個奇妙地向我啟示出來，從當初唯一的「千元支持一隊（短宣隊）」(One Thousand One Team) 到如今五條管道，加上一個宣教訓練學校。每條管道都走上了不少的羊兄羊姐，並接觸了不少迷羊；每樣宣教事工也都由認真盡責的同工做得有聲有色。

幾年來，最令我欣慰的是看到參與或支持台灣宣教者當他(她)們切實遵行了愛的誡命及大使命後，那燦爛亮麗的笑臉。也在這個時候，「台灣宣教基金會」全體同工的一切勞苦都不徒然了！感謝上帝奇異恩典揀選一群平凡的人來為祂成就不平凡的使命。也感謝所有海內外致力於台灣宣教的教會與組織，因為我們是一起同工一起為主當兵效命的。

寫到此，要特別感謝最近一波海外台灣宣教先鋒 ── 林華山醫師。他不但二十年來到處奔走帶動海外的台灣宣教，2008年並協助出版了海外第一本台灣宣教書籍《福音天軍降寶島》。本會尚在萌芽階段即經常獲其誠摯的關照，並因著他的鼓勵，今天才得以出版這第二本《台灣宣教展翅飛》。這本超過六十篇的寶貴文集是以半年時間接觸了三百個教會及兩百個基督徒而得。目的是要收集台灣移民這半世紀海外的台灣宣教故事。為讓讀者一覽台灣宣教歷史的軌跡及來龍去脈，特邀台灣教會及宣教史教授鄭仰恩牧師精簡撰述一百五十年的台灣宣教史，又請林華山醫師記下二十餘年來，他所親歷目睹的海內外台灣宣教事蹟。

另外，感謝多位作者們，以現身說法寫下他們數十年來各國各地各宗各派各類各式多元多樣的台灣宣教經歷。這些文章也讓我們看到掌管歷史的上帝如何興起一群忠僕，而他們不分男女老幼熱切回應祂的呼召，奮力奔往海內外台灣各

宣教區傳揚福音。最後，為了讓我們後代子子孫孫以及各國信徒都能認識「台灣宣教」，全書以中英雙語出版。由於文多，一群天賜的中英翻譯校訂志工自2010年初即不分日夜埋頭趕工。象徵希望及充滿動力的書名《台灣宣教展翅飛》，也是集思廣益而得。多少話都不足以感謝總編輯亦台灣文學家楊遠薰姐，謝謝她為上帝國及台灣同胞靈魂所作的奉獻犧牲。她與副執行編輯黃文秀姐加上上帝及時差來的天使楊毓清牧師、韋瑪俐退休宣教師和張音音律師、廖安怡，一起再作最後繁重的中英文潤稿及編排。尚有其他志工參與各類瑣事。凡此種種，集多人血汗而成的結晶，才能如此豐美多姿地呈現在你的面前。

當你雙手捧著它、翻讀它，願你知道它得來不易而倍加珍惜！也希望你把它多多介紹給各地的朋友，歡迎為出版費奉獻。萬分感謝2010年一月郭正義長老電告其所屬辛城台灣長老教會長執會已通過贊助一千美元。這第一筆捐款給編輯同仁帶來很大的激勵。深盼這本書能激發更多基督徒投入「台灣宣教」，不論國籍、不分宗派，一起努力突破現狀。讓我們一起期許「台灣宣教展翅飛」。

[12]文中一群貴人：張玉明牧師、林華山醫師、莊澤豐牧師、關榮根牧師以及 Rev. Douglas W. Fombelle [3]「台灣宣教基金會緣起」的奇蹟式故事，請參考本書最後一篇第361-371頁或參考「台灣宣教基金會」網站：www.TaiwanMissionFoundation.Org
[4] 翻譯校訂志工： 楊毓清牧師、韋瑪俐-退休宣教師、張音音律師、 廖安怡、黃志貞、林青瑤、林繼義、杜立欣、何理美、楊玠之、施旭傑、陳宏文牧師、何采穎、張敏鈺、何佩青、李秀明、Angel Chuang、蔡佳翰、Danny/Grace Hsieh Murphy夫婦、葉介庭律師、Joanne Tseng、陳維民、林正堅、楊淑婉、翁彩薰牧師、葉文德牧師和黃韻蓉。

6/9/07 TMF首次董事會於作者楊宜宜會長(前中)及夫婿張富雄董事(二排中)紐約的家舉行
TMF first Board Meeting held at President Eileen (mid) couple's home in New York

11/1/08第二屆宣教感恩大會-作者楊宜宜會長分享, 主題是：我們要接棒
President Eileen shared TMF vision at 2nd Annual Convention in New Jersey FPC with the theme of "We Will Seize The Baton"

A Wish : Taiwan Mission Taking Off

Rev. Eileen YiYi Chang
Founder and President of Taiwan Mission Foundation in New York

The percentage of Christians in Taiwan has not exceeded 3% in the last 150 years. Some overseas Taiwanese Christians despairingly criticize the Taiwanese churches as being full of problems, or even blame Taiwanese Christians for not being zealous enough and not caring about evangelism.

In 1998, the Chinese Coordination Center of World Evangelism and Great Commission Center co-published a book, "21st Century New Strategy for Chinese Ministry," which discussed the issue and the breakthrough of Chinese mission. The manifesto on the front page stated, "The largest stumbling block for the church to fulfill its Great Commission is not external but comes from the internal conflicts, dilemmas, and splits of the church." Rev. Li-Shan Yu, in his article explaining the challenges of world evangelism, mentions that, "The beginning of the 21st century will be a blossoming era of evangelism. Many parts of the world are geared up for the Gospel, especially the churches in the Third World. "Yet why are most Chinese churches still hesitating?"

Moreover, Rev. Joseph W. Kemp (1872-1933) who experienced the Welsh Revival from the 19th to 20th centuries said in his sermon, Revivals and Evangelism, "Evangelism is for the nonce suffering an eclipse. It has passed under a cloud. I do not suppose evangelism will ever become popular." Sadly, the Church also saw the task of evangelism as an ancillary work of the Church in those days. Thus, the lack of zeal for evangelism is not a problem solely existing among Taiwanese churches and Christians.

During the 19th and 20th centuries, when the "Comfort Zone Theory" described populations living in booming economic regions as content with maintaining the status quo, the Christian Church debated internally whether Christians were similarly affected, causing them to become less willing to move beyond their comfortable church pews, and thereby negatively affecting the fruits of evangelism. Robert Johnson, journalist for the Wall Street Journal, also wrote an

article, "A Hard Question: Should Church Pews Be a Comfort Zone?" based on the fact that many American churches added cushions to their pews because of the booming economy and improved living standards. While the Western Church was engaged in a lively discussion on "comfort vs. evangelism," the Third World Church, which was not affected by the issue of comfort, had quietly begun a wave of evangelism, especially in Africa. Today, the percentage of Christians in China has reached 10%.

Entering seminary at age 50, I never wanted to believe that Taiwanese Christians were lackadaisical. Christians who have been baptized, have studied the Bible, and listened to sermons, should know they need to share the Gospel which is the good news of Jesus Christ. They should have heard that "Sheep are birthed by sheep and not by the shepherds." Christians who have not shared the Gospel must have a great sense of guilt and grief. What on earth is the reason that the sheep cannot birth more sheep? Indeed, those Christians and missionaries who are aggressive and active in sharing the Gospel and testimonies are among the minority.

After more than 20 years of earnest prayers, meticulous observation and deliberation, I deeply realized that "the lack of mission channels" is the major factor. Church conflicts, comfortable pews, and abundant materials more or less affect the quality of the Christian zeal and service; nevertheless, "the lack of mission channels" is the critical problem. Without proper channels, one cannot even move out with zeal and passion. Sheep need a path to walk on, even if it's a narrow path, and sheep need to be guided too. Establishing diverse channels for the sheep to walk on mission paths is the immediate task for mission work in Taiwan.

God called me at the opportune time. God also led me to meet several saints toward the later stage of my life journey. Through their help and encouragement, Taiwan Mission Foundation was established. I would like to pay special tributes to Pastor Joseph Chang, who was my professor and also showed me all the mission fields around Taiwan. One by one, God amazingly revealed the mission channels to me, from the beginning with "One Thousand One Team (short-term mission team)" to today's five different mission channels and a mission training school. Every channel has many sheep who meet the lost sheep. Every mission is carried out fully by diligent and responsible co-workers. What has been most comforting to me in the last few years is to see the brightening and beautiful smiles of those Taiwan mission participants. Peace, joy, and contentment gush out endlessly from those who have followed faithfully the Great Commandment and Great Commission. In such moments, all the labor of TMF co-workers are no longer futile. Thanks be to God for His amazing grace in choosing ordinary folks to accomplish His extraordinary commission. I am also grateful for all the churches and organizations in Taiwan and overseas that devote themselves to Taiwan mission because we are comrades for the Lord.

What is more, I have to offer a special word of gratitude to Dr. Howshan Lin, the pioneer of the most recent wave of the Taiwan mission movement. Dr. Lin has mobilized the overseas efforts in Taiwan mission in the last 20 years. In 2008, he also assisted with the publication of the first book on Taiwan mission, Heavenly Messengers Descend Upon Formosa. Though TMF is still in its budding stage, we have received much honest and passionate attention and advice from Dr. Lin. As a result, we are able to publish this second book, "Taiwan Mission Taking Off."

This collection of more than 60 valuable articles is the result of our connection with 300 churches and 200 individual Christians. To enhance the readers' understanding of the origin, legacy, and future of Taiwan mission history, we are privileged to have Dr. Yang-En Cheng, professor of Church History in Taiwan Theological Seminary, provide us with an overview of the 150-year history of Taiwan mission. We also invited Dr. Howshan Lin to write on many events that he personally witnessed during the last 20 years regarding Taiwan missions. Additionally, we appreciate the many writers who shared their experiences in Taiwan missions from many countries, locations, and denominations. These articles demonstrate how throughout history, the sovereign God has been able to raise a cadre of faithful men and women of all ages who have fervently responded to God's call and strived to share the Gospel with Taiwanese people all over the world.

Lastly, in order that our descendents and non-Taiwanese speakers will be able to learn about Taiwan mission, the book is published bilingually in both Chinese

and English. A group of God-given volunteer translators and editors have worked day and night since the beginning of 2010. The title "Taiwan Mission Taking Off" – a hopeful symbol full of forceful dynamism – is a collective effort of many people's ideas. Words cannot express my gratitude to Editor-in-chief Carole Hsu, a Taiwanese literary woman, who made the sacrifice for the kingdom of God and our beloved Taiwanese people. Together with Wenly Hsieh, God-sent angels Rev. Eunice Yang and retired missionary Marie Wilson worked diligently through the final editing details. Because of many people's toils, you are able to see this exquisite and abundant volume. When you hold it in your hands, please remember that it did not come about easily and thus we hope you cherish it even more!

Moreover, we hope you introduce it to or share it as a gift with people of all races and cultures, we welcome donations to help cover the publishing costs. A word of thanks is due to the Cincinnati Taiwanese Presbyterian Church whose Session, led by Elder Cheng-Yih Kuo, approved a contribution of $1000.00 for the publication of the book in its 2010 January meeting. This first contribution brought much encouragement to the editorial board. Our hope is that this book will inspire and move many Christians into "Taiwan mission" regardless of their citizenship or denomination so that we may break through the status quo. May we jointly look forward to see "Taiwan Mission Taking Off!"

[6]The saints mentioned in the article include Rev. Joseph Chang, Dr. Howshan Lin, Rev. Tse-Feng Chuang, Rev. Henry Kwan, and Rev. Douglas W. Fombelle.
[7]Please find the Chinese article, "Origin of Taiwan Mission Foundation," in the appendix in this book p.361-378, or on our website : www.TaiwanMissionFoundation.org.

TMF deeply appreciates the help of its translating & editing volunteers: Rev. Yuching Eunice Yang, Marie Wilson (retired missionary), Karen I. Wu, Esq., Sharon Liao, Cindy Dillard, Gary Lin, Li-hsin Tu, Li Wang, Sarah C. Wang, Jack Shih, Pastor Thomas H. Chen, Jenny Yang, Kathy Chang, Pei-Chin Faison, Elisa Law, Angel Chuang, Hans Tsai, Danny Murphy, Grace Hsieh Murphy, Chieh-Ting Yeh, Esq., Joanne Tseng, Fred Chen, Victor Lin, Shu Wan Yang Ting, Pastor Anna Ueng Wang, Pastor Philip Yeh and Zoë Huang.

特邀稿 A Special Invited Article

台灣宣教史的回顧與展望
The Review and Outlook of Christian Mission in Taiwan

鄭仰恩牧師
台灣教會史教授、台灣神學院副院長
Dr. Yang-En Cheng
Professor of Taiwan Church History,
Vice President of Taiwan Theological Seminary

本文簡要提及台灣宣教史中的幾個面向，因篇幅關係，將跳過十七世紀荷蘭改革宗教會的宣教經驗，集中探討十九世紀起以長老教會為主體的宣教運動。

一、 台灣現代化的功臣 － 英加長老教會的宣教

自十九世紀下半葉起，英國長老教會和加拿大長老教會分別通過醫療、傳道、教育、社會服務、文字傳播等工作，在台灣開啟一波帶有「現代化」特質的新教宣教工作。自1912年起，這兩個宣教運動的成果因共同組織「台灣大會」而逐漸匯聚合流，成為現今長老教會的前身。

當時長老教會宣教運動的開創，是基於兩個契機性的因素才成為可能：一是基督教本身的因素，即十九世紀由西方基督教（特別是新教）所展開的海外宣教運動；另一則是政治性的因素，亦即在英國和大清帝國交戰後於1858年所簽訂的天津條約中規定台灣必須開放雞籠、滬尾、安平、打狗為通商口岸，也因此「在租界內自由傳教」才成為可能。不幸的，基督教因而被視為西方殖民勢力的一部份，是「外來宗教」，基督徒也被台灣民眾視為西方帝國主義的「同夥人」。

這種殖民情境是台灣宣教的主要場合，也是必須突破、克服的地方。我們較常聽到的是「落教，死無人哭」或「多一個基督徒，少一個台灣人」的悲哀感嘆，早期的台灣宣教史也成為已故黃武東牧師所主張的「迫害及殉道史」。這些帶有「焚而不燬」見證的歷史經驗包括埤頭事件及莊清風的殉教(1868)、甘為霖的白水溪遭難事件(1875)、清法戰爭(1884)中北部教會遭受的嚴重迫害事件，甚至還包括後來日本佔台時(1895)的許多的誤解和迫害（例如麻豆事件）等。

因此，在福音和本地社會的對立與衝突中，教會努力以「現世化」的宣教語言－醫療、教育、文字、社會服務－來實際關懷人的需要，並藉著「本土化」的作法來減輕台灣社會對教會的敵意。有趣的是，這些努力一方面讓教會在敵視的環境中尋求「被接納」和「被認同」，但另一方面也在「聖/俗對立」的世界中呼召人脫離世俗社會，進入教會。事實上，真正吸引人接受福音的，往往是信徒生活的聖潔和純真。這種努力進入社會但又刻意表現出不同價值體系的態度，也使得當時的台灣教會成為一種具排他性、只對內論及婚嫁的孤立小社會。

提到對台灣現代化的貢獻，比較常被提起的宣教師有下面幾位：將現代西洋醫學及現代化教育引入北台灣、推廣公共衛生、提升婦女地位及角色的馬偕 (G. L. Mackay)；深具現代建築理念和數理才能、引介民主化議會制度的吳威廉 (William Gauld)；對教會音樂和西洋音樂的介紹不遺餘力的吳瑪利 (Margaret Gauld)；在推廣白話字（普及教育）、聖經翻譯、神學教育、大眾傳播（創辦聚珍堂及台灣首份報紙《台南府城教會報》）等方面貢獻良多的巴克禮(Thomas Barclay)；帶動荷蘭學研究、編撰台語字典、關懷盲啞人教育的甘為霖 (William Campbell)；一生致力於痲瘋病人關懷工作的戴仁壽(George Gushue-Taylor)夫婦；對中部地區台灣民眾展現「切膚之愛」的蘭大衛(David Landsborough)父子夫婦兩代等。

這些都是值得紀念且一提再提的「美善之事」(《腓立比書》4:8)。

二、 二次大戰後的宣教情勢及挑戰

二次大戰後成立的台灣基督長老教會，重新強調教會的「宣教」本質與使命，所以推動一連串的宣教運動，其中最具代表性的就是1965年慶祝「宣教百週年」前後的「倍加運動」和「新世紀宣教運動」。回顧起來，「倍加運動」的宣教形態和對福音的了解比較停留在個人靈魂得救、教堂的興建、主日禮拜的出席、會友人數的增加等，是典型的「福音派」觀點。因為重量不重質，未重視「後進」的信仰教育工作，加上傳道人和經費的不足，在時代局勢改變後反而呈現衰退現象。然而，倍加運動是第一個「本土」宣教運動，有寶貴的「上山下鄉」經驗，也為第二世紀宣教運動打下基礎。

相對的，自1960年代末期起，台灣社會開始轉型，由傳統農業社會逐漸轉向以「加工出口」及「家庭工業」為主的工業社會，農漁村社區逐漸解體，教會的宣教面臨工業化、都市化、現代化、全球化社會的衝擊和挑戰。於是，「新世紀宣教運動」以「多角宣教」為原則，關懷特定的宣教場合和沒落中的社區（如山地、農村、都市、海外移民等）並強調平信徒的信仰職份，以

及自立與互助的夥伴精神，在宣教理念和形態上和普世教會運動的「上帝之宣教」的宣教觀比較接近。遺憾的是，「新世紀宣教運動」立意雖佳，但在人力及資源無法充分支援的情形下，加上台灣政治局勢丕變，以致未能持續，非常可惜。

1980年代起，台灣教會的宣教模式大都傾向「向外取經」，欠缺宣教神學的深刻反省，以致造成宣教觀上的困擾與混亂。簡略來說，1980年代後期的教會大多採用美國福音派的「教會增長」理論，不過成效不佳。

1990年代以後更因為靈恩派團體的成長，且逐漸進入都會地區，開始引進韓國、新加坡和北美洲的不同宣教模式：從南韓，特別受到趙鏞基牧師(David Yonggi Cho) 所領導的中央純福音教會的衝擊；從新加坡，紛紛熱烈仿效注重成功神學和市場策略導向，且具有高科技裝備的超大型教會；從北美洲，則深深受到主領神醫特會、權能事奉和教會增長運動的靈恩領袖或神醫佈道家所影響。因為這些新興運動喜強調「特殊性」的靈恩教導及獨斷性的評論，往往帶來衝突、困惑，甚至分裂。

面對當前「全球化」的宣教模式和以「市場」為取向之作法的衝擊和挑戰，台灣教會尤其需要好好深思、重整其宣教理念。

三、委身鄉土與民主發展的宣教典範

1970年代以後，台灣基督長老教會在面臨新的處境（台灣被迫退出聯合國、外交孤立、中國和美國邁向關係正常化、台灣的政治社會呈現前所未有的危機感）的情形下，基於信仰的良知以及認同鄉土、人民的態度，前後發表三個宣言，提出「自決」的主張，要求政治革新，強調教會的先知職份，主張講母語的權利和文化的自主性，期待教會間的和諧和互相尊重，注重和世界教會的關係，並強調社會公義是教會的宣教使命。

1977年的「人權宣言」更進一步主張「人權和鄉土是上帝所賞賜」，台灣人民的安全、獨立和自由應得著保障，並基於自決的原則，促請政府建立台灣為一「新而獨立的國家」。

為了表明自己的信仰立場，總會更在1985年通過《台灣基督長老教會信仰告白》，其中有關「教會觀」的部分可以說最精彩的理念結晶：「阮信，教會是上帝百姓的團契，受召來宣揚耶穌基督的拯救，做和解的使者，是普世的，復
定根在本地，認同所有的住民，通過愛和受苦，來成為盼望的記號。」

由於台灣人長久受到外來政權的統治，不但必須面對「自我身份認同」的問題，更欠缺「當家做主」的主觀意願。結果，台灣人追求「出頭天」的願望和長老教會所主張「自決」的權利重合，形成新的「台灣人基督徒」認同。教會所遭受的苦難也讓台灣人民能夠認同，在「共同受苦」的歷史經驗中被接納，並表達對人民和土地的認同。

事實上，歷經1947年的二二八事件以及1950年代的「白色恐怖」後，台灣社會在國民黨「粉飾太平」的專制戒嚴體制下可以說毫無聲音，早自1960年代起，許多英美宣教師勇敢為台灣人發出先知的聲音，成為民主政治發展的先鋒，並為此付出艱辛代價，或被驅逐出境或拒絕居留，例如美國衛理公會的唐培禮 (Milo Thornberry) 和唐秋詩 (Judith Thomas) 夫婦、美國長老教會的韋禮遜 (Donald J. Wilson) 和郭大衛 (David Gelzer)、美國歸正教會的嘉偉德 **(Wendell Karsen)**、萬益士 (Rowland van Es)，以及英國長老教會的彌迪理 **(Daniel　Beeby)** 等牧師。這些宣教師認同自己為「台灣人」，並且因為實際參與了台灣教會對自身之歷史和社會經驗的反省，所以具有強烈的本土認同。

這些委身鄉土、參與民主發展的運動，當然是近代台灣宣教史的重要部份。

四、走出本位主義，致力宣教的新課題

1985年以後,由於台灣社會激變,解嚴後的社會一方面繼續呈現國家認同危機、心靈腐化、族群對立、生活物化、道德敗壞、生態污染等現象,另一方面卻又充斥著自力救濟式的「我群」意識。教會面臨「新興文化」的衝擊,不知所措,在無以回應的情形下,遂轉向「本位主義」的教會觀。確實,台灣教會目前遭遇一個相當大的危機,即其會友多由中產階級所組成,而大部分中產階級的教會所型塑出來的基督徒是一種習慣舒服地坐在自己教堂座椅上的基督徒。也就是說,在心態上、動機上是一種內向的,習慣很自在地活在自己覺得舒適的位置上 (comfort zone)。這種本位主義可以說是宣教課題的最大挑戰。

當代宣教學者 David J. Bosch 對宣教下一個簡單的定義:宣教就是願意跨越你所感到安逸舒適的領域的邊界,走出去,願意邁向一個不可知的挑戰的可能性。因此,我認為,我們除了理解宣教的本質外,可能必須先思考「宣教動機」的問題。其實今天台灣教會(特別是長老教會等主流教會)所遇到的挑戰在於大家都習慣靜態的、內向的思考,所以如果我們的教會無法有一種新的動機或心態,即一種我們要勇敢地邁出去、邁向一個不可知的領域的動機,如果沒有這種動機的話,那麼,用什麼宣教方法或策略可能都沒有用。

今天的西方教會似乎具有一種將宣教「內化」為生活價值觀、文化運動或社會運動的傾向。換句話說,如果基督徒作任何事都算是一種宣教,那麼宣教意識也可能會隨之消失!也因此,對許多過去慣於接受宣教的所謂「後進教會」(younger church) 和「接受教會」而言,參與海外宣教、跨文化宣教或各種短期、長期宣教的經驗似乎是一個體驗、覺醒、認知、教育的必要過程!

[結論] 宣教理念的再思

我相信也期待,台灣教會需要在宣教觀上進行深刻的反省,以期建立一個更齊全的宣教或信仰見證模式。過去,我們喜歡強調《馬太福音》28章18-20節所指明的「大使命」。這個範型並非不好,但它僅是宣教模式的一環。我們若

將多元豐富的聖經內涵和信仰傳統簡化為「領人信主」或「搶救靈魂」，那將會是對基督教信仰的大誤解。

相對的，現今宣教學者喜歡同時強調《約翰福音》13章34節所主張的「大誡命」的範型。確實，宣教學者David J. Bosch所著《更新變化的宣教》一書早已成為普世神學教育的主要教科書，書中列出十多種宣教模式，明白昭示宣教典範在教會歷史中不斷地轉移。

「大誡命」的範型提醒我們，即使台灣基督徒必須長久扮演「少數人」的角色，我們仍能為基督信仰的社會實踐與本土見證奮力不懈！但願台灣眾教會和基督徒都能積極培養宣教意識，並在台灣處境裡辨認「時代的徵兆」，最重要的是，勇敢地跨出腳步，邁向未知的信仰旅程！

[參考書目及延伸閱讀]

1. 博許(David Bosch)，《一路上奔走》，林鴻信譯（台北：禮記，2003）。

2. 《信仰的記憶與傳承—台灣教會人物檔案（一）》，鄭仰恩主編（台南：人光，2001）。

3. 《信仰偉人列傳》。楊士養編著，林信堅修訂（台南：人光，1989）。

4. 鄭仰恩，《歷史與信仰：從基督教觀點看台灣和世界》（台南：人光，1999）。

5. 鄭仰恩，《定根本土的台灣基督教》（台南：人光，2005）。

6. 陳南州，《台灣基督長老教會的社會、政治倫理》
（台北：永望，1999再版）。

7. 陳南州，《宣教的神學與實踐》（台北：永望，2003）。

8. 陳南州，《認同的神學》（台北：永望，2003）。

9.《「感恩與巡禮」國際友人對台灣民主與人權奮鬥的回顧》，Vol. I & II（台北：財團法人台灣民主基金會，2003）。

10. A Borrowed Voice: Taiwan Human Rights through International Networks, 1960-1980, written and edited by Linda Gail Arrigo and Lynn Miles (Taipei: Hanyao Color Printing Co., 2008).

11. 鄭仰恩，〈基督教歷史中的文化脈絡—看基督教何去何從？〉，《原住民文化與福音的對話》，台灣世界展望會編著
（台北：台灣世界展望會，2004），頁41-50。

12. Yang-en Cheng,"Calvinism and Taiwan,"Theology Today, vol. 66, no. 2 (July 2009), pp. 184-202.

13.賴永祥教授網站：http://www.laijohn.com/Index.htm

【編註：十分感謝鄭仰恩牧師提供本文中所有的照片】

原住民教會
Aboriginal Church

戴仁壽夫婦
Dr. George Gushue-Taylor and wife Marjorie Miller

原住民教會
Aboriginal Church

李庥牧師
Rev. Hugh Ritchie

台灣宣教史的回顧與展望　　31

甘為霖
Dr. William Campbell, MD

教士會
Mission Council

早期台灣宣教師合影
Group picture of early missionaries

巴克禮牧師
Thomas Barclay

樂山園教堂
Happy Mount Colony Church

淡水女學
Tamsui Girls School

淡水女學堂
Tamsui Girls School

淡水女學校
Tamsui Girls School

開創護理部的女宣教師
Lady Missionaries and Founders
of the Department of Nursing

台灣宣教史的回顧與展望

淡江中學八角塔
The Octagonal Tower At Tamkang High School

樂山園同工
Co-worker of Happy Mount Colony

馬偕所建 艋舺教堂
Mackay's Church in Bangka Branch

牛津學堂
Oxford College

馬偕旅行傳道
Mackay's Itinerant Mission

馬偕醫療工作
Mackay's Medical Mission

馬偕訪問東部
Mission trip to Eastern Formosa (Taiwan)

馬偕
George Leslie Mackay

馬偕醫院
Mackay Memorial Hospital

台灣宣教史的回顧與展望　　35

蘭大衛醫生夫婦及學生
Dr. & Mrs. David Landsborough and their students

唐培禮
Milo L. Thornberry

馬雅各醫師全家
James Laidlaw Maxwell and his family

孫雅各牧師夫婦
Rev. James I. & Lillian Dickson

A Special Invited Article

The Review and Outlook of Christian Mission in Taiwan

Dr. Yang-En Cheng
Professor of Taiwan Church History
Vice President of Taiwan Theological Seminary

This article briefly describes several aspects of the history of mission in Taiwan. Due to limited space, I will pass over the 17th century Dutch Reformed mission and focus on exploring the Presbyterian-centered mission movement in the 19th century.

I. The Major Contributors of Taiwan Modernization: The Missions of the Presbyterian Churches in England and Canada

Beginning in the second half of the 19th century, the Presbyterian Church in England (PCE) and the Canada Presbyterian Church (CPC) embarked on a series of Protestant missions in Taiwan using modern methods of ministry that included medicine, evangelism, education, social work, and literary communication. Since 1912, the missions of the two churches converged in co-organizing the "National Synod in Taiwan," which later became today's Presbyterian Church in Taiwan.

The inauguration of the Presbyterian mission movement in the 19th century became possible because of two critical factors. The first factor was intrinsically Christian, that is, the 19th century overseas mission movement initiated by particularly the Protestant Church. The second factor was a political one associated with the postwar 1858 Tianjin Treaty signed by both Britain and the Ching Dynasty. The Treaty forced open the Taiwanese ports in Kelang (Keelung), Hoboe (Tamsui), Anping (Tainan), and Takao (Kaoshiung) for foreign trade which accordingly made viable "uninhibited evangelism within concession."

Unfortunately, Christianity was therefore seen as a part of the Western colonial power – a foreign religion. Consequently, Christians were perceived as partners of Western imperialism. The mission in Taiwan was situated in this kind of a colonial context, and needed to be overcome. We have often heard expressions of regrets like "A Christian believer dies without any mourners," or "One more Christian means one less Taiwanese person." The early history of Taiwanese mission was as late Rev. Huang Wu Tong puts it, "a history of persecution and martyrdom." This part of the history was marked by the witnesses of "Nec tamen consumebatur (yet it was not consumed)" including but not limited to events such as: Pi-tau Incident and the martyrdom of Chuang Ching Fong in 1868, the White Water Creek Assault on Rev. William Campbell in 1875, the Sino-French War in 1884 that triggered persecutions among churches in northern Taiwan, and persecutions during the Japanese occupation in 1895 (such as the Matau Incident).

As a result, in the midst of rivalries and conflicts between the Gospel and local culture, the church made every effort, using "modernized methods" of mission – medicine, education, literature and social services – to meet the practical needs of the people. Moreover, contextualizing Christianity became a way to alleviate the animosity shown by the Taiwanese society toward the church. These efforts not only paved the way for the church to be accepted and identified in a hostile environment, but it also called people to separate from the secular society and join the church in a world that is marked by "divine-secular conflicts." As a matter of fact, what often drew people to accept the Gospel was the holiness and purity exemplified by the Christian way of life. The attitude of attempting to connect with society while intentionally displaying a different set of values, nevertheless, made the early church in Taiwan an isolated social group that confined marital partners exclusively to insiders.

The following missionaries are often mentioned as the major contributors to the modernization of Taiwan: Rev. Dr. George L. Mackay, who brought Western medicine and education system into Taiwan, and helped advance public health and enhance women's role and status; Rev. William Gauld, a gifted architect and mathematician, who brought in the democratic representative system; Ms. Margaret Gauld who tirelessly introduced Church music and Western music; Rev. Dr. Thomas Barclay who was famous in promoting Romanization of Taiwanese language – a way of public education, biblical translation, theological education, and mass media (instituting Chu-Tin Printing Press and first Taiwanese newspaper, Tainan Church News); Rev. William Campbell initiating the Dutch studies, compiling Taiwanese dictionary, dedicating to education for the deaf and the blind; Mr. and Mrs. George Gushue-Taylor who devoted their lives to caring for lepers; Dr. and Mrs. David Landsborough and their son and daughter-in-law who manifested "A Skin-Graft with Love" in middle Taiwan. Such are deeds "admirable and commendable" (Philippians 4:8) worth telling again and again.

II. The Situation and Challenges of Missions after the Second World War

After World War II, the Presbyterian Church in Taiwan reemphasized the church's essence and call of mission, and thus launched a series of mission movements beginning with the centennial celebration of church mission in 1965, among which the most representative were the Church Doubling Movement (1955-1965) and the New Century Mission Movement (1965-1978).

In retrospect, salvation of soul, church planting, worship attendance, membership growth, etc… which was typical of the perspectives of the evangelical church tradition remained the core of the mission concept and the understanding of the nature of the Gospel in the Church Doubling Movement. However, the emphasis on number rather than quality, the neglect of faith formation of new believers, and the lack of clergy and finance, the movement faded after a dramatic shift of the spirit of an age (zeitgeist) in Taiwan. The Church Doubling Movement which offered pragmatic experiences nonetheless was the first "indigenous" mission movement that took root on the soils of Taiwan and built a firm foundation for the mission movement of the second century.

In contrast, the end of 1960s, Taiwan began experiencing rapid social changes, moving gradually from an agricultural society to an industrialized society with concentration on export processing and domestic manufacturing. The agricultural and fishing communities were gradually disintegrating. The mission of the church faced the wallops and challenges of industrialization, urbanization, modernization, and globalization. The New Century Mission Movement principled on "Multi-angled Mission," therefore, paid attention to particular mission contexts and dwindling communities, for example, aboriginal and rural communities, urban and overseas immigrant contexts. The Movement also emphasized the vocational calling of lay believers, self-reliance and mutual partnership. The concept and model of the Movement was similar to the concept of "missio Dei" of the recent ecumenical movements. Unfortunately, the New Century Mission Movement despite its sound foundation ceased to continue due to insufficient manpower and resources, and the abrupt changes of Taiwan's political landscape.

Since 1980s, the missions of Taiwanese churches tended to "import" foreign mission strategies and lacked in-depth missiological reflection, thus contributed to missional confusion and chaos. In summary, churches in Taiwan since the 80s generally adopted the "church growth" model of the evangelical churches in America with very little success. With the growth of the charismatic movement and its influence in the urban areas in the 1990s, churches started bringing in evangelization strategies from Korea, Singapore, and North America. The thrash from Korea came from the Yoido Full Gospel Church led by Rev. David Yonggi Cho. Churches also imitated the prosperity-gospel-oriented, market driven and high-tech-equipped mega churches in Singapore.

The influence of North America was brought about by the charismatic leaders or miracle-working evangelists and their healing and power ministries. These new movements tended to champion special charismatic gifts and bring on absolute judgment, and thus often caused conflicts, confusion, and splits in the churches. Facing the challenges of globalization of the mission paradigm and market driven evangelization, the church in Taiwan had dig deeply and reintegrate the concept of mission.

III. The Mission Paradigm of Committing to the Home Land and Democratic Development

In the 1970s, Taiwan was ousted from the United Nations, and the normalization between the United States and China isolated Taiwan from the world communities and global stage. Thus, Taiwan and its people were grasped by an unprecedented sense of political and social crisis. Under such milieu, the Presbyterian Church in Taiwan, based on its faith conscience and its identification with the land and the people, issued a series of three declarations. The major themes of these statements include: self-determination, political reform, prophetic role of the Church, the right to speak one's mother tongue, cultural autonomy, the accord and mutual respect among the churches, staying connected with the ecumenical communities, and social justice as mission of the church. The Declaration on Human Rights (1977) further asserts "human rights and the homeland as the gifts of God" that the security, independence, and freedom of the Taiwanese people shall be protected. Moreover, based on the principle of self-determination, the declaration urges the government to establish Taiwan as a "new and independent country."

In order to profess its beliefs and stance, the General Assembly in 1985 approved The Confession of Faith of the Presbyterian Church in Taiwan. The section on ecclesiology is ingeniously stated, "We believe that the Church is the fellowship of God's people, called to proclaim the salvation of Jesus Christ and to be an ambassador of reconciliation. It is both ecumenical and rooted in this land, identifying with all its inhabitants, and through love and suffering becoming the sign of hope." Taiwanese people, long governed by alien regimes, not only faced the dilemma of self-identity, but did not have the will power for self-autonomy. The Taiwanese people's desire to "rise above one's head" (*a Taiwanese slang meaning transcending one's unfavorable circumstances*) and the declaration on "self-determination" by PCT went hand in hand and formed a new identity for Taiwanese Christians. The suffering endured by the Church enabled the Taiwanese people to identify with and accept the Church through the historical experience of "co-suffering" and thus strengthened the church's identity with the people and the land.

As a matter of fact, through the 228 Incident in 1947 and the "White-Terror Rule" of the 50s, Taiwanese were voiceless under the totalitarian Martial Law instituted by Kuomingdang's "sweeping under the rug" policy. From the 1960s and onward, many Western missionaries fearlessly became the prophetic voice for the Taiwanese people and the harbingers of democratic development. They paid a high price for doing so. They were either expelled from Taiwan or refused reentry visa. Among them were Michael Thornberry and Judith Thomas of the United Methodist Church, Donald J. Wilson and David Gelzer of the (former entity of) Presbyterian Church USA, Wendell Karsen and Rowland van Es of the Reformed Church in America, and Daniel Beeby of the Presbyterian Church in England (later United Reformed Church). These missionaries regarded themselves as Taiwanese and, after participating in the historical and social reflections of the Church, were filled with a strong sense of indigenous identity.

These movements of identifying with the land and participating in democratic development surely have become an important part of the history of mission in Taiwan.

IV. Beyond Parochialism and Focusing on the New Challenges of Mission Since 1985

Taiwan began experiencing rapid social changes. After the lifting of the martial law, the society continued to experience critical issues such as national identity crisis, spiritual corruption and distortion, ethnic conflicts, materialism and consumerism, moral depravity, and environmental pollution. Yet, on the other hand, the society was filled with the self-help ideology of "I/We Group." The church was lost in confronting the tides of the "New Cultures." Not knowing how to respond, the church turned toward the parochialism oriented ecclesiology. Without a doubt, the church in Taiwan was faced with an enormous crisis. Most of the believers were middle class. Most of the middle class churches had molded Christians who were sitting comfortably in the church pews. Both mentally and behaviorally, these Christians were inward looking and had accustomed to their comfort zone. Such parochialism is indeed the most urgent challenge in today's mission of the church.

Missiologist David J. Bosch defines mission as "the willingness to cross over the boundary of one's own world," that is, to cross over the comfort zone, the willingness to step beyond and march towards the possibility of being challenged by the surprises and unknowns. Consequently, I believe except for understanding the essence of mission, we must reflect on the issue of "the motives of mission." Today's churches in Taiwan, especially the mainline churches like the PCT, are faced with the challenge of a habitual way of static and introvert thinking and acting. Without a new motive or new attitude of being willing to audaciously move toward an unknown territory, any mission method or strategy may be futile.

Today's Western churches have a tendency to internalize mission as a value of life, a cultural movement or social movement. In other words, if everything that a Christian does can be considered mission, we may lose the distinctive mission consciousness. Hence, for younger church and receiving church that used to be the recipients of Western missions, participation in overseas and cross-cultural missions in various short or long-term formats seems to be an indispensable process for mission experience, awakening, cognition, and education!

CONCLUSION: THE RETHINKING OF THE CONCEPT OF MISSION

I believe and hope that the Church in Taiwan will develop an integrated mission paradigm and witness through in-depth deliberation on missiology. In the past, we preferred focusing on the Great Commission of Matthew 28:18-20. This paradigm, though not necessarily defective, is not the only paradigm for mission. Simplifying the multivalent and diverse biblical content and faith tradition as "evangelizing the nonbelievers" or "saving souls" can be the major misinterpretation of Christianity. In contrast, modern missiologists also emphasize the paradigm of the Great Commandment of John 13:34. In reality, the book Transforming Mission written by missiologist David J. Bosch has become the classic text in theological education of the universal church. The book delineates more than 10 different mission paradigms which illustrates the continuous transformation of missions throughout the church history. The mission paradigm of the Great Commandment reminds us that Taiwanese Christians may always be the minority; nonetheless we continue to strive for the social practice and indigenous witness of Christian faith. May the churches and Christians in Taiwan actively develop a mission consciousness – a deeper awareness and deeper sense of mission – to be able to discern the signs of the time in the Taiwanese context. Most importantly, may we make a bold stride and march toward an "uncharted" journey of faith!

REFERENCES AND FURTHER READINGS

Arrigo, Linda Gail and Lynn Miles, ed. A Borrowed Voice: Taiwan Human Rights through International Networks, 1960-1980. Taipei: Hanyao Color Printing Co., 2008.

David Bosch. Transforming Mission: Paradigm Shifts in Theology of Mission. Orbis Books, 1991.

David Bosch. A Spirituality of the Road. Eugene, Or.: Wipf & Stock Publishers, 2001.

Chen, Nan-Chou. Social and Political Ethics of the Presbyterian Church in Taiwan. Taipei: Yung-Wang, 1999.

Chen, Nan-Chou. Theology and Practice of Mission. Taipei: Yung-Wang, 2003.

Chen, Nan-Chou. Theology of Identification. Taipei: Yung-Wang, 2003.

Cheng, Yang-En. "Calvinism and Taiwan." Theology Today, Vol. 66, No. 2 (July 2009): 184-202.

Cheng, Yang-En. "The Cultural Contexts in Church History: The Future of Christianity,"

The Dialogue between Aboriginal Culture and the Gospel. Taipei: World Vision, 2004.

Cheng, Yang-En. History and Faith: A Christian Perspective on Taiwan and the World. Tainan: Jen-Kuang, 1999.

Cheng, Yang-En. Contextualizing Christianity in Taiwan: Collected Essays on the History of Christianity in Taiwan. Tainan: Jen-Kuang, 2005.

Cheng, Yang-En, Ed. Memory and Heritage of Faith: Profiles of Christians in Taiwan, Vol. 1. Tainan: Jen-Kuang, 2001.

Lai, Yun-Hsian. www.laijohn.com/Index.htm.

Thanksgiving and Pilgrimage: The Review of International Comrades on the Struggles of Democracy and Human Rights in Taiwan. Volumes 1 and 2. Taipei: Foundation for Democracy in Taiwan. [2003].

Yang, Shi-Yang, ed. Biographies of Faith Giants. Tainan: Human Light, 1989.

【Editor's Notes：A lot of thanks to Rev. Yang-En Cheng for all the historical photos in this article.】

第二篇
台灣宣教篇
II. Missions in Taiwan

台灣宣教之門大開
Taiwan Mission: The Door is Wide Open

台灣宣教之門大開

張玉明牧師
靈糧神學院北美分院院長

2004年二月二十九日，我開始擔任愛恩台福基督教會的主任牧師。愛恩教會是一個到台灣作短期宣教的先驅。數年來的每年寒暑假，都由林華山與劉碧珠醫師夫婦推動、莊澤豐牧師組團，共同到台灣基層鄉村教英文或向民眾宣教。

我於2005年首次帶領愛恩的年輕人到台灣作短宣。當時，我們全家六口加上來自美國各地的其他熱心人士，一共五十九人參與。我們在嘉義縣太保鄉集訓後，分別前往台東、新竹寶山、員林、彰化、台中、花蓮、宜蘭、台南、新竹與基隆等十八個工作站，分別作為期三星期的宣揚福音事工。那年的主題以介紹美國的節日為主。

這些從沒教過書的美國大孩子在宣教工場上，頓時都成了美麗的親善大使。他們的熱情與純真贏得了台灣學校師生們的心。這一年的成功堅定了我們暑期短宣的心志，也清楚地看到幾個短宣可行的方向：

一、短宣最好在學校舉行。因為學校裡可以接觸到不少需要福音的人，也方有足夠的場地可容納超過一百名學生的營會。

二、需在台灣進行師資集訓。在台集訓三天可以讓美國來的小老師們瞭解台灣的環境，並且彼此認識，建立良好的團隊默契。

三、需要一套活潑生動的英文教材。一套好的教材是英文營成功的一半，每年都需及早設計，並且內容年年不同。

四、需有在地的同工與各學校作良好的聯絡，俾使每一位飛越大半個地球到台灣短宣的教師們都有教學、見證與分享的機會。

五、要有安排良好的作息表，方能讓每一位同工覺得不虛此行。

六、年輕教師們一天要到兩個學校輪教，每日教學六小時，加上往返交通、早晚靈修、準備教學、為學生禱告等等，工作相當繁重，因此隨隊父母的照顧與鼓勵成為不可或缺的後援力量。

2006年，我再次帶隊到台灣短宣。此次營會以「品德」為主題，全團六十三人來自全美十六所教會。台福在台灣與基福、工福、客福和鄉福等四個福音團體同工，所以被人稱為「五福臨門」，顯示神真確愛台灣。

美國老師在台灣越來越受歡迎，我們也意識到在台灣的學校宣教的時期不會太長，因此必須及時徵召更多的老師。但徵師著實不易，神因此讓我想起紐約的楊宜宜牧師。宜宜是我在台福神學院教書時的一位極出色的學生，做事很有魄力，又兼具文采，自畢業後，即在紐約幫神學院作三年的拓展事工，為延伸部奠下美好的根基。2005年，台福神學院因改組與調整方向，收回美東的事工，也因此促使宜宜到美國伯特利神學院美東分院攻讀教牧博士學位。

就在這時，我邀請她到台灣宣教。我於2006年5月1日打電話給她，她在七月初就抵達台灣，隨後到嘉義作為期一星期的短宣。自第二星期開始，我帶她與另一位同工作一次環島觀摩之旅，讓她經歷不同地區與不同教學的特色。

該年冬天，宜宜接受吳三連基金會的邀請，回台舉行新書發表會，又參加冬季短宣。她於2007年夏季，再度參加短宣。然後，她回紐約，創立「台灣宣教基金會(TMF)」，結合眾人的財力、心力與人力，共同推動台灣的宣教事工，成為台灣短宣成長過程中一個令人欣慰的成果。

雖然「台灣宣教基金會」不直接徵師帶隊到台灣，卻以「千元支持一隊(One Thousand One Team)」的方式，鼓勵更多教會徵師到台灣短宣。該會成立未及三年，即已支助將近二十團的短宣隊到台灣宣教，儼然成為另一型式的宣教據點。我連續三年帶隊到台灣短宣後，於2008年轉任「矽谷生命河靈糧堂」教牧領袖學院院長。原以為從此將與我所熱愛的台灣宣教告別。但這一年，台灣靈糧堂首次邀請北美靈糧堂回台短宣，我於是再次帶隊回台短宣。這次參與的人數並且超過一百二十人。

我曾在過去幾年，多次祈禱回台短宣人數能超過一百人，結果神在差遣我離開台福後，意外地應允了這項禱告。這年，我把所組的台灣短宣隊取名為「ADVENT TAIWAN」，即「Americans Dedicated for Voluntary English Teachers in Taiwan」的縮寫，網址為www.adventtaiwan.org。事實上，「Advent」一字就是主耶穌再來的意思。

主使用年輕人開拓台灣這塊福音荒涼之地，並賜下神蹟與祝福。我們感謝神讓台灣宣教的規模在短短幾年間迅速擴展，也衷心盼望在主耶穌再來時，台灣的多數人都已歸順為基督徒。最後，我們誠心祝福「台灣宣教基金會」能在台灣全國歸主運動裡，扮演一個極重要的角色。

作者張玉明博士與夫人
Author Rev. Dr. and Mrs. Joseph Chang

2008作者張玉明博士與夫人(三排右7 & 8)帶領夏季短宣隊回台
7/1- 8/9/08- Taiwan Mission Team led by Pastor Joseph Chang and wife (3rd row 7th & 8th from right)

Part 2 : Missions in Taiwan

Taiwan Mission : The Door is Wide Open

Rev. Yueming Joseph Chang
President of Bread of Life Theological Seminary of North America

I became the senior pastor of the Evangelical Formosan Church (EFC) of Irvine on February 29, 2004. EFC Irvine is a church that pioneered short-term Taiwan mission trips. For several years during the winters and summers, under the direction of Dr. Howshan and Mrs. Eunice Lin, and Rev. Tse-Feng Chuang, we would go to villages in Taiwan to teach English and spread the Gospel to the villagers.

In 2005, I led our first short-term mission team to Taiwan. A total of 59 young people from EFC Irvine, including six from my family, and people from all over the U.S. participated. After our training in Taipao of Chiayi, we proceeded with our Gospel mission for three weeks in about eighteen locations, such as Taitung, Hsingchu, Paoshan, Yuanlin, Changhua, Taichung, Hualien, Yilan, Tainan, and Keelung. The main theme of this mission tour was to introduce American holidays.

As far as mission is concerned, these American teenagers who had never taught before suddenly became beautiful ambassadors. Their sincere passion and love for the children won the hearts of teachers and students alike. This year's success confirmed our determination to do more summer short-term missions. It also helped us identify our mission directions:

1. Events should take place in schools. We can reach many people who need the Gospel, and the facilities enable us to hold camps for more than 100 students.
2. Tutor trainings should be held in Taiwan. Three days of concentrated trainings help the U.S. tutors understand the local context and allow tutors to get to know one other and establish effective teamwork.

3. English teaching materials should be dynamic, creative and different every year. Good materials are half of the way to a successful English camp. They should be designed as early as possible.
4. We need co-workers in Taiwan to keep in touch with every school so that all the tutors will have the opportunity to teach and share their testimonies.
5. A well-organized schedule is the key to a meaningful mission trip.
6. The tutors' schedule are very tight. They teach in two different schools for six hours each day, plus time is spent on commute, preparation for classes, and spiritual disciplines. The accompanying parents' encouragement and support are indispensable.

I led a mission team again in 2006 with 63 participants from 16 churches. The theme was virtues. EFC Irvine cooperated with the Grass Root Mission, Industrial Mission, Hakka Mission, and Village Gospel Mission.

【Note: All 5 organizations have the word "Gospel/Blessing (same word in Chinese)" We called this mission "The Dawning of Five Blessings." God truly loves Taiwan.】

Tutors from the U.S. are in greater demand, yet it is not easy to recruit enough candidates. We realize that the door to this type of mission in Taiwan won't stay open for long. We need more teachers. God reminded me of Rev. Eileen Yi-Yi Chang in New York, who was an outstanding student while I was on the faculty at Logos Evangelical Seminary (LES). She has exceptional abilities and excellent communication skills. After graduation, she volunteered for three years to establish a firm foundation for the Extended Course of LES Training Institute in New York. However, due to LES' restructuring and redirection in 2005, this program on the East coast was brought to an end. Subsequently Rev. Eileen Yi-Yi Chang began her studies at the Doctor of Ministry program of the Bethel Seminary of the East.

That's when I invited Eileen to join me in Taiwan mission. Shortly after I talked to her on May 1, 2006, she came to Taiwan in July. We spent the first week in Chiayi. During the second week, I took her and another co-worker on a field trip around the island so that they could experience the different teaching situations in different locations. Next winter, Eileen was invited to Taiwan by "Wu San-Lien Foundation for Taiwan Historical Materials" for the publication of her book. Thus, she participated in the winter and again the summer short-term mission trips. Afterwards, Eileen founded Taiwan Mission Foundation (TMF) in New York, uniting and consolidating the finances, capabilities, and passion of many to promote Taiwan missions, which has become an encouraging fruit of Taiwan short-term missions.

TMF does not bring mission teams directly to Taiwan. It encourages churches to recruit teachers for short-term Taiwan missions through the program "One Thousand ($1000) One Team." In less than three years, TMF has supported almost 20 teams. TMF has become another archetype of mission approach.

I brought short-term missions teams back to Taiwan for three consecutive years. In 2008, I became the dean of River of Life Pastoral Leadership Institute in Silicon Valley. I thought I would have to say good-bye to my beloved Taiwan mission. Surprisingly, for the very first time, the Bread of Life Church in Taiwan invited the Bread of Life Churches in North America for a short-term mission, and I was able to bring back a team that had over 120 participants. I had been constantly praying for teams that exceeded 100 participants. God brought me away from EFC, but answered my prayers at the same time. So I called this short-term Taiwan mission team "ADVENT TAIWAN," abbreviated from Americans Dedicated as Voluntary English Teachers in Taiwan. The website is www.adventtaiwan.org. Advent means the second coming of Jesus Christ.

God used a generation of youth to cultivate the gospel-starving land, Taiwan, and gave us abundant wonders and blessings. We are grateful that God has rapidly expanded the scale of Taiwan mission in recent years. We truly hope that when our Lord Jesus returns, most of the Taiwanese will be Christians by then. Last but not least, I sincerely pray for abundant blessings upon Taiwan Mission Foundation, for this organization to play an extremely important role in the movement of Taiwan missions, and for all Taiwanese to declare that Jesus is Lord.

回台宣教
Taiwan Mission

林華山醫師與劉碧珠夫婦
北美路加傳道會前董事、鄉福基福北美代表 - 洛杉磯
Dr. Howshan Lin & Mrs. Eunice Lin
Former Board Member of Luke Medical Mission in North America
North American Liaison Officer of
Village Gospel Mission & Taiwan Grass-Roots Mission

回台宣教

林華山醫師與劉碧珠夫婦
北美路加傳道會前董事、鄉福基福北美代表 - 洛杉磯

1989冬天，我們夫婦自紐約赴華府，參加「基督使者協會」所舉辦的華人差傳大會。在會中，我們從聽了陳昌和牧師有關台灣鄉村福音的演講後，才知道自己的家鄉竟是一個福音未得之地，不禁十分傷感。

陳牧師以一個非河洛語為母語的人，為了服事鄉間百姓，到菜市場學河洛語。而「鄉村福音佈道團（鄉福）」更是由一對「內地會」的宣教士魏德凱牧師夫婦騎著鐵馬，逐鄉繞村地禱告成立的。至於我們這兩個自稱基督徒的「正港台灣郎/娘」，竟對家鄉的福音事工「朦喳喳」，因此往後連續三個晚上，我們為台灣的福音事工流淚禱告。

自差傳大會歸來後，我們夫婦開始寫信、打電話，「不見笑」地毛遂自薦，請各教會賜予機會，讓我們分享與傳遞。此後，我們便常帶著自製的看版與文宣，在紐約附近城鎮的小組聚會、主日學、退修會等各種場合傳遞台灣鄉村福音的需要，也邀請鄉福的同工到美國來，真人實事地見證與分享。他們的委身、屬靈的爭戰和對鄉村百姓認同的心，不但感動也喚醒許多北美教會的兄姐，成立鄉福北美董事會，在各地委託負責的弟兄如紐澤西吳啟政長老、華府許辰召弟兄、北加州陳仕展長老等等，就近傳遞異象。

1995年，我們和蔡青陽長老、郭惠美醫師等共同成立「大紐約區醫療團契」，在大紐約區義診或舉辦醫療講座等等，服務當地華人。我們所隸屬的紐約史德登島恩光教會的張景祥牧師也開始帶領教會的青年回台短宣，開設「美語營」迄今。

1997年，我與內人搬到南加州，就近照顧孫兒，並加入台福教會的大家庭。由於發現加州有一大群小留學生，也承續對台宣教的挑戰，並回應台福「台灣宣教」的異象，我們夫婦在2001年親自帶領一群一點五代的青年回台短宣，開設「美語營」，往後由愛恩台福教會的莊澤豐牧師主領，就這樣走上「回台宣教」之路。

感謝神，祂為我們開了一扇奇妙的門。由於當時台灣政府正大力推行學童學英語，使年輕的一點五代有機會進入國中、國小教英文，並傳講福音。他們藉著道具與演啞劇，解說神的創造與人的罪，讓觀眾體會神的愛，我們夫婦則以醫生的身份，隨隊在全台各地舉辦健康講座。結果參與宣教回來的人，不論老少（最高齡者八十二歲，最年幼者只有六歲）皆靈命更新。每個人都能見證神的奇妙作為，因此事奉的心益加謙卑堅定。

2002年，神奇妙地安排我們接待「基層福音差傳會」的秘書長陳士廷牧師，開啟我們對台宣教的另一扇門。2004年，「工業福音團契」總幹事蔡國山牧師訪美，分享勞工福音事工。隔年，客家宣教神學院溫永生院長亦訪美，傳遞客家福音倍增運動。因此，我們的宣教從台灣南部沿海的鄉村伸展到北部的客家庄，甚至「翻山越嶺」到宜蘭、台東、花蓮的原住民部落。

因著醫療講座，我們也與「路加傳道會」同工，走遍全臺灣，甚至遠走至金門。2006年，愛恩教會莊澤豐牧師和詩班指揮黃長老也帶領詩班團，走遍台灣監獄，聖靈大大作工，使獄犯紛紛舉手決志。近年來，我們看見在美國的台福教會、靈糧堂、浸信會、長老教會等都紛紛投入回台宣教，甚至澳洲、紐西蘭的教會也利用南半球的暑假，回台和台灣的小朋友們一起慶祝聖誕，使「回台短宣」的聲勢大為壯大。

2007年，我們更欣見神感動了美國東岸的楊宜宜牧師，讓她在紐約成立了超教派的「台灣宣教基金會」，而張玉明牧師則在美國西岸的北美靈糧堂繼續推動對台宣教。有感於八年來回台短宣隊的腳蹤何其佳美，我們在2008年將它匯集成書，出版了《福音天軍降寶島》。

福音確能改變人心。只要投入更多的愛心與時間，在福音保守的鄉鎮，口嚼檳榔的阿公、賣菜的歐巴桑、討海的捕魚人、穿制服的學生，都願意接受福音。上帝必使臺灣這塊島嶼蒙福。

我們的回台短宣，正如保羅（羅馬書9：2-3）的心境，為我骨肉之親，我心也憂愁也傷痛----，重重的負擔---。求主賜福台灣！

Taiwan Mission

Dr. Howshan Lin & Mrs. Eunice Lin
Former Board Member of Luke Medical Mission in North America
North American Liaison Officer of
Village Gospel Mission & Taiwan Grass-Roots Mission

In the winter of 1989, my wife and I went from New York City to Washington DC to attend the Chinese Mission Convention held by Ambassadors for Christ. After attending the workshop of Taiwan Village Gospel Mission (VGM) given by Rev. Timothy Chen, we realized that our home country Taiwan still has a lot of room for the Gospel. Even though Taiwanese was not Rev. Chen's native dialect, he learned it in market places in order to serve the locals. VGM was founded by China Inland Missionaries Rev. and Mrs. Richard Webster as a result of their fervent prayers while riding their bicycles around villages. By contrast, as Taiwanese Christians, we were so ignorant about the mission work happening in Taiwan. For three nights, we wept and prayed for the mission in Taiwan.

After the conference, my wife and I unabashedly introduced ourselves and requested opportunities to share our vision for Taiwan evangelism at different churches. We made posters and flyers and visited small groups, Sunday schools and church retreats in nearby cities throughout the Greater New York area to share the needs of the Gospel movement in rural Taiwan. We also invited VGM coworkers to come to the United States to share their testimonies. Their spiritual battles as well as their commitment to villagers moved and awakened many in North America. Accordingly, we established a North American board to help spread the vision of VGM in North America (with Elder Dhi-Cheng Wu in New Jersey, Brother Chen Hsu in Washington D.C., Elder Chris Chen in Northern California).

In 1995, we founded the Greater New York Medical Mission Fellowship with Elder Chin-Yang Tsai and Dr. Amy H. Kuo to offer free health clinic for Taiwan ese/Chinese people in New York. Around the same time, Rev. John Chang of Staten Island Grace Christian Church, the church to which we belonged, started taking young people to Taiwan for short-term English mission camps. We moved to Southern California in 1997 to be closer to our grandchildren and joined Evangelical Formosan Church (EFC). California had a large number of "1.5 generation" teenagers from Taiwan. In response to the Taiwanese mission started in New York and the "Taiwan Mission" vision of EFC, we led a short-term mission team of the "1.5 generation" Taiwanese-Americans to Taiwan in 2001 to teach at English camps. Eventually, Rev. Tse-Feng Chuang from EFC Irvine took over the leadership of this mission.

Thanks be to God, an amazing door was opened at the same time. The Taiwanese government started heavily promoting English language education. As a result the 1.5 generation mission team members were easily able to enter the elementary, middle, and high schools to teach English. They shared God's love and the Gospel through dramas and other venues to illustrate God's creation and the fall of mankind. We as medical professionals offered health-related workshops. Many of those who participated in the mission, from ages 6 to 82, all felt spiritually revived. They all shared testimonies of how God worked in their lives, and their determination to serve was strengthened.

In 2002, God brought us a special guest, Rev. Shi-Ting Chen, the general secretary of Taiwan Grass-Roots Mission. In 2004, we met Rev. Kuo-Shan Tsai, the general secretary of Taiwan Industrial Evangelical Fellowship, when he came to the U.S. to share the ministry with manufacturing laborers in Taiwan. The next year, Rev. Peter Yung-Sheng Wen, Dean of Christian Hakka Seminary, came to share the "Gospel Multiplication Movement" among the Hakkas. As part of this Movement, our Taiwan mission was extended from Southern Taiwan to Northern Taiwan, Hakka villages, and over the mountain to Yi-Lan, Tai-Tong, as well as the aboriginals in Hualein. We also collaborated with Chinese Christian Medical Mission sponsoring workshops in many places, even Kinmen. In 2006, Rev. Chuang and Elder Huang from EFC Irvine also led a choir to visit prisons in Taiwan. Through the work of the Spirit, many prisoners decided to accept Christ.

In recent years, EFC, the Bread of Life Church, Baptist Church and Presbyterian Church have all participated in Taiwan mission. Even churches in Australia and New Zealand have gone to Taiwan to celebrate Christmas with Taiwanese children. The number of people going to Taiwan for short-term missions has increased so much.

In 2007, God moved Rev. Eileen Yi-Yi Chang to establish an inter-denominational organization, Taiwan Mission Foundation, on the east coast. Rev. Joseph Chang from the Bread of Life Church continues to lead Taiwan mission on the west coast. We have been so touched by all the efforts of missions to Taiwan in the past eight years; therefore, we published a book <u>Heavenly Messengers Descend upon Formosa</u> in 2008.

There is no doubt that the Gospel can change people's lives. With the outpouring of love and time, even in the reserved rural Taiwan, the betel nut chewing gentlemen, the peddling women, fishermen, students in uniforms all will be won by the Gospel. God's blessings will shower over the island of Taiwan. Our short-term mission efforts in Taiwan reflect what Paul says in Romans 9:2-3 "I have great sorrow and unceasing anguish … for the sake of my own people, my kindred…" May God bless Taiwan!

2007作者林華山醫師/ 劉碧珠夫婦在嘉義縣六腳鄉蒜頭村廟口的健康講座
Health forum at the temple yard in Suantou, Chiayi

宣教的態度與抉擇
The Attitude and Choices about Taiwan Mission

蔡國山牧師
台灣工業福音團契總幹事
Rev. Kuo-Shan Tsai
General Secretary of Taiwan Industrial Evangelical Fellowship

宣教的態度與抉擇

蔡國山牧師
台灣工業福音團契總幹事

談起台灣的宣教，許多教會幾乎都把注意力放在教會人數的增長、教會數量的增加、以及建堂的花費與規模等等。這些正反應今日教會流行的宣教觀。

我們必須回歸聖經，藉著耶穌的教訓與榜樣、同時通過教會的歷史與見證，以建立正確的宣教態度，並作出正確的思維判斷與抉擇。

一、釐清正確的宣教目標

聖經的宣教目標是要實現上帝對萬民的救恩計劃及上帝永恆的國度。根據舊約《創世記》，上帝在人類墮落之後，宣告祂對人類的救恩計劃，並且藉著「女人的後裔」，預言耶穌基督十字架的救恩。到了《出埃及記》，上帝要以色列人作上帝國度的新百姓。

到了新約時代，上帝親自差遣愛子耶穌基督到世上，來實現上帝對萬民的救恩計劃。上帝的國度，也從以色列家擴展到萬民中。耶穌一方面傳佈上帝國的福音，醫治各樣的病症，另方面造就門徒。當時法利賽人的宣教是到處拉人入教，增加教派人數。耶穌則要人作祂的門徒和上帝國的新百姓。因此，台灣宣教務必以上帝的國度為念，不要落入數字的迷惑，一味追求人數的增長。

二、信守正確的宣教角色：

過去三十多年，不少基督教的宣教方式已逐漸演變成「以人為主導」的運動。但我們發現不論是早期聖經中的宣教史、日後聖法蘭西斯時代的宣教運動、莫拉維教會的普世宣教、十九世紀英國的亞非洲宣教、二十世紀美國的宣教運動、甚至近代中國大陸家庭教會的復興，都是由「上帝」展開並主導宣教。使徒保羅亦將自己的宣教定位為蒙主呼召，表明他完全是領受天上來的異象與使命。

至於台灣宣教，不論是撒種、收割、栽種或澆灌，主的工人都不應逃避或誇口。惟有忠於主所託付的宣教角色，才能完成今日台灣宣教的使命！

三、傳揚正確的宣教信息

耶穌要人奉祂的名傳「悔改赦罪之道」，從耶路撒冷到萬邦（路加福音 24：47）。綜觀今日教會盛行的宣教信息，主要偏重在滿足人現實的需要，如強調「病得醫治」、「神蹟奇事」、「成功見證」等。但耶穌到世上宣教的第一句話則是：「日期滿了，神的國近了。你們當悔改、信福音！」（馬可福音1：15）而且在最後升天前，也命令門徒要傳「悔改赦罪之道」，即「基督十字架的福音」，讓人能真正得到釋放與自由(哥林多前書2：2）。

早期的使徒不但親身經歷福音的大能，也放膽傳這大能的福音。許多教會史上忠心的宣教士包括威廉克理、約翰衛斯理、戴德生、馬偕、巴克禮、宋尚節等等，也都奉主的名勸人悔改、信福音！因此，今日談台灣宣教，絕不可忽略所傳的信息及見證人。

四、學習正確的宣教態度

今日宣教的潮流也較忽略約翰福音的真理。《約翰福音》第一章強調耶穌「道成肉身」，住在我們中間。 耶穌自始至終強調祂是父所差來的，是從天上降到人世中成為卑微的奴僕。這種道成肉身的宣教態度，顛覆了今日瀰漫的世俗宣教心態，包括羨慕成為有名的傳道人。

耶穌也一再提醒門徒，務必效法祂受差遣的榜樣，「父怎樣差遣了我，我也照樣差遣你們」（約翰福音20:21）。

今日面對台灣的宣教，除了關心宣教的能力、事工與策略，更重要是要檢視我「這個人」，是否願意像一粒麥子，效法「道成肉身」的基督，降卑捨己順服到底。惟有更多的麥子落地而死，才能結出更多的種子，讓台灣這塊宣教的禾場開滿美麗的宣教花朵！真誠盼望台灣宣教能經歷上帝的復興與拯救的作為！

The Attitude and Choices about Taiwan Mission

Rev. Kuo-Shan Tsai
General Secretary of Taiwan Industrial Evangelical Fellowship

Today as we discuss Taiwan Missions, many Christians are concentrating on the growth of membership and the number of Taiwanese churches, and the cost of building church facilities. These reflect the importance of mission won in Taiwan.

We should go back to the Bible. Through Jesus' teaching and model, as well as the history and testimonies in church history, we can establish the correct attitude for mission and make correct judgments and choices accordingly.

1. To keep the biblical objectives in mission-

The goal for mission according to the Bible is to fulfill the plan of God's salvation and establish His kingdom. In Genesis, after man's fall, God reveals His plan of salvation and uses "the woman's descendent" to prophesy "salvation through Jesus being nailed on the cross." In Exodus, God makes the Israelites His chosen people.

In New Testament times, He sent His beloved Son, Jesus, to the world to carry out God's plan of salvation for the world; to extend the kingdom of God from the Israelite people to all people. Jesus preached the gospels and healed many sick people. At the same time, He taught his disciples. While the Pharisees were busy recruiting people to increase their numbers, Jesus wanted people to follow Him and be His disciples and citizens of God's Kingdom.

2. To play the correct role in mission-

In the past 30 years, many Christian mission movements have changed to be "led by man solely." However, we will find from the mission teaching in the

Bible, the Franciscan-era missionary movement, the Moravian Church's universal mission, the nineteenth-century British mission in Asia and on Africa mainland coasts, the twentieth-century American missionary movement, or even the China house church revival in the 1970's, that God leads missions Himself. Paul was very sure that God's calling for him was in missions; he received the vision and obeyed God's calling to accomplish the mission.

As for the mission in Taiwan, whether it is seeding, harvesting, planting, or watering, we worked as God's servants and there is nothing to brag about. We must be faithful to God's calling for our roles in mission so that we can accomplish today's mission.

3. To preach the correct message in mission-

Jesus wanted us to preach "the message of repentance and forgiveness of sin" in His name, from Jerusalem to all nations (Luke 24:47).

The message given in today's church often emphasizes satisfying the needs of materialism or earthly success. For instance, healing from sickness, miracles and wonders were a testimony of earthly success. However, the first message that Jesus told the world was, "The time has come. The kingdom of God is near. Repent and believe the good news!" (Mark 1:15). Also, before He went back to the Heaven, He commanded His disciples to share "the message of repentance and forgiveness." That's the "Gospel of the Cross" that can truly set people free.

Early disciples not only witnessed the power of "the message of repentance and forgiveness," they were also empowered to preach boldly. Reflecting on church history, a lot of faithful missionaries, such as William Carey, John Wesley, Hudson Taylor, George Leslie Mackay, Thomas Barclay, and John Sung Shang Chieh all preached "the message of repentance and forgiveness of sins." Therefore, the success or failure of missions in Taiwan depends on the message we preach and on our being witnesses for the Lord.

4. To learn the correct attitude in mission-

Today, the trend of missions neglects the truth in the gospel of John regarding missions. According to the first chapter in the Book of John, "The Word became flesh and made His dwelling among us." Jesus emphasized that He was sent by the Father; He was willing to humble Himself descending from heaven and taking for Himself in the nature of a servant. This kind of missionary attitude is quite opposite to the popular mission attitude today. Many admire and envy the famous preachers.

Jesus reminded His disciples over and over again to follow His model of being sent, "…As the Father has sent me, I am sending you." (John 20:21).

As we face the mission in Taiwan nowadays, we not only care about the capability, work and strategy of the mission, we especially need to evaluate ourselves: Are we willing to become like a kernel of wheat that falls to the ground in the same way that Jesus was the Word who became flesh and made Himself nothing? Only when many seeds die, will there be more seeds growing up to make the mission field of Taiwan filled with beautiful mission blossoms. We sincerely hope that the mission in Taiwan can experience God's revival and His almighty power.

作者蔡國山牧師
Author Rev. Kuo Shan Tsai

台灣外勞長宣

Foreign Labor Long-term Mission

陳玉春
國際差傳協會 (加拿大) 宣教師
Rita Chen
Missionary of SEND International of Canada

台灣外勞長宣

陳玉春
國際差傳協會(加拿大)宣教師

我居住加拿大，迄今近四十年。1972年基於求學順利、工作穩定，又得到不少基督徒的關心，乃於復活節受洗。此後我熱心參與事奉，也常邀請一些台灣來的青少年學生到家裡用餐，盼能播下福音的種子。

神同時讓我在職場上常跟同事一起午餐靈修。這些年，共有三位同事因獻身當牧師而離職。看到這些高職高薪的朋友為福音捨棄世上的榮華，令我產生不少省思，也開始到神學院修課，裝備自己，盼為主所用。

2005年夏天，我帶領五位大學生到中國青海短宣。2006年，我開始關心台灣外籍勞工的配偶，覺得這些離鄉背井的台灣新移民需要關愛，是個福音的新禾場。因為神的呼召，我也毅然辭職，踏上台灣宣教之途。

久居國外，回台難免需要調適，有時甚至感到挫折。然而上帝的恩典夠用，祂差我跟潭子工業福音陳淑英傳道配搭服事，在外勞福音中心傳播福音，領受許多奇妙的經驗。

外籍事工自關懷、探訪、傾聽心聲，到解決工作、勞資、法律、婚姻等問題，可說包羅萬象。我們幸運得到國外短宣隊的協助，使福音的觸角延伸到外勞工廠、宿舍、監獄、移民局、拘留所等地方。我們也舉辦一些節慶活動與郊遊，譬如：中秋節烤肉、新竹綠世界之遊、情人谷農場餐敘等等。有一次，在「粽子飄香」的端午節餐會中，我們詢問來參加的越南、印尼、菲律賓⋯等五十多名外籍勞工：我們能為他們做什麼？多數人答以他們盼望學中文。所以會後，我們著手開辦中文會話班。剛開始，來的人並不多，但感謝主，祂讓一位佳能電子廠的越勞阿旺興起了渴慕的心。

阿旺很用心地學習一對一陪讀的「基要真理」，漸漸敞開心懷，接受救恩，同時成為宣教的好幫手。他常常帶短宣隊的同工到工廠的宿舍探訪，並廣邀同事與朋友參加中文班及節慶活動。

此外，有一位越南新娘也透過一對一的陪讀，慢慢經歷 神的愛。她信主後，參與服事，特別在我視網膜開刀期間，主動擔任中文班老師。她因與學生們的母語相通，所以很能吸引越勞來上課，使學生一度多達五十人。可惜2008年許多外勞因金融海嘯被遣返，人數就起伏不定。幸好她不灰心，繼續用心帶學生，還為他們煮好吃的越南點心。

2009年九月，我返加拿大工作。待再度回台後，主又開啟福音之門，經由吳啟民醫師的幫助，使我們得以每週一次地到外勞配偶就讀的國小教導外籍配偶有關婦女保健、親子關係、夫妻相處之道等課程。

我們也邀請這些外籍配偶與他們的家人一起參加每月一次的福音茶會，目前的人數正在慢慢增加中。我們期盼福音的種子能蒙神澆灌，早日在他們之間萌芽、成長。

上帝實在是一個良善、慈愛、又看顧卑微人的神(詩篇136：1、23)。祂透過工福，使許多異國朋友聽到福音，並且把福音帶回母國。我們所做的著實有限，但神能使五餅二魚的服事餵飽許多失喪的靈魂。

Foreign Labor Long-term Mission

Rita Chen
Missionary of SEND International of Canada

I lived in Canada for almost 40 years: first to study, then to work. My life in Canada went well and I received much support from Christians along the way. I was baptized on Thanksgiving of 1972 and have been actively serving others enthusiastically since then. Often I have invited international students from Taiwan for meals, hoping that they might receive the gospel.

In the workplace, God led me to gather with a few colleagues for lunch and devotion time. Three of them later quit their jobs and became ministers. They inspired me to change my life direction, too, since they all gave up their lucrative jobs for the sake of the Gospel. Therefore, I also went to seminary to take classes to prepare myself for the Lord.

In the summer of 2005, I led a short term mission team with five college students to Ching-Hi, China. In 2006, I was called to minister to the spouses of foreign workers in Taiwan. They left their homes to immigrate to Taiwan for work, and they need much love and care. It is a new field of harvest for the Gospel. Obedient to God's calling, I left my job and started my mission in Taiwan.

It took a lot to get used to life in Taiwan after living overseas for a long time. It could be frustrating sometimes. However, God's grace is sufficient. He sent me to work with Missionary Phoebe Su-Yin Chen in the Tanzu Industrial Mission. I had a wonderful experience working in the mission.

The missionary work includes visitation, listening and helping resolve problems with jobs, wages, laws, marriage, etc. I have found that, with assistance from short-term mission teams from overseas, the gospel can reach out to where foreign workers are: factories, dorms, prisons, immigration service, and detention centers.

To accomplish this, we hosted many activities in the Gospel Center during special seasons: a BBQ for the mid-autumn festival, Green World trip in Sing-chu, a picnic in Valentine's Valley Farm. One time during the Dragon Boat Festival, more than 50 people from Vietnam, Indonesia, the Philippines and other countries joined us. Often when we asked what we could do for them, their answer was, "Help us to study Chinese," so we started a Chinese conversation class. Few people came in the beginning, but that changed when the Lord gave us Awang, a Vietnam worker who had moved to the Chi-non Factory.

We thank the Lord greatly for him! After walking through a one-on-one study of "Basic Truth" with him, he opened his heart to accept the Lord and became an excellent helper in the mission. He often took short-term mission workers to the factory dorm for visits. He also invited colleagues and friends to participate in Chinese classes and special outreach activities.

A Vietnamese bride also accepted the Lord and is helping to serve in the mission after experiencing God's love through one-on-one Bible study. She even volunteered to be the teacher for our Chinese class when I had my retinal surgery. Because she speaks the students' language, she was able to attract many Vietnamese workers to classes. For a while attendance exceeded 50 people. But in 2008, due to the financial tsunami, many foreign workers were forced to go back to their countries or change jobs. Therefore, the number of students in class began to fluctuate. She was not discouraged but continued to reach out to her students, even cooking delicious Vietnamese food for them.

In September of 2009, I came back to Taiwan after reporting to my mission organization in Canada. God again opened the door for the mission- we were able to enter into the school that foreign spouses attended. With family doctor Wu Chi-Ming's help, we were able to teach them about parent-child relationships, marital relationships, healthcare for women, etc…

We also invited these women and their families to attend our monthly tea gospel party. The number of attendants is gradually increasing. May God make these gospel seeds grow!

God is good. His love endures forever… (He) remembered us in our low estate (Psalm 136:1, 23). He brings the gospel to many foreign friends through Industrial Gospel Mission; they then bring the gospel back to their home countries. What we can do is very limited, but through "our five loaves of bread and two fish", He feeds so many foreign lost souls. Amen!

尚待耕耘的台灣客家教會
Ongoing Work for Hakka Mission in Taiwan

曾政忠牧師
客家福音協會前總幹事
Rev. John Cheng-Chung Tseng
Former President of Christian Hakka Evangelical Association

尚待耕耘的台灣客家教會

曾政忠牧師
客家福音協會前總幹事

有人問：「為什麼台灣的客家教會長期處在弱勢中？」這是因為派入客家的精兵少，正如一畝地，倘若缺少耕種的好工人，收成自然少。

福音進入台灣已有一百四十多年的歷史，台灣最近一波的福音宣教運動是從AD.1865年開始。但在最初的一百年，幾乎沒有會講客家話的宣教師到客家庄傳教。客家人信主，如同「沾醬油」，僅沾到一點，全靠神的憐憫。目前台灣約有一百間客家教會，大多數教會的聚會人數約在三十至五十人。2012年九月論壇報朱三才牧師的報導，台灣基督徒的人口比率為5.44％。而客家的統計，在2011年客家宣教神學院的溫永生院長報告僅0.4％，還不到基督徒的1/10。我們怎能坐視這樣的情況繼續下去？直到三十餘年前，一群關心台灣客家宣教荒涼景況的牧長同工成立了「客家福音協會」，向全球客家教會呼籲，此後方有近百名宣教師陸陸續續地來，目前尚有二十餘位留在客家庄服事。

1.早期向客家人宣教事工的忽略：
客家人在台灣是弱勢，約五分之一的人口。宣教的前九十年，沒有一位海外宣教師學客語。過去在客家庄宣教，就是有客家人歸主，要讀聖經靈修，也需學會台語及羅馬拼音白話字，要通過兩道關口。感謝神！ 2012年4月客語聖經翻譯出版，客語聖詩陸續出版。客家宣教神學院成立於2000年於新竹縣竹東鎮，2005年發動十年倍加運動。期盼許多台/華教會能積極響應組織短宣隊到客庄：
- 或做全職宣教師
- 或在教會成立客家小組
- 成立客家團契
- 多多向客家人傳福音

2.究其原因：傳統喪葬禮儀和祭祖帶來很大的攔阻，在客家人中特別嚴重。2010年桃園新屋鄉葉姓家族祭祖約6-7000人。為解決這個問題，1991年出版基督徒喪禮手冊，2010年出版基督徒喪禮與敬祖手冊。

3.基督教在台灣/客家社會中的認同度不高？

基督教＝洋教
客家傳統的喪葬禮儀和祭祖成了惡者的營壘—讓基督教冠上了「不忠、不孝」的惡名。 台灣人及客家人把孝，推到死後的葬禮和祭拜。但是，基督信仰則認為，人死，靈魂歸天，安息主懷，等候末日的復活與審判。靈魂不存在於地上人間，自然沒有祭拜禮儀，外國宣教士來台面對客家/台灣人的祭祖文化，直認為是偶像崇拜而大加反對，可惜沒有深入的瞭解並提出合理的回應。以致傳統宗教中的華人，以為基督教是「不忠、不孝」的宗教。

4.祭祖問題是宣教者必要面對的課題與省思。申命記34:8 以色列人在摩押平原為摩西哀哭了三十日，為摩西居喪哀哭的日子就滿了。路加福音3:38該南是以挪士的兒子，以挪士是塞特的兒子，塞特是亞當的兒子，亞當是上帝的兒子。基督教應有合真理、合民情的對策。一方面要傳講真理，破除錯誤的敬拜。一方面要有合真理，合民情的紀念禮儀。

5.目前我們提出「追思三禮」、「致敬禮」和「祖先紀念表」來取代傳統的喪葬儀式和祖先牌位

A.追思三禮
    a. 倒水禮--（意指飲水思源）—由長輩行禮
    b. 獻花禮--（意指祖德流芳）—由中年人行禮
    c. 點燭禮--（意指光宗耀祖）—由少年人行禮

B.致敬禮
我們以捻花行禮來代替捻香，我們以尊敬人的方式來紀念尊重先人。

C. 祖先紀念表

二十年前，台灣客家福音協會，提出了更新喪禮和敬祖的儀式。至今，許多不是全家歸主的基督徒家庭，多能接受。許多參加過的非基督徒也蠻能認同，認為基督徒的紀念祖先方式雖不太一樣，但簡單隆重，很有意義，很能安慰遺

族。每年清明節前的週末，我們舉行教會全體對先人的敬祖感恩禮拜。漸漸的破除了「不要祖先」、「不孝」的謊言。但願客家/台灣人在惡者營壘被攻破之後，可以更積極的傳福音，帶下新一波客家/台灣人歸主的浪潮，教會得以大大復興。

「客家福音協會」的同工們在2005年發起「台灣客家教會十年倍加運動」，期盼客家教會在這十年間，藉神的憐憫與眾教會同工的禱告、支持，很快地加倍成長。各教派也開始注意到客家宣教的需要，紛紛在客庄拓植。這些年，台灣開始重視客家。政府機構設立了客家委員會，客家電視台相繼成立，學校也開始教授客語，客家菜更處處流行。2000年，教會設立客家宣教神學院，台灣基督長老教會成立客家中會，顯示神正在台灣的客家做大事。

感謝神！五年來，已多成立了五間以客家人為主要宣教對象的教會，並有六家都市教會開創客語崇拜。2008年，「客福」成立聖樂團，並出版新的客語詩歌和CD。台灣聖經公會也預定於2011年出版客語新舊約聖經。

客家宣教工作正興起新的一波浪潮，願眾教會一起來代禱。我們祈求莊稼的主，打發工人來收割，並希望有更多主的精兵受召前來一起奮鬥，使台灣客家能快快建立差傳的教會，和眾教會一起負起向普世宣教的使命。願主的國度早日降臨！

1. 敬祖禮拜—追思三禮
Service to honor the ancestors -Three Memorial Services

2. 倒水禮--意指飲水思源—由長輩行禮
The elder of the family to perform the service of water pouring

尚待耕耘的台灣客家教會

3. 獻花禮--意指祖德流芳—由中年人行禮
An adult to perform the service of flower presentation

4. 行禮後讀啟應文
Response reading after the service of flower presentation

5. 點燭禮--意指光宗耀祖—由少年人禮
A young family member to perform the service of candle lighting

6. 追思心語
Words of Remembrance

尚待耕耘的台灣客家教會

7. 我們以捻花行禮來代替捻香，
我們以尊敬人的方式來紀念尊重先人。
We use flowers presentation to replace burning of incense. We pay our respect to deceased human being the way human being deserved to be respected.

8. 祖先紀念表
Record of Ancestry

9. 祖先紀念表
Record of Ancestry

曾政忠牧師
客家福音協會前總幹事
Rev.John Cheng-Chung Tseng Former President of Christian Hakka Evangelical Association

Ongoing Work for Hakka Mission in Taiwan

Rev. John Cheng-Chung Tseng
Former President of Christian Hakka Evangelical Association

Some asked "Why is the Hakka Church in Taiwan so weak?" Simply put, there are not enough soldiers of the Lord fighting for it. If you don't have good farmers to work on the land then the crop will be scarce.

The Gospel has been spread in Taiwan for over 140 years. The most recent wave of evangelical missions to Taiwan started in 1865 AD. However during the first 100 years there were very few missionaries who could speak the Hakka dialect. Just like dipping the soy sauce, Hakka people dipped into the Gospel because of God's mercy. There are about 100 Hakka churches in Taiwan right now, and the average atten dance at most Hakka churches is around 30 to 50 people. In September of 2012, Rev. Zhu San Cai reported in Christian Tribute that 5.44% of Taiwan's population is Christian. In contrast, Dean Yong Sheng Wen of Christian Hakka Seminary reported in a 2011 study that only 0.4% of the Hakka population is Christian, less than 1/10. It cannot continue like this.

A group of concerned ministry workers in Taiwan established the Hakka Evangelism Association 31 years ago and invited Hakka churches around the world to send missionaries to Taiwan. There were about 100 missionaries who came through this call and now there are about 20 left.

1. Oversight of the early mission to Hakka community:
Hakka people are a minority in Taiwan, consisting of only about one-fifth of the population. In the past, even if some Hakka people became believers and wanted to read the Bible, they would first need to overcome two obstacles: to learn Taiwanese and the Roman Phonetic. In the first 90 years of mission, not a single foreign missionary learned the Hakka language.

Praise the Lord! Publication of The Hakka Bible and Hakka Hymns were published in April of 2012.

The Christian Hakka Seminary was established in Zhudong of Hsinchu County in the year 2000, and in 2005 started a movement to double the number of Hakka Christians in 10 years. We hope the Taiwanese/Chinese churches actively support the movement by:

1.   organizing short-term missions to Hakka villages
2.   becoming full time ministers or
3.   establishing Hakka fellowships in church

2. Traditional funeral services and ancestor worship is an obstacle to mission; this is especially problematic in the Hakka community. In 2010 roughly 6000-7000 members of the Yeh Clan worshipped their ancestors in Xinwu of Taoyuan. To solve this problem, we have published the Handbook of Christian Funeral Service in 1991 and Handbook of Christian Funeral Service & Honoring Ancestor in 2010.

3. Why does Taiwanese/Hakka community have low acceptance of Christianity?
- Christianity = Foreign Religion

Traditional Chinese funeral service and ancestor worship became the base of the evil one. The Christian faith is seen as a religion that teaches disloyalty and disrepsect toward parents. Taiwanese and Hakka extend respect for the parents beyond death in the form of burial service and worshipping of the deceased. In contrast, Christians believe that when one dies, the soul goes to heaven and rests with God to await the resurrection and Jjudgment of the end times. Souls do not exist on earth, naturally there is no ancestor worshipping.

When the missionaries encountered the Taiwanese and Hakka culture of ancestor worship, they saw it as idol worship and strongly opposed it. Unfortunately, they did not truly comprehend it nor provide a reasonable alternative. Therefore, Chinese that grew up in traditional culture perceived Christianity as a religion which is "disloyal" and "disrespectful" of the parents.

4. Ancestor worship is an issue that earnest missionaries need to face and give serious consideration. In Deuteronomy 34:8, the Israelites grieved for Moses in the plains of Moab thirty days, until the time of weeping and mourning was over. In Luke 3:38, it was noted that Kenan was "the son of Enosh, the son of Seth, the son of Adam, the son of God. Christians should have a strategy that is befitting with the Biblical truth and human compassion. One one hand we need to teach biblical truth and teach against incorrect forms of worship. On the other hand, we need memorial services that are consistent with both biblical truth and Chinese culture.

5. Currently we propose "Three Memorial Services", "Service to Show Respect" "Record of Ancestry", to replace traditional funeral services and ancestor worship.

A. Three Memorial Services
    a. The service of water pouring- The elder of the family to perform the service of water pouring.
    b. The service of flower presentation- An adult to perform the service of flower presentation.
    c. The service of candle lighting- A young family member to perform the serice of candle lighting.

B. Service to show respect
We use flowers presentation to replace burning of incense. We pay our respect to deceased human beings the way human being deserve to be respected.

C. Record of Ancestry

Twenty years ago, Taiwan Christian Hakka Evangelical Association proposed a new funeral service and memorial service for ancestors. Today, many families , in which not all members are Christians, accept implementing these funeral service and memorial service. A number of non-Christians that have participated in these ceremonies also accept it, they recognize that although these practices are different, it is simple yet serene and it provides comfort to the surviving family members. Every year, the weekend before the Chin Ming Festival, our entire church conduct services to honor the ancestor or worships dedicated to thanking and honoring the ancestors. Gradually we are dispelling the lies that Christians "abandon the ancestors" and "be disrespectful to parents." It is our hope that after the base of the Evil one are overcome, Chinese Christians can spread the gospel more actively and earnestly, to bring about the next wave of Chinese to believe in Christ and the revival of the church.

In these past few years, there have been more awareness in Taiwan of Hakka people. The Government has set up a special Hakka commission, Hakka dialect is being taught in school, a Hakka TV station has been set up (even Hakka dishes are gaining popularity). In the year 2000, churches set up a Christian Hakka Seminary. The Presbyterian Church in Taiwan, the largest denomination, also set up a Hakka Presbytery. God is working in the Hakka community in Taiwan.

The members of the Hakka Evangelism Association started a movement in 2005 to double the number of Hakka churches in ten years (2005-2014). We pray that during these years, with the support and prayers of all churches involved, and under the mercy of God, that the Hakka churches will grow rapidly in number.

Praise the Lord! We have seen five newly established churches aimed at the Hakka community in the past five years. Six churches have added in Hakka dialect to their worship. A Worship Choir group started in 2008 and published a CD of new Hakka Hymns. The Taiwan Bible Society is aiming to publish Hakka Bibles in 2011.

Through intercession and support, waves of the Hakka mission movement continue. We pray for more warriors to join in the battle of spreading the Gospel and to send out more missionaries into the field to establish healthy and strong Hakka churches. May the Kingdom of God come in the near future!

來自台灣客家的呼聲
Call for Prayer from the Hakka People

蔡希晉
北美客家歸主禱告事工創辦人
大費城三一華人基督教會差傳委員會委員
Hsi Chin Tsai
Founder of Hakka for Christ Prayer Ministry
Mission Committee Member of Trinity Christian Church of Greater Philadelphia

來自台灣客家的呼聲

蔡希晉
北美客家歸主禱告事工創辦人
大費城三一華人基督教會差傳委員會委員

我是台灣客家人，出生在新竹縣竹東鎮，於1964年留學美國，1978年因患腸癌蒙神醫治，自此認識基督，接受耶穌作我個人的救主。

信主後，我每隔幾年便回台探訪親友，也向親人傳福音，可惜卻沒有人決志信主。我為此感到內疚，深覺愧對主與家人。

2007年初，我在《中信》雜誌上讀到「客家福音協會」的網址，欣然進入網站，但接著便被台灣只有0.3%的客家人信主的數字所震憾！台灣有四百萬的客家人，0.3%才不過一萬兩千人，連賓州州立大學的足球場都裝不滿。我不禁淚流滿面，彷彿聽到有個聲音說：「信主的客家人那麼少，你有什麼感受？」

我當時毫不猶豫地在內心回答：「倘若主接我回天家時，信主的客家人仍只有0.3%，我實在無顏以見上帝。」

同年十二月，「使者差傳大會」在費城召開。我因左眼視網膜脫落，剛動手術，無法前往。正準備在家靜養時，我們的組長一再邀請我參加大會，為大會禱告。感謝神，也感謝這位愛主的組長，使我再度聽到主對客家宣教的呼召。

在會中，神的僕人遠志明鼓勵大家到中國傳福音。他希望福音在中國傳開後，再傳至邊疆回族，繼而由邊疆回族傳至歷代拒絕福音的回教國家，然後傳回耶路撒冷。那時，主就要榮耀地再來！

當弟兄姊妹紛紛擁向主席台前，回應呼召時，我感到福音由中國傳回耶路撒冷的工作一定會成就。主就要來了，而且也會很快地到來。但同時，我更感到向客家人傳福音的機會已不多，於是碰碰坐在身旁的妻子，說：「我現在沒有離

座，走向主席台，因為那是回應向中國傳福音的呼召。我回應的地點不同，我要向台灣的客家人傳福音。」

向主回應後，我不知該如何走「下一步」，但「使者」為我們預備了「下一步」。 2008年五月，「下一步退修會」在「使者農莊」舉行。我在那次的退修會中，得到兩項重要的幫助：

一、下一步該怎麼作？
由於我對教會禱告聖工向來懷著使命，因此回應主的呼召後，我求問主：「我下一步該作甚麼？」

「禱告！在北美成立客家歸主禱告會。」

「主啊，我是什麼人？敢作這些事工？」

然後，在「下一步退修會」中，我與一位屬靈長輩提起這項使命。我說我不敢踏出第一步。他說他一向是個點火的人，還鼓勵我說：「先作點火的人，以後再讓主所興起的僕人或使女來接替你。」

我欣然同意。我知道自己的恩賜有限，但我可以作一個點火的人，如同巴拿巴把保羅引出來，我開始求神把客家人中的保羅引出來。

二、究竟何時該展開這項禱告事工？
我與另外四位參加「下一步」的弟兄姊妹分享我的關心。當他們知道我只要作一個「點火的人」後，馬上說：「今天就開始吧！」

感謝主，感謝「使者」與這四位有使命感的弟兄姊妹，「北美客家歸主禱告協會」於2008年5月17日晚正式成立。 上述四位弟兄姊妹於是成了禱告會的首批成員。禱告會成立的宗旨在激勵對客家福音有使命的北美洲客家基督徒，期待更多弟兄姐妹以禱告來支持台灣客家的福音工作。

自從禱告協會成立後，感謝神的恩典，「台灣基督客家協會」及時提供了禱告

的事項，使客家歸主的禱告信得以順利發出。迄今，我們已經寄出了十六封禱告信。然後，下一步究竟該如何走？我們目前尚不知道，也不敢自作主張。我們完全把它交在恩主手中，求祂引領。與此同時，我們也必須努力裝備自己。

主耶穌說：「我實實在在地告訴你們，我作的事，信我的人也要作，並且要作比這更大的事，因為我往父那裡去，你們奉我的名無論求什麼，我必成就，叫父因兒子得榮耀。」（約翰福音14:12-13）

讓我們一起奉耶穌基督得勝的名，恆切地禱告。使恩主在台灣客家人中行大事：「我們在天上的父！願客家人都尊祢的名為聖。願祢的國降臨，願祢的旨意行在客家人的地上，如同行在天上。阿門！」

（附記：若您對台灣客家宣教覺得有任務，請與 Hakkaforchrist@gmail.com 聯絡。 非常歡迎您加入為台灣客家人禱告的事工，願神賜福您！）

作者蔡希晉與夫人於2010使者差傳大會的下一步退修會訓練
Hsi Chin & Helen Tsai undergoing Next Step Training at the AFC 2010 Retreat

Call for Prayer from the Hakka People

Hsi Chin Tsai
Founder of Hakka for Christ Prayer Ministry
Mission Committee Member of Trinity Christian Church of Greater Philadelphia

I was born in Hsin Chu, Taiwan. I came to the United States in 1964 to further my studies. I was diagnosed with cancer in 1978, and because of the healing power of God, I came to know Christ Jesus and accepted Him as my Savior.

Since then, I have returned to Taiwan every few years to visit and share the Gospel with my relatives and friends, but I have not led anyone to God and I am deeply saddened by this.

How God got my attention about the Hakka Mission

In spring 2007, I read a missions journal article that brought tears to my eyes. The Hakka Chinese, an ethnic group in Taiwan and China, are largely unreached. Just 0.3% of Hakka in Taiwan are Christians– about 12,000 out of a population of four million. That does not even fill up the football field of Penn State University. I am a Hakka. God spoke to my heart. "How do you feel about the low number of Hakka Christians?"

I cried. "If I die and go to heaven, I will be ashamed if such a low number of my people know Christ."

In December 2007, because I had just undergone retinal detachment surgery, I decided not to participate in the AFC's Chinese Mission Convention (CMC) in Philadelphia. CMC's Logistics Team director, Brother Jack Hwang, nevertheless encouraged me to take part in CMC that year, and by God's grace, I did. During a plenary session, speaker Zhi Ming Yuan challenged participants to evangelize to the Chinese, particularly those who live along bordering Muslim countries. When the Gospel reaches the Muslim countries and comes around back to Jerusalem, that will be the moment of the second coming of Christ.

Many listeners stood up and committed themselves to that important work. I know the Gospel will spread from China back to Jerusalem in the near future. Yet the Hakka people burdened my soul. I turned to my wife. "My heart is telling me to go forward," I said. "My call is to the unreached Hakka people in Taiwan."

God confirmed my call at Next Step

After I made that commitment, I consulted with my pastor, my church missions committee, AFC's staff, and those connected with the Next Step program.

The Next Step retreat in May confirmed that call.
1. In the months that followed, I felt God leading me to start a prayer ministry in the U.S. for the Hakka people. "How, Lord?" During small group and one-on-one mentoring sessions at the retreat, I shared my burden. "I don't want to be the leader of this prayer ministry," I explained. "But I feel the need to get it started."

"You can light the fire and let others take over when it catches on," suggested one participant. I knew my limitation but I could ignite the small fire just like Barnabas brought out Paul. I prayed that God would bring out a "Paul" among the Hakka people.

2. When should I start this prayer mission?
I shared my burden with four other people at the retreat and said, "Why not

start tonight? " So on May 17, 2008, at AFC's Next Step retreat, four other Next Steppers joined me as charter members of the Hakka for Christ Prayer Association.

Our purpose is to encourage Hakka Christians in North America through prayer and to intercede for more Hakka people to know Christ. I send weekly prayer emails to the group, so far sixteen, with the group with the latest onsite information from the Christian Hakka Seminary and the Christian Hakka Evangelistic Association (CHEA).

What is our next step? We are not sure but we leave it to the guidance of our Lord and at the same time continue to equip ourselves.

"Very truly I tell you, whoever believes in me will do the works I have been doing, and they will do even greater things than these, because I am going to the Father. And I will do whatever you ask in my name, so that the Father may be glorified in the Son." (John 14:12-13)

Let us pray earnestly in the name of our Christ the Lord to work miraculously among the Hakka people: "Our Father in heaven, may all Hakka people glorify Your name. Thy kingdom come, Thy will be done among Hakka people as it is in Heaven. Amen."

(P.S. If you feel the call for Hakka people, please contact us at: Hakkaforchrist@gmail.com. We welcome you to be part of the prayer mission for the Hakka people in Taiwan. God Bless you.)

台灣客家短宣
Journey of Taiwan Hakka Mission

周志忠
波士頓西區聖經教會
George Chou
Boston Metro West Bible Church

台灣客家短宣

周志忠
波士頓西區聖經教會

我是波士頓西區聖經教會的會友，也是道地的客家人，到美國之前，一直在苗栗基督長老教會聚會。

承蒙林贊煜牧師的栽培，我擔任過不少教會的事工，也對客家福音一直懷著使命感。自2004年開始，我連續參與四年的台灣短宣，尤其在2006年與2007年時，與妻子玉娥及吳鴻銘執事、蔣永青姊妹兩度回苗栗宣教，見證了許多真實感人的事蹟。

以下是我們2007年六月回台短宣略記：
六月五日，我們到戒毒中心的「晨曦會」，關懷與鼓勵曾耽溺毒品的弟兄們。此行印象最深的是認識一位彈得一手好鋼琴、還擅長吉他與打擊樂器的斯文青年。他不幸受毒品危害，正期盼被主差使，我們殷切地為他禱告。感謝慈悲全能的天父垂聽，他終於在2008年擔任教會青少年組的吉他手，熱心服事主。

隔天，我們探訪由家扶中心支助的婦幼館，安慰曾受過家庭暴力或親人拋棄而誤入岐途的少女們。我們藉著動聽的詩歌與福音的真理，與她們分享信主耶穌的平安與喜樂。許多少女首次接觸到福音，才明白上帝原來如此愛她們。臨行前，有兩位少女決志信主。哈利路亞！

六月九日，我們到台中市平安堂教會宣揚福音。我分享見證，玉娥教剪紙手工，永青姊妹獻唱詩歌。當晚，一位數個月未到教會的姊妹聽到與她同樣來自中國的永青姊妹要獻詩，就來參加聚會，重回主的懷抱。

在台灣短宣兩星期後，我們參加妻妹聚會的台中市平和長老教會主日崇拜。我在前兩年都到此分享見證。感謝主的關愛，妻妹夫張國榮弟兄終於回到教會，在2008年聖誕節前受洗，並熱心輔導學童們的課後英文，甚至開放家庭，讓一

些孩子們在放學後到他家聚會。讚美主！

臨回美國前，有人對我們短宣隊的成效抱著懷疑的態度。我們也自問：只有四個人，真會有效果嗎？但主對我說：「我的恩典夠你用的， 因為我的能力是在人的軟弱上顯得完全。」(哥林多後書12：9)，而且「我們得幫助，是在乎倚靠造天地之耶和華的名。」 (詩篇124:8)

感謝主，讓我們全家大小得有機會回故鄉，投入台灣短宣，實地體驗「至於我和我家，我們必定事奉耶和華」(約書亞記24：15)」的真諦。

作者周志忠全家回母教會苗栗基督長老教會宣教(前左起：夫人玉娥， 長老陳瑪麗，後左起：兒恩福、恩賜，作者周志忠)
Author George Chou's family during Taiwan Missions trip in 2007 at hometown church-Maio Li TPC. From front left: wife Anna & Elder Mary Chen; from back left: John, Daniel & author George Chou

Journey of Taiwan Hakka Mission

George Chou
Boston Metro West Bible Church

I am a member of Boston Metro West Bible Church, and also a full blooded Hakka. I coordinated and served in numerous church activities under the training and care of Pastor Zanyu Lin. Before coming to the U.S., I attended Miaoli Christian Presbyterian Church in Taiwan. I always had a burden for spreading the gospel among the Hakka people. From 2004 until 2008, I participated in a few Taiwan short-term mission trips. In particular, in 2006 and 2007, my wife Anna and I, along with Deacon Jeremy Wu, and Sister Jiang Yongqing, returned to Miaoli. We witnessed many testimonies.

On June 5, 2007, we went to Operation Dawn Drug Rehabilitation Center to provide encouragement to those who had been abandoned by society, the convicted, those brothers and sisters controlled by their drug addictions, including one brother Sin Hong, a young man with a gentle demeanor who no one would ever suspect of being a drug addict. Not only did he play the piano and guitar beautifully, but he was also an outstanding drummer. He longed to be used by God one day. Thank God for answering our prayers.

In 2008, he began to serve in the youth ministry as a guitarist. On June 6, 2007, we visited the Taiwan Fund for Children and Families which supported the House of Women and Children, in order to comfort those young women who had experienced domestic violence, were abandoned by their loved ones, had lost direction in life, were emotionally wounded, or felt lonely and hopeless. Through wonderful hymns and the truth of the gospel, we were able to share with them the hope, peace, and joy that comes with Christ Jesus.

Many of the young women had never been exposed to the gospel, but now were able to learn how much God loves them. Before we left, two young women accepted Christ as their savior. On June 9, 2007, I went to the Peace Church in Taichung to provide testimony and sharing. Anna taught arts and crafts and Sister Yongqing sang hymns. The biggest reward that evening was being able to see one of the sisters from China, who had not attended church in several months, return to attend fellowship upon hearing that Sister Yongqing from China would be singing hymns. This lost sheep finally returned to the Lord's arms.

Two weeks later, we attended my sister-in-law's Sunday service at Peng-Ho Church in Taichung. For the past two years, I had been sharing my testimonies. After our honest and spirit-led conversations with our brother-in-law Chang Guorong, his life was transformed and he was willing to return to Christ and be baptized during Christmas of 2008. He even willingly opened his home to assist kids with English afterschool. Hallelujah!! Praise the Lord!!

Before we left for the short-term mission, people had cast their doubtful eyes on us. We even asked ourselves, "would such a small group of four people be able to provide an effective ministry?" In 2 Corinthians 12:9, the Lord said to me, "My grace is sufficient for you, for my power is made perfect in weakness." Also in Psalms 124:8, "Our help is in the name of the Lord, the Maker of heaven and earth." Thanks to the Lord for giving our whole family the opportunity to participate in a short-term mission to Taiwan and to be able to experience Joshua 24:15, "But as for me and my household, we will serve the Lord."

更生團契的事奉

Christian Born Anew Fellowship

黃明鎮牧師
台灣基督教更生團契總幹事
Rev. Ming Cheng Huang
General Secretary of Christian Born Anew Fellowship in Taiwan

更生團契的事奉

黃明鎮牧師
台灣基督教更生團契總幹事

1971年，我在擔任三年警官後，到美國深造。原想拿了學位，回台灣比較容易升遷。沒想到神的意旨高過人的意念，我在「犯罪制裁」研究所畢業後，即去讀神學院，然後在美國加州帶職事奉十幾年。1988年，我受神的差遣，攜家帶眷回台灣，此後全職事奉「更生團契」。

更生團契係由一位退休的典獄長陸國棟先生所創設。我因是他警察大學的學弟，便接續他的服事迄今。目前，我們的工作重點有三：

1. 犯罪預防
更生團契常到校園宣導菸酒毒害，並設立少年之家與少年學園，收容邊緣青少年。我們鼓勵他們讀書，也藉騎獨輪車操練他們的心性，同時引導他們經由每日讀經與禱告，脫離犯罪邊緣，成為社會上有用的人。

2. 犯罪矯正
更生團契到全台五十多個看守所，向監獄裡約六萬多人犯傳播福音，每年都帶領六、七百人受洗歸主。有些長期接受栽培，出獄後成為同工，回頭堅固其他的弟兄。

3. 犯罪被害人的關懷
台灣每年約有十萬刑事被害人，躲在陰暗角落哭泣。我們藉由關心，引領他們信主，並與加害人和解，實踐舉世推動的「修復式正義」的精神，既可消彌再犯，並能營造社會的和諧。

更生團契目前共有八十幾位同工與數百名志工。此外，北美短宣隊每年暑期都回來幫忙。我們的工作遍佈全台灣，歡迎各地有志之士隨時與我們搭配，一起投入這項搶救靈魂的事工。

更生團契的事奉

黃明鎮牧師基督教更生團契總幹事，成為台灣宣教基金會的顧問
Rev. Ming Cheng Huang of Christian Born Anew Fellowship in Taiwan is the TMF Advisor on Prison

作者更生團契黃明鎮牧師，正在高雄女子監獄勉勵受刑人
Author Rev. Ming Cheng Huang speaking to the inmates in Kohsiung Women's Prison

Christian Born Anew Fellowship

Rev. Ming Cheng Huang
General Secretary of Christian Born Anew Fellowship in Taiwan

I moved to the United States in 1971 for further study after being in the police force for three years. I thought a degree would improve my chances of getting a promotion. God's will is certainly greater than mine. Once I graduated from studying criminal justice, I went on to study theology and served in California as a tent-making pastor for more than 10 years. In 1988, I was called to go back to Taiwan with my family to serve full-time at Christian Born Anew Fellowship.

Christian Born Anew Fellowship was established by a retired Warden Mr. Kao Tong Lu. I was a fellow alumnus at a lower grade from the Police Academy and I have served as the organization's General Secretary until the present.

There are three key points of our work:

1. Crime Prevention – We go into schools to teach about the harm of alcohol and drugs. We set up Youth Home and Youth Academy to house those wandering around, encourage them to study, and use the exercise of the unicycle to train their minds. By leading them in Bible study and prayer, we hope they will be delivered from sinful temptation and become useful people in society.

2. Crime Correction – We share the Gospel with more than sixty thousand inmates at more than 50 prisons. Every year, there are six to seven hundred prisoners who are baptized and some of them go through more training, and eventually became our comrades after they are released, and help to strengthen others.

3.   Crime Victims Caring – There are more than 100,000 judicial victims hiding in the dark, suffering. Through the care of our community, they are led to know our Lord and reconcile with the ones who inflicted their pain. We work on the spirit of "Restorative Justice," minimizing recidivism and help to establish harmonized relationships among people.

Christian Born Anew Fellowship has about 80 co-workers and hundreds of volunteers. We also have many short-term mission groups from North America who come to help us in the summer. We welcome all sorts of help and involvement, long or short-term because our work is in every corner in Taiwan. Let's work together for the salvation of souls.

更生團契的少年學園事工 - 騎獨輪車的孩子不會變壞
Unicycling Ministry- Youth Home/Youth Academy of Christian Born Anew Fellowship

監獄宣道的感想

Reflections on Prison Ministry

黃清源
加州柑縣愛恩台福教會
Chinyuan Huang
Evangelical Formosan Church of Irvine in S. California

監獄宣道的感想

黃清源
加州柑縣愛恩台福教會

教會的林華山醫師夫婦向來非常熱心回台宣教的事工，每回見了我，就鼓勵我帶領詩班回台巡迴宣教，我卻屢次以各種理由搪塞。

然而到了2005年年底，詩班的幾位團員提及回台宣道的呼應，那年正好內人淑貞擔任詩班班長，也有同樣的感動，我覺得上帝的時辰到了，因此在年底詩班聚餐時，向所有團員提出這項構想。

由於來自聖靈的感動，詩班團員的報名很踴躍，接下來的過程也進行得非常順利。但要去什麼地方？向什麼人宣道？卻遲遲未定案。我與莊澤豐牧師起初計劃到台灣的安養院、孤兒院、晨曦會、戒毒中心、醫院及監獄等一些地方宣道，但聯絡了幾個地方，都沒有得到肯定的答覆。

2006年六月初，我回台南探親。在探望看西街教會的蔡長老夫婦時，長老娘知道我們有意回台宣教，便問我有沒有明確的目標。我說：「工場很多，但都無著落。我個人比較喜愛到監獄宣道。」蔡長老一聽，當場打電話給陳淑蘭老師。原來陳老師是「台南市監所收容人關懷協會」的會長，長期致力監獄輔導的事工，我們於是約好隔天見面。就這樣，我們展開了連續三年、走遍台灣所有監獄的福音事工。

上帝說：「我必在曠野開道路，在沙漠開江河。」(以賽亞書43:19)。誠然是個信實的真理。連續三年，我們都有超過四十位以上的團員參與，年齡從四歲到八十歲皆有。有時一天連趕三場，非常辛苦。有的團員甚至累到病倒，但大家都沒有怨言。我們都自費參加，上班的人還得請假。然而感謝主，參加的同工年年增多，其中竟有二十四位連續三年都參與，真令人感動。

為什麼參加的人如此熱烈呢？因為我們一次又一次地領受到監獄受刑人的破碎

心靈得到撫慰、饑渴心田得到滋養的奇妙經歷。印象最深的是桃園女子監獄的副典獄長在結束致詞時，感動得淚流滿面，久久說不出話。澎湖監獄的教誨師亦說，他每年接待五十個左右的探訪團體，但三年來，從沒見過一場像我們的詩班所帶來的那種「平安與祥和」的氣氛。

有時當牧師呼召時，幾乎所有收容的人都舉手，表示願意接受耶穌為他們的救主，那情景真令人動容！

我們在監獄裡，看到一群渴慕上帝的愛、需要主耶穌救恩的人。上帝已將這使命託付予我們，希望更多的人能回應神的呼召，說：「主啊！我在這裏，請差遣我！」（以賽亞書6：8）

在此，我誠摯地呼籲主內的牧長兄姊們，讓我們一起去參加監獄宣道，共同經歷聖靈的奇妙大能與作為。

10/25/10 -11/05/10 愛恩台福教會詩班的台灣監獄巡迴音樂宣道為受刑人演話劇:"浪子回頭"
"Prisons Mission in Taiwan by the Choir of EFC Irvine
10/25- 11/5/10- Drama: The Return of the Prodigal Son

Reflections on Prison Ministry

Chinyuan Huang
Evangelical Formosan Church of Irvine in S. California

Dr. and Mrs. Howshan Lin are passionate about missions in Taiwan. They return to Taiwan every year and encourage people to do the same. Every time he ran into me, he tried to persuade me to lead the choir to do traveling concerts in Taiwan. I always tried to avoid him. Yet, by the end of 2005, several choir members mentioned their desires to do missions in Taiwan. My wife shared the same desire at that time. I knew it was God's timing. My wife was the choir chairwoman that year and we announced the mission plan to the whole choir at the dinner gathering at the end of the year.

Since God moved us first, many choir members volunteered to participate. The preparation and planning process went smoothly. Yet, we still did not know the "where" and the "who" of our mission. Rev. Tse Feng Chuang and I planned on visiting retirement homes, orphanages, Operation Dawn, addiction treatment centers, hospitals or prisons. We contacted a few places but did not receive any response. In June of 2006, I went back to Tainan and visited Elder Tsai of Khoan-Sai-Koe Church. Mrs. Tsai, knowing our Taiwan mission plan, asked me if we had any target group in mind. I said to her, "There are many choices but we have not settled on one. Personally, I'd love to go to prisons."

Elder Tsai immediately called Ms. Chen Shu-Lan, a teacher. Ms. Chen is the President of the Association of Tainan Prisons and Rehabilitative Care which focuses on providing counseling for prisoners. I met with Ms. Chen the next day and thus began a three-year journey of sharing the gospel in all of the prisons in Taiwan.

Indeed, God does make a pathway in the wilderness and create rivers in the desert. Thanks be to God! Each year, more than 40 choir members from ages

4 to 80 participate. Some days, we performed three concerts a day. Some people fell ill because of the intensity of the mission work, but no one complained. The spirit of mutual support was evident. The number of participants increased every year despite the fact that people had to take vacation time and support themselves financially for these mission trips. Twenty-four members participated for all three years. Why would people volunteer in this way? Because we witnessed that the prisoners' broken hearts were healed and their spiritual hunger was fed.

The Vice-Deputy Warden of Taoyuan Women's Prison was moved to tears at the end of our visit. The counselor of Penghu Prison told us that among the 50 different groups visiting his prison every year, he had not experienced such peace and reconciliation as that brought by our choir. It was indeed very touching to see so many prisoners respond to the minister's call for repentance to accept Jesus Christ as their Savior.

In the prisons, we saw a group of people who hungered for God's love and who needed the redemption of Christ. God has called us to act. May more people respond to God's call by saying, "Lord, Here I am! Please send me!" Brothers and sisters in Christ, I encourage you to participate in prison ministry from which you will experience the wonderful work and transformative power of the Holy Spirit.

10/27/10 莊澤豐牧師於台灣高雄女子監獄傳講，全體受刑人決志信耶穌。
10/27/10- Kaohsiung Women's Prison- after hearing the message from Pastor Chuang, all prisoners accepted Jesus as their Savior.

她們是我們的姊妹
— 台灣宣教基金會監獄事工 —
They are Our Sisters
-Prison Mission of TMF-

楊玓之
大波士頓台灣基督長老教會
Sarah C. Wang
Taiwan Presbyterian Church of Greater Boston

她們是我們的姊妹
— 台灣宣教基金會監獄事工 —

楊玖之
大波士頓台灣基督長老教會

在台灣宣教基金會（TMF）2007年11月17日的第一次年會裡，長島蕭淑蓉姊報告了TMF的監獄事工，並分享她在2007年十月到龍潭桃園女子監獄探訪的故事。我當時聽得心動，加上TMF會長楊宜宜的鼓勵，便趁2008年3月26日回台探親之便，參與TMF的監獄事工，和周清芬、蕭淑蓉兩位姐妹作了桃園監獄三人行。

TMF的監獄事工做得相當上軌道，得歸功在台灣開創監獄事工的溫媽媽及台北同工周清芬姊的忠心奉獻。清芬姊每週一次在台北馬偕醫院門口接志工前往監獄傳播福音，然後在回程時再停留各捷運站，讓志工們搭捷運回家。

桃園女子監獄是吸毒犯的戒治所，大多數的女犯人都年輕且秀氣，因為在監獄裡不自由，渴望和外界接觸，也願意接受訊息。

我們探訪那日，先由清芬姊帶領傳講神拯救的道理，再由我們分組禱告。受刑人都聽得十分專注，也一起呼叫神的名，羨慕神的話語，還請我們在離開前，為她們代禱。

紐約的廖沈壽美阿嬤在2009年3月11日探監時，看到那些可愛的少女，心疼得還沒說出話，就哭了起來，受刑人也跟著哭。事實上，只要出自內心的真情，她們都感受得到，探訪的人其實不必擔心要說甚麼或做甚麼。

四月時，TMF的董事張富雄亦和加州的姊姊張惠真一起去探監兩次，並見證五十位受刑人接受洗禮的喜悅。富雄說，戒治所預留寬裕的時間給外界探訪，在所裡可以看到很多宗教界的刊物。

她們是我們的姊妹 — 台灣宣教基金會監獄事工

8月19日，TMF楊宜宜會長回台時，親自往獄中帶領這些吸毒少女唱歌表演，帶給她們不少歡樂及鼓勵。12月16日，紐澤西的楊純貞姐回台，帶給獄中姊妹們聖誕蛤鐘（Jingle Bell調）的愉快信息。純貞姐向她們見證神的慈愛恩典，勉勵她們學習服從神的旨意。

我一向同情叛逆的孩子。八十年代初期，我在美國電話電報公司的「肯定行動」工作坊裡，看過一部短片《你是時空的產物》，讓我學習到終生受用不盡的功課。的確，人是時空的產物，我們和孩子的成長時空是多麼不同啊！我們小時候，過新年才得以享受雞鴨美味和新衣新鞋，而今天的孩子要什麼有什麼，大魚大肉吃到膩，怎能理解我們那種期待的興奮？他們無從學習知足，於是在毒品與奇裝異服中尋找刺激。願我們能以同理心來關切他們的失落，並幫助他們尋回生命的方向與意義。

從此事工，我看到的不是犯人，而是我們的姊妹。她們讓我想起神的話語：「我實在告訴你們，這些事你們既作在我這弟兄中一個最小的身上，就是做在我身上了。」(馬太福音25：40)

4/2009本會董事張富雄,TMF同工, 及海內外監獄宣教勇士, 探訪桃園女子監獄 ,見證受洗大典。
US TMF board member Morgan Chang, TMF Taiwan co-worker and US/Taiwan prison mission warriors, witnessing the Baptism ceremony in Taoyuan woman prison.

They are Our Sisters
- Prison Mission of TMF -

Sarah C. Wang
Taiwan Presbyterian Church of Greater Boston

Sou-Yung Hsiao of Long Island gave a report on the TMF prison mission during its first annual meeting on November 17, 2007, and shared her experience of visiting Taoyuan Women's Prison (TWP) in Lung-Tan in October 2007. The TMF prison mission is organized through Wen Mama – Mother of the Prison in Taiwan, and is coordinated by a devoted TMF co-worker Ching-Fen Chou. Once a week, Ching-Fen picks up volunteers from the front door of Taipei MacKay Hospital and drives them to Taoyuan Prison. On the way back, she drops them off at subway stations.

Moved by Sou-Yung's speech and encouraged by TMF President Eileen YiYi Chang, I participated in the TMF prison mission when I visited Taiwan in March of 2008. Ching-Fen, Sou-Yung, and I went to TWP together. The prison is a drug rehabilitation center for mostly young women. Because they do not have freedom, the prisoners are eager to meet visitors and willing to listen to our message. On the day of our visit, Ching-Fen shared God's saving grace with them. When we prayed together, they opened up their hearts to God and asked us to pray for them before we departed.

When May Liao of New York visited the prison on March 11, 2009, she cried at the first sight of these young women and they cried with her. When visiting prisoners, we do not need to fret over what to say or what to do. They are touched by what comes through our hearts. In April 2009, Morgan Chang of New York and his sister Emma Lee of California visited TWP twice, and witnessed the baptisms of 50 prisoners. Morgan said the prison made religious materials available and was generous in granting them visitation time.

They are our Sisters - Prison Mission of Taiwan Mission Foundation -

On August 19, 2009, President Eileen visited the prison, and sang with the women, and it brought them much joy and encouragement. Chue Jen Huang of New Jersey also went there on December 16, 2009 to bring the gift of Christmas music. She illustrated God's love and grace and encouraged the women to trust and obey God.

I always have great sympathy for rebellious children. In the early 1980s, AT&T, in an Affirmative Action workshop, showed a short film entitled "What you are is Where you are and when," which taught me a great life lesson. Indeed, we are affected by where and when we live. Our children grew up in a totally different world from ours. In our upbringing of them, they only feast on meats and enjoy new clothes and shoes during the Lunar New Year celebration. Our children are materially overfed. How do we expect them to understand our upbringing? Where do they find their contentment in life? Thus they turn to drugs and odd fashions to fill their emptiness. May we become empathetic with our children and help them find their direction and meaning in life.

In the TMF prison mission, I saw not inmates but our sisters. They reminded me of Jesus' words in Matthew 25:36-40 "...Truly, I tell you, whatever you for one of the least of these brothers and sisters of mine, you did it for me."

3/11/09 本會同工廖沈壽美和周清芬探訪桃園女子監獄
TMF coworker May Laio and Ching Fen Chou at Taoyuan woman prison

3/26/08 桃園女子監獄宣教-左起:作者楊玫之, 蕭淑蓉, 台灣同工周清芬
TMF coworker Ching Fen Chou (right) helped arrange Sou-Yung Hsiao/Long Island (middle) and author Sarah Wang/ Boston (left) visit to Taoyuan woman prison.

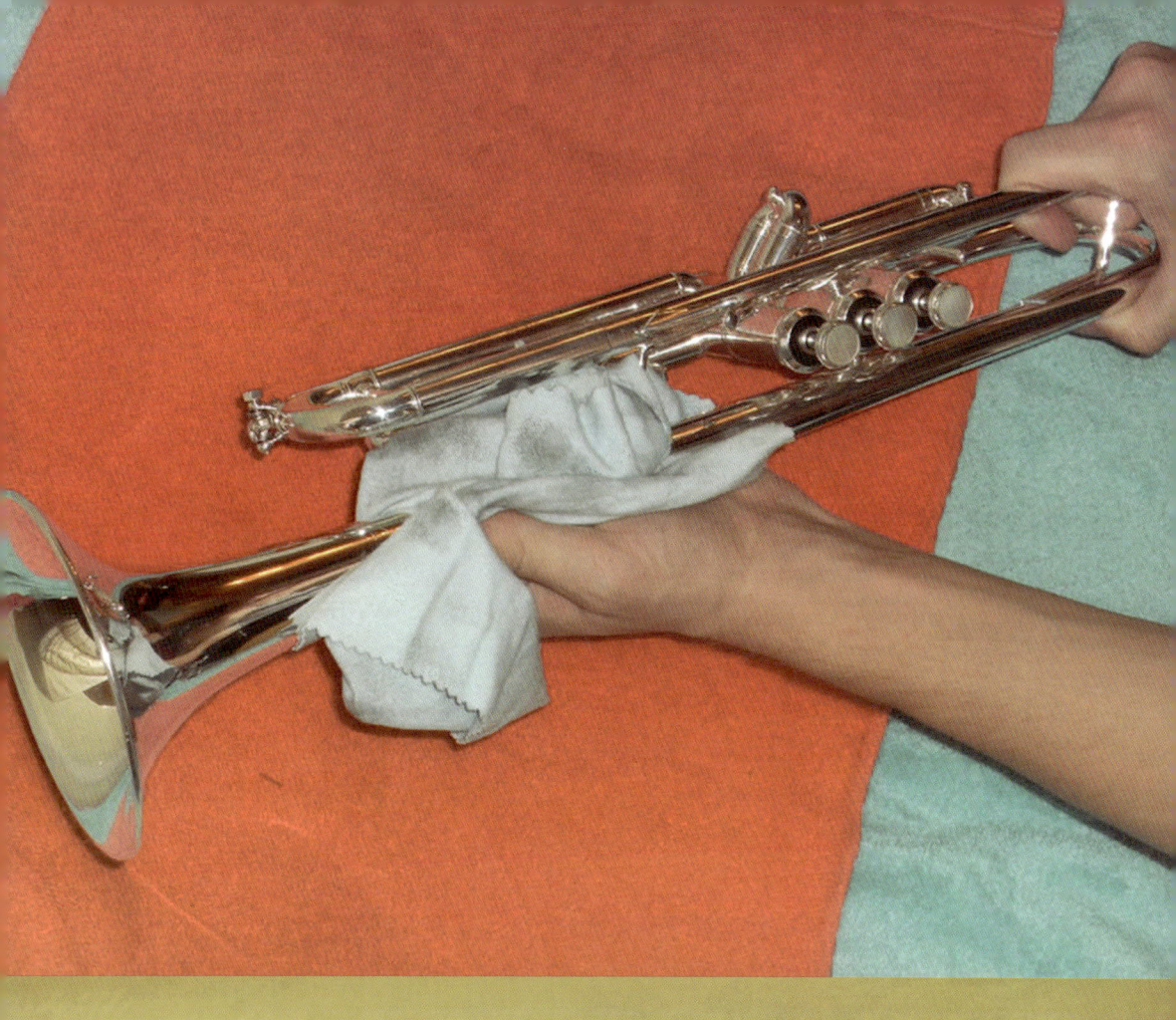

更新！發光！
- 一次珍貴的短宣經驗 -
RENEWED! SHINE!
A PRECIOUS EXPERIENCE OF SHORT-TERM MISSION

潘暉醫
台灣基督協會 - 維吉尼亞州
Jate Pan
Taiwanese for Christ, Inc. in Virginia

更新！發光！
- 一次珍貴的短宣經歷 -

潘暉啓
台灣基督協會 - 維吉尼亞州

幾年前，「基督教更生團契」總幹事黃明鎮牧師前來華府，分享監獄福音事工，並邀請「台灣基督協會(簡稱基督協會)」返台參與福音事工，我們都十分心動。然而，基督協會的同工都是帶職事奉，而且分散在不同的行業，很難全部湊在同一時間返台，因此雖然心動，卻多年來不見行動。

2007年，基督協會成立屆滿十年。同工們回顧十年來的服事，才驚覺這項最初也是最重要的返台宣教心願竟未達成，因此下定決心，決意在這年年底之前排除萬難，返回故鄉台灣，參與福音宣教的事工。

感謝神！經由更生團契總幹事黃明鎮牧師的協助，基督協會的同工一行十六人終於在十一月成行，前往多所監獄、教會、醫院和更生團契花蓮少年學園，向鄉朋親友分享耶穌救贖的大能，並且接受福音戰場的操練。

「更新！發光」是我們此次短宣的主題。同工們期盼透過此次操練，參與故鄉的福音事工，並使每個團員的靈命得到更新的造就。因此，密集的禱告會、練詩背詞、棒鐘器樂訓練等成為團員們的行前裝備。

返台宣教後，我們在幾處教會的見證分享上，看到主內兄姊熱切耕耘福音的心志。台北濟南教會婦女詩班的獻詩與提供台灣小吃、慕義堂兄姊們的親切款待、以及花蓮馬太鞍教會充滿熱情活力的載歌載舞的敬拜，都讓同工們體會到返家的溫馨與無盡的主愛！

我們每到一處監所，都感受到門禁森嚴的「牆」隔開了監所的裏外，使之成為兩個截然不同的世界。然而，「主是平安，祂已拆毀中間隔斷的牆…」、「耶

穌愛你，在你一生中最大的福份就是耶穌永遠愛你…」的詩歌，不只開啟受刑朋友的心門，也讓我們從他們臉上的淚水與舉手決志看見神的愛和大能。

前往台南新樓醫院、新樓麻豆分院以及斗六靜萱療養院的詩歌分享，讓我們看見另一群需要福音的鄉親，也更能體會身心靈醫治的精神與特色。誠如黃牧師所說，監獄的受刑人和家屬及醫院的病患可說是最需要關懷與支持的人群。

少年學園同工們的付出則不只見證主的愛，也讓我們看見這些年少同學的希望。「這些事你們既做在我這弟兄中一個最小的身上，就是做在我身上了。」(馬太福音25:40)

神的豐盛恩典超乎人的想像。密集的短宣行程幫助我們調適時差。更生團契各區會同工的愛心接待，更讓我們親嚐主愛的溫馨。我們由衷向神獻上感謝與讚美！願神加添能力，裝備每位在福音戰場上的同工，使之成為高舉基督廣傳福音的精兵。

基督協會的同工願藉此機會向黃牧師與師母的安排、聯絡與帶領，表達深深的謝意。他們為神委身的心志與喜樂，實是我們同工學習的榜樣。此外，我們也感謝華府地區主內兄姊的代禱與奉獻。願主繼續成就我們的宣教事工。

台灣基督協會手鐘團，作者潘暉瑩(二排右一)
TFC Handbell Mission Team
(author, 2nd row 1st right)

2007台灣基督協會男聲合唱團以詩歌鼓勵受刑人要堅強
2007- The TFC Rock Men's Choir presented "Be Strong in the Lord" to encourage the inmates in Taiwan

Renewed! Shine!
- A Precious Experience of Short-term Mission -

Jate Pan
Taiwanese for Christ, Inc. in Virginia

A few years ago, Pastor Huang (Rev. Ming Cheng Huang), the general director of Christian Born Anew Fellowship, came to Washington, D.C. to share the prison gospel ministry and its needs. They also invited Taiwanese for Christ (TFC) to return to Taiwan to participate in evangelical ministry. Co-workers in TFC were very much inspired and encouraged. However, because we all have jobs in different professions, it was a challenge to schedule the same time to go to Taiwan. For many years, although we were inspired, we never took any action.

TFC reached its tenth anniversary in 2007. Recalling a decade of service, co-workers discovered that the first and the most important wish, which was not yet fulfilled, was to return to Taiwan for mission. Against all odds, therefore, we determined to return to Taiwan before the end of the year to participate in the gospel mission ministry. Thank God! Through the support and arrangements of Prison Fellowship and the Director-General Huang, Rev. (Rev. Ming Cheng Huang), 16 co-workers from TFC finally took the trip in November. We visited many prisons, churches, hospitals, Prison Fellowship Taiwan, and Boys Ranch in Hua-Lien to share about Jesus and salvation. We exercised discipline in the Gospel battlefield.

"Be Renewed and Shine" was the theme of this short-term mission. Co-workers hoped that through this trip, we would not only participate in hometown evangelism, but also be revived spiritually ourselves. Therefore, we had many intensive prayer meetings, we memorized hymns, and practiced hand chime music; but we never felt that preparation for this trip was hard work.

In several Gospel ministries in local churches, we witnessed that many brothers and sisters in the Lord have much passion to follow the Lord to preach the gospel. The Chi-nan Church in Taipei, the TPC Women's Choir, the Taiwanese snacks, the warm hospitality from Mu-Yi Church brothers and sisters, as well as Hua-lien Ma-Tai-An Church worship, praise, singing, and dancing, all made co-workers feel at home. God's love is really abundant!

Every time we visited prisons, we sensed the "wall" that separated the prison from the outside world. However, "God is peace and He has torn down this wall…." and "Jesus loves you. …The greatest blessing in your life is that Jesus loves you forever." These hymns opened the hearts of prisoners, since we saw God's love and power touch them to shed tears and raise hands to accept Christ.

We went to Tainan Sin-Lau Hospital, its branch hospital in Matou, and Tou-Li-ou Ching-Shuan Mental Hospital to share praise songs. Seeing another group of people who needed the gospel, we came to a deeper understanding of the nature and character of spiritual healing. Just as Pastor Huang has said, "The prisoners in jail and patients in the hospitals, as well as their families, are the people who need support and care the most. "Workers from Youth Academy testified to God's love and gave us hope in these young people. "…Whatever you did for one of the least of these brothers and sisters of mine, you did for me." (Matt. 25:40)

God's grace is beyond man's imagination. Our intensive schedule actually helped us recover from our fatigue and jetlag. The passion and love from Prison Fellowship Taiwan helped workers from TFC experience God's love. We could only offer our thankfulness and praise to God. May God give strength and equip every coworker in the Gospel battle field, so everyone will become a good soldier to raise Christ high while preaching the Gospel.

TFC workers also want to express our appreciation to Pastor and Mrs. Huang for their hard work in arranging every detail of our trip. Their joy and commitment to God is also our model. In addition, the prayer support and offerings from brothers and sisters in Washington D.C. area are also part of the great support for this short-term mission.

將心歸祢
To You My Heart Belongs

葉俊明 詩歌創作專輯一・James Yeh Vol.1

台灣音樂短宣
Short term Music Mission in Taiwan

葉俊明牧師
威明頓主恩堂 - 德拉瓦州
Pastor James Yeh
Wilmington Community Evangelical Church in Delaware

台灣音樂短宣
-將心歸祢-

葉俊明牧師
威明頓主恩堂 - 德拉瓦州

我過去總以為回台短宣是一個遙遠的夢。畢竟在美國工作的事務繁多，回台宣教的願望便一年拖過一年。幸好神憐憫我，為我的台灣短宣之行開了路。

2009年年初，在台灣從事音樂宣教的謝鴻文傳道請我回台，與他們的磐石樂團配搭服事，在台灣作巡迴各地的音樂佈道。這對我來說，真是一個千載難逢的好機會，便欣然答應。

當飛機抵達桃園機場，我心中激盪的情緒油然而生，目光也被周圍的一景一物所震撼，我不由地深深吸了一口氣，明白自己猶然深愛著這塊土地。

這趟宣教任務一共七站，分別是台中的大甲與大里、台南鹽水、嘉義、彰化與台中市等地。首站選在我的母會─大甲基督長老教會。我的任務是傳講信息，見證神如何在艱困的環境中，感動我寫下《將心歸祢》創作專輯中的詩歌，並且在磐石樂團伴奏下，親自獻唱。

然而，當我看到不少過去看我長大的親友和教會裡屬靈的長輩們專程前來，竟突然緊張地說不出話，而且拼命咳嗽，心裡真是著急萬分，擔心首場在家鄉服事就搞砸，接下來到外地服事，真不知該怎麼辦？

於是，我在聚會前禁食禱告、全然交託給上帝。沒想到當我開始分享時，聖靈大大地動工，咳嗽奇妙地停止，樂團的成員也很有默契地展開服事。我們的分享感動了台下的聽眾。我看見許多人頻拭眼淚，尤其最後呼召時，不但有人決志要信耶穌，而且台下的大部分基督徒都將手舉起，願意將心歸主，讓生命重新獻在主前，一生成為別人的祝福。感謝主！

有了第一場的順利服事，我明白神會繼續保守。 果然，我們在往後的音樂巡迴佈道中不斷地見證相同的情況。我終於明白上帝要幫助眾多處境艱難的台灣人得到聖靈的安慰，並重新獲得力量。

我也相信神促成我這一趟台灣短宣行。祂在我生命最低潮、面對生離死別、軟弱無助、幾乎放棄一切的時候，賜我靈命，寫下《將心歸祢》專輯裡的詩歌，安慰自己，也安慰同樣遭遇苦難的人。

原來過去攔阻我的，不是各樣的藉口，而是我的不順服。誠然，外在的環境或個人的欠缺都會阻撓我們的宣教行動，但神若要用你，就會為你排除困難。只要我們持著對台灣宣教的熱忱，勇於嘗試，就能夠經歷神的大能，完成上帝的託付。

2009葉俊明牧師與磐石樂團在台南鹽水夜市的音樂宣道
2009- Rev. James Yeh with Music Stone Ministry at night market in Tainan

Short-term Music Mission in Taiwan
-To You My Heart Belongs-

Pastor James Yeh
Wilmington Community Evangelical Church in Delaware

In the past, I always thought it was just a hard-to-fulfill dream to go back to Taiwan for a short-term mission. My work in America has kept me very busy so my mission trip to Taiwan was delayed year after year. Eventually, God showed mercy to me and opened a way for my short-term mission trip to Taiwan.

In the beginning of 2009, I was invited to go to Taiwan by Pastor Steve Hsieh, who has been doing music ministry for many years. He asked me to serve with his band of Music Stone Ministry to tour several locations in Taiwan. I happily accepted this once-in-a-lifetime opportunity.

When the airplane finally arrived in Tao-Yuan International Airport, I felt a rush of uncontrollable emotions burst out inside of me, and I was deeply touched by every single thing in my sight. I couldn't help taking a deep breath, and realized that I was still deeply in love with this land.

We had seven locations for this mission: Ta-Chia and Ta-Li in Taichung, Yien-Sui in Tainan, Chia-Yi, Chang-Hua, Taichung city, etc. The first location was my hometown church – Ta-Chia Presbyterian Church. My main mission was to share the testimony of how God moved me to write these praise songs while I was in the midst of difficult situations. The Music Stone Band accompanied me while I sang.

When I saw that all of my family and friends came out of their way to see me, and even the elders who watched me grow up, I became so nervous. I could hardly talk, and I suddenly started to cough intensely. I couldn't help but think: If I end up ruining this first sermon in my own hometown, what would it be when I go to other touring locations?

So I made up my mind to fast and pray before the meeting, leaving it all to God. To my own surprise, when I started sharing my testimony, the Holy Spirit came upon me, and I stopped coughing miraculously. The band members stayed perfectly in tune with me, and the audience were all touched.

Many people kept wiping their tears away. When I gave the altar call, not only were there people raising hands to accept Jesus as their Lord and Savior, but most of the Christians also raised their hands to show their willingness to give their hearts to the Lord. People rededicated their lives to God, to be a blessing to others.

After this first successful mission experience, I was convinced that God would continue to watch over our mission tour. As I predicted, the same results kept showing in every location during this music mission. I finally realized that God wanted to help many Taiwanese people who have suffered much; He gave them comfort and strength through the Holy Spirit.

God made this Taiwan mission trip possible. When I was in the lowest point of my life, facing death and departure from loved ones, being in my weakest and most helpless moments, I was inspired to write these praise songs, not just to comfort myself, but to comfort many people who were suffering. The real past hindrance to my mission in Taiwan was not the excuses, but my disobedience in overcoming difficulties. I agree that hindrance for us to take action in evangelism can come from both outward situations and personal lacking in certain areas. But if God wants to use you, He will make a way. As long as we continue to have a heart for Taiwan mission and dare to try, we will experience God's mighty power and accomplish the mission bestowed on us.

讚美之泉
Stream of Praise

謝秉哲
讚美之泉音樂事工 - 加州
Eric Hsieh
Stream of Praise Music Ministries in California

讚美之泉

謝秉哲
讚美之泉音樂事工 - 加州

一個單純的異象：「讓讚美的聲音在台灣的大街小巷響起」，使我在過去十五年間，年年帶領「讚美之泉」團員，回到台灣這片神所愛的土地，藉著敬拜的歌聲，播下福音的種子。

「讚美之泉」係由一群愛主的台灣留學生於1993年在洛杉磯成立，並於1995年在美國加州登記為非營利團體，然後於1997年在台灣登記為「讚美之泉文化事業基金會」。

十五年來，「讚美之泉」一共出版了三十多張敬拜的音樂專輯，每年舉辦五十至七十場的大型讚美聚會，接觸將近十萬的民眾，巡迴腳蹤遍及東南亞、北美、澳洲、紐西蘭及歐洲等地區，而台灣則是「讚美之泉」服事的最主要地區。

一首《耶和華祝福滿滿》讓我們從台灣頭唱到台灣尾。我們用詩歌不斷地為台灣祈福，也在屬天的詩歌中，看見上帝對台灣的應許與疼惜。

至於與「讚美之泉」同名的敬拜歌曲《讚美之泉》，更道出神如何引領我們在台灣，以敬拜轉變新世代生命的見證。其4句歌詞如下：

1. 從天父而來的愛與恩典，把我們冰冷的心溶解 -
神藉著屬天的詩歌，闡明祂對我們的愛，使原本沒有笑容的民眾聽到詩歌和見證，都敞開胸懷，領受到主的愛和恩典。

我們帶著單純的心，相信神會在人心作工，一年又一年地到台灣各地服事，果然看見人們的笑容變多了，愁眉苦臉的人少了。神藉著《讚美之泉》，溫暖了許多台灣人憂傷的心。

2. 讓我們獻出每個音符，把它化為讚美之泉 -
音樂是神給人一份非常美好的禮物，許多年輕人也都很喜愛音樂。我們年復一年地鼓勵台灣教會的弟兄姐妹，將他們音樂的恩賜獻給神使用。

藉著音樂的敬拜，也藉著對台灣這片土地發聲的詩歌，我們影響一些新世代的年輕人，在教會組織敬拜讚美的樂團，開始以創作的詩歌讚美主，感謝主。

3. 讓我們張開口、舉起手，向永生之主稱謝 -
我們剛開始到台灣帶領敬拜讚美聚會時，許多人還不習慣向神「張開口、舉起手」的敬拜方式。多年來，「讚美之泉」在聚會中教導並呼籲大家自由地向神傾心敬拜，終於逐漸見證台灣弟兄姐妹在敬拜中的更新和蛻變。尤其近年來，台灣的敬拜更自由，對神的渴慕更熱情，讓年年到台灣服事的我們得到極大的鼓勵。

4. 使讚美之泉流入每個人的心間 -
「讚美之泉」的使命是以敬拜讚美和聖樂創作來宣揚福音，並激勵更多的年輕人為神發揮潛力、多結果子。十五年的服事期間，我們從不敢鬆懈從神而來的呼召和託付。

我們看到神在台灣興起許多愛神、又願意用音樂服事神的年輕一代，並且大大地用他們來祝福台灣。我們會不斷地回到這塊土地，服事神所愛的百姓，讓讚美的泉源不斷地流入每個人的心靈深處。

我們大聲歌頌，因為我們知道這是神賜的恩典。我們勇敢宣告，因為我們被神的愛轉化。我們四處見證，因為我們要高舉主的名！我們感謝神使用我們見證祂在台灣的奇妙作為，盼望繼續在台灣喚醒一群全方位的屬靈軍隊，建立一個屬神榮耀的國度！

Stream of Praise

Eric Hsieh
Stream of Praise Music Ministries in California

"Let Taiwan be filled with the sound of praise and worship"-this was my simple vision.

Born from this vision to see Jesus lifted high, Stream of Praise music ministries (SOP) has been returning to Taiwan each year for the past 15 years. Through our songs of praise and worship, the seeds of the Gospel are sown in this land that God loves. Located in Los Angeles, California, Stream of Praise Music Ministries was established in 1993 and registered as a 501(c)(3) non-profit organization in California in 1995. In 1997, we registered in Taiwan as the "Taiwan Stream of Praise Music Ministries Foundation."

In the past 15 years, SOP has published 30+ praise and worship albums. Footprints of our praise and worship evangelical events can be found in countless places in Asia, Southeast Asia, North America, Australia, New Zealand, and Europe. Each year, we hold anywhere from 50 to 70 large evangelical events, and we have served about 100,000 brothers and sisters. Taiwan is a main and focused territory of our service.

Our namesake song, "Stream of Praise," is now a very familiar tune in all Taiwanese churches. We have prayed and blessed Taiwan continuously with songs and we have witnessed the love and care of God for Taiwan. The four-line lyrics of this song speak of how God longs to raise up a new generation of worshippers who are transformed by the power of worship:

1. The love and grace of our Heavenly Father gently melts our hard hearts

God gave us songs from heaven to show how much He loves us. Through the transforming power of worship, people are able to open their hearts and taste the sweetness of God's goodness. We do not rely on ourselves but we simply serve this generation with a pure and sincere faith, trusting that God will surely do His work in this land, and each year we have seen Taiwan being transformed, joy restored, compassion found and hope rediscovered.

2. May each note of music be a stream of praise

Music is a gift from God and we have a generation of young people who love music with a passion. Our prayer and mission is to raise up worshippers who long to utilize their musical gifts for the glory of God. We are witnessing to people more and embracing this vision and calling. More and more praise and worship bands are being formed, and also more and more anointed original compositions are being created.

3. Let us open our mouths, raise our hands, and give thanks to our living God.

When we first started leading praise and worship concerts in Taiwan, many were not used to singing aloud and lifting their hands in worship. Throughout these 15 years, we have been encouraging and teaching people to worship with abandon, and we are seeing the fruits of our labor. There is a radical transformation of worship in Taiwan, and nowadays we are seeing people express their love and yearn for God in new and creative ways. The anointing and unity that is born from such worship greatly blesses us.

4. And may this stream of praise overflow into all hearts.

We do not take our divine calling lightly. Our mission has been and continues to be to utilize praise and worship, music composition, and training as a vehicle to spread the gospel, motivate, equip, and empower Christians, and declare God's kingdom. We aim to inspire and enable all young people to realize their full potential in God as productive and responsible individuals. God is raising up a new generation of His army, people who totally commit themselves to the Lord and serve Him with music. We know that God will greatly use these gifts to become a channel of blessing to Taiwan. There are still many who do not know the Lord and we will continue to return to this land to serve His chosen ones. We want to see the stream of praise continually overflow into everyone's heart.

By His grace we sing, by His love we serve. We lift up the name of Jesus and glorify Him with all our hearts, minds and strength. It is our honor to be part of God's plan for His people and we will continue to pray and work towards the revival of Chinese communities all over the world.

香柏樹的音樂宣道
Cedar Music Ministries

吳英俊
美國香柏樹音樂宣道機構 – 加州
Bach Ying Chun Wu
Cedar Music Ministries in California

「香柏樹」的音樂宣道

吳英俊
美國香柏樹音樂宣道機構 – 加州

大約四年前，我到「愛修園」上神學課，聖靈開啟我創作敬拜音樂的心門。我愈創作，愈覺得接近主，於是向上帝祈求說：「主啊！我願意獻上我的恩賜，成為見證耶穌的器皿。」

其後數個月，我與「愛修園」的蘇恩慈牧師同心禱告、懇求。有一天，我讀到詩篇九十二篇第12至14節：「義人要發旺如棕樹，生長如利巴嫩的香柏樹。他們栽於耶和華的殿中，發旺在神的院裡。他們年老的時候仍要結果子，要滿了汁漿而常發青...」，頓時領悟到服事無需停留在專業的領域，而是願意被神栽種在祂的殿中，做為有用的器皿。

我那時方才明白：神的啟示又真又活，叫我這渺小又膽怯的人，無可推諉地直呼讚美主。因此不久，我照著祂的應允，成立了「香柏樹音樂宣道坊」(www.cmmmusic.org)。

我們以洛杉磯為本壘，開始到美國各地作福音演唱，並且多次回台灣作音樂短宣。我們到過長老教會、聖教會、神召會、醫院、民間醫療診所、讀書會、神學院和各大學等許多地方，向許多未信主的大學生、病人與民眾傳遞福音的訊息。

2009年暑假，主甚至為我們開啟南半球之窗，使我們的福音事工能延伸到紐西蘭與澳洲等地區。神的作為何等奇妙！

自「香柏樹音樂宣道坊」創立於2006年至今，我們殷切期盼能成為聖殿裡的香柏樹，長得高大壯碩，充滿汁漿，天天發出讚美主的聲音！

「香柏樹」的音樂宣道　　125

作者吳英俊
Author Bach Ying Chun Wu

作者吳英俊11/3/2009於佳里培訓台南玉井長老教會詩班. 其宣教亦及於阿根廷, 巴西與馬來西亞
2009- Cedar Music Ministries founder Bach Wu's music mission in Tainan, Taiwan. His music mission also reached out to Argentina, Brazil and Malaysia.

Cedar Music Ministries

Bach Ying Chun Wu
Cedar Music Ministries in California

About four years ago, an opportunity arose that allowed me to study theology at Agape Bible Institute where I felt God touch my heart, using the Holy Spirit to inspire me to create praise and worship music. The more I wrote, the richer the music became and the more I seemed to comprehend God's will. Through this music ministry, I've experienced God's never-ending blessing. After praying together with Rev. Angelina Su from Agape Bible Institute for a few months, I finally said to God, "My Lord, I am willing to use the gifts you have given me to become a vessel of witness for Jesus Christ."

One day I was reading Psalm 92:12-14, which says, "The righteous shall flourish like a palm tree: he shall grow like a cedar in Lebanon. Those that be planted in the house of the Lord shall flourish in the courts of our God. They shall still bring forth fruit in old age; they shall be plump and green." This passage reminded me that I should not continue to serve God with simply my profession or skills, but I should be willing to be planted in the house of the Lord and be a usable vessel. Just like a cedar, when I grow older, I can still be fruitful and flourishing.

I am very grateful that God, through His love and kindness, entered His will into my heart and led me to start "Cedar Music Ministry" (www.cmmmusic.org). I pray for a continually clear vision from God, and ceaseless motivation and musical inspiration.

Since our founding, based in Los Angeles, we have held praise concerts in

U.S. States as well as in Taiwan. We have appeared in different denominational churches as well as hospitals, clinics, reading clubs, seminaries and universities, ministering to college students and hospital patients – most of whom were non-Christians.

In 2009 summer, God amazingly opened the door in the southern hemisphere in New Zealand and Australia. Praise God and please pray for us.

Since Cedar Music Ministry's founding in 2006, we have been bringing the Gospel all over the world. Our name reminds us that we should be like the cedar trees in Lebanon, built big and strong, meant to eternally praise and be fruitful in God's house.

作者吳英俊所出版的音樂CD 千萬個祝福
The music CD published by author Bach Ying Chun Wu - Unlimited blessings

長宣在屏東
Long - term Mission in Ping -Tung

黃輝銘
東灣台灣基督教會 - 北加州
Hwe-Ming Huang
East Bay Formosan United Methodist Church (UMC) in N. California

長宣在屏東

黃輝銘
東灣台灣基督教會 – 北加州

基於信仰的使命，我決定在退休後趁身體還健壯時，回臺灣傳福音，向未信主的鄉親介紹耶穌基督。為了尋找宣教區，我向東灣台灣基督教會的周宏毅牧師請教。真巧，周牧師不久前在臺灣遇見一位在屏東縣長治鄉繁華村開拓「繁華教會」的黃素娥牧師。黃牧師一生為主差用，前些時因體力漸衰，乃託周牧師代尋適當人選，來延續事工。

2008年三月初，我接受周牧師的建議，前往屏東縣長治鄉，協助當時剛接辦繁華教會的陳郁芬牧師。

繁華村的民間宗教信仰普及，道壇林立，幾乎沒有傳福音的空間，但我們還是想辦法接觸群眾。於是陳牧師和我兵分兩路，她從學校與醫療機構切入，我由菜市場和社區單位着手。然後，我們在教會開設免費的學生課後輔導班、鋼琴、直笛和英文班。起初，參加的人不多，但我們並不氣餒。我們相信藉著禱告和信心，以愛心待人，終會出現曙光。

感謝主，祂引導我們到不同領域去聽取民眾的心聲，並贏取他們的信任。首先，繁華國小主動與教會合辦夏令營。接著，繁華社區中心的老人會要求教會為他們安排節目。然後，附近兩座安養院期待我們去辦活動，而「羅滕園」殘障服務中心也歡迎我們去關懷。

就這樣，教會與社區建立起關係，往後互動益加密切。2009年，兩家安養院歡迎我們，尤其「椰子園」安養院更自今年五月的第二個禮拜天開始，提供該院大廳，讓繁華教會帶領園內的殘障人士做主日禮拜，感謝主的大能。

這幾年的義工經驗，讓我覺得從事福音事工，無法求立竿見影，而是要以實際的行為慢慢感化人，引導人進入神的國度，領受神的愛。

Long-term Mission in Ping-Tung

Hwe-Ming Huang
East Bay Formosan United Methodist Church (UMC) in N. California

With the Great Commission in mind when I retired, I decided to go back to Taiwan to spread the Gospel by introducing Jesus Christ to unbelievers while my body was still healthy. I consulted with Pastor William Chou of East Bay Formosan UMC about finding a mission field. Through Pastor Chou, I met Pastor Chu-Uo Huang, who has dedicated her life to the Lord as a missionary at the Prosper Church in Ping-Tung. As it turned out, Pastor Huang had asked Pastor Chou to help her search for a candidate to continue her ministry at the church.

In March 2008, I accepted Pastor Chou's recommendation to go to the Prosper Church in Chung Chi Village at Ping-Tung County to assist the new pastor, Yu-Fen Chang, with the church ministry.

Traditional Taiwanese folk religions and temples saturated the area, making it extremely difficult to share the Gospel. Nevertheless, we still wanted to connect with the people as much as possible. Pastor Chang worked with schools and healthcare organizations, while I went to markets and community organizations. We also hosted a free after-school program at church to teach academic subjects, as well as piano, flute and English. Even though there were very few participants initially, we were not discouraged. We believed that through faithful prayers and kindness, hope will rise.

Praise the Lord! He led us to different places where we learned how to listen to people's stories and eventually earn their trust. The result was that we were able to host a summer camp at the local elementary school. The community senior center and nearby nursing homes also asked the church to help them plan events. Lo-Ten Disability Center also welcomed us to visit their clients.

The church and the community began to develop a close relationship. In 2009, we received invitations from two nursing homes. In May, we were able to start Sunday Service at Coconut Garden Nursing Home's meeting hall to worship with the disabled friends. Praise the Lord for His might!

After some years of volunteer experience, I learned that the best approach to sharing the Gospel is not merely by words. Rather, it is through life and action that we can touch hearts and point people to the kingdom of God, where they can receive His love.

壯圍中宣的回顧
Reflection on Mission in Zhuang-Wei

黃政俊傳道/黃碧輝夫婦
新澤西主恩堂/台語堂
Minister Cheng-Chun (CC) & Faye Huang
Chinese Christian Church of New Jersey/Taiwanese Congregation

壯圍中宣的回顧

黃政俊傳道/黃碧輝夫婦
新澤西主恩堂/台語堂

2009年，我們第四次到「台灣基層福音差傳會」所在的宜蘭縣壯圍鄉壯圍教會從事中宣。

2006年我們回台灣參加親戚的婚禮，返美前到壯圍教會做禮拜，發現這裡迫切需要人手。經過禱告，我們夫婦一同感動，決定呼應教會魏正德牧師所說的：「這次來參觀，下次來同工」的徵召，於是在二月中回美國處理一些家務後，將房子委託紐澤西主恩堂的弟兄姊妹看管，就帶著大家的祝福，在三月中回到台灣傳福音。

我倆這些年能回蘭陽服事，確是神的美妙安排。雖然我們生長在宜蘭，但對壯圍一向陌生，這下總算有機會目睹故鄉美麗的田園，也較能深入瞭解這純樸鄉間所隱藏的痛苦、辛酸與無奈。

我們探訪的家庭，有不少是患重病、家暴、吸毒、離婚、單親或隔代教養的案例。由於鄉下資源少，能力較強的年輕人往往到城市謀生，留下來的有許多是低收入或靠救濟金度日的家庭。這些家庭就是教會關心的對象。由於「要收的莊稼多，工人少」，壯圍教會的劉雅貞牧師特別需要短宣與福音隊的協助。

我們在壯圍除了探訪與事奉主日崇拜外，還帶領週三與週六的查經與家庭禮拜，並教孩子們彈鋼琴及協助宜蘭大學生從事兒童課後輔導的活動。我們甚至數次到國小教英文，還每週兩次在鄉立圖書館教授美語。

由於此地甚少見到從國外回來宣教的人，所以我們在學校的安排下，接受記者的訪問，上了報紙，無形中替教會增添一些傳福音的接觸點。

壯圍教會的會友不多，卻都很愛主。幾位常來聚會的伯母雖不識字，查經不用翻聖經，唱詩不用看詩本，但都能將經文與歌詞背得滾瓜爛熟，唱得真情流露。我們與這些弟兄姊妹的溝通既單純又甜蜜，也體驗主內都是一家人的意境。就憑這些，我們所得的已比付出的多。

每次要離開壯圍，我們都覺得依依不捨。盼國外能有更多弟兄姊妹回來，帶領這裡的弟兄姐妹們查經，教他們用羅馬字讀台語聖經，鞏固他們的信心，為福音打美好的仗。

Reflection on Mission in Zhuang-Wei

Minister Cheng-Chun (CC) & Faye Huang
Chinese Christian Church of New Jersey/Taiwanese Congregation

We went on our fourth mission to Zhuang-Wei Christian Church with Taiwan Grass-Roots Mission in 2009. We found out about the great needs of Zhuang-Wei Church four years ago when we went back to Taiwan for a wedding. After praying together, we felt moved to respond to Pastor Junter Way's words of challenge – "This time, you come for a visit; next time, please come as co-workers." In February, we returned to New Jersey in the United States to make arrangements and then went back to Taiwan in March.

It is indeed God's blessing for us to serve in Lanyang all these years. Although we grew up in Yilan, we were not familiar with Zhuang-Wei. So we finally got the opportunity to see the beauty of the place and to gain a deeper understanding of the simplicity, as well as the toils and sufferings of rural life. Besides visitations and Sunday worship, we also led Bible studies and small groups on Wednesdays and Saturdays. We also taught piano and assisted Yi-Lan University in running the after-school program for children. We even had the opportunity to teach English at the elementary school and public library. Since the city did not have many opportunities to work with overseas missionaries, the elementary school arranged interviews with newspaper reporters, which also gave the church an opportunity to share the Gospel.

Although Zhuang-Wei Church is not big, our brothers and sisters love the Lord very much. Despite their illiteracy, they know the Bible verses very well and sing worship songs with very sincere hearts. Their love is very genuine and sweet, which allowed us to experience the meaning of "family in Christ." Based on this alone, we have gained more than we have given. It is difficult for us to say good-bye to our brothers and sisters in Zhang-Wei every time we leave. It is our hope that more people will be willing to visit Zhuang-Wei to teach Bible study and Roman Pin-Yin so they can read the Bible and be built up in their faith to fight the good fight.

鹿港短宣
Lu-Kang Mission

陳明敏
紐約台美基督教會
Michael Ming-Min Chen
Taiwanese American Christian Church in New York

鹿港短宣

陳明敏
紐約台美基督教會

我的故鄉鹿港保存著豐富的歷史遺產與寺廟文化，但卻是一塊對福音冷漠的硬土。

近年來，無論官方或民間，都大力推廣鹿港，使之成為台灣文化遺產的旅遊焦點。因此，偶像供奉和寺廟慶典不僅是宗教，也是重要的觀光經濟來源。但感謝主，鹿港基督徒雖是少數，並沒有忘記他們的神聖責任。2006年，我的父母到紐約探望我們。他們在回台灣的前四天，受洗歸主。然後，他們渴望與鄉親分享福音的願望，成了我們紐約台美基督教會鹿港短宣計劃的催化劑。

2007年7月，台美基督教會展開第一次的〈鹿港心，鹿港情〉短宣。靠著主豐富的恩典，我們迄今已持續三年的鹿港短宣。

在過去三年裡，我們的短宣隊不僅將耶穌基督帶給美語夏令營的數百位學生，同時也到重度殘障中心、精神病院、老人醫療中心及中途兒童青少年之家傳播福音。

我們的美語夏令營的主題是「讓美國出生的ABC教您的孩子ABC」，對鹿港的孩童有很強的吸引力。台美青年們的音樂才華、舉止、語言與信仰，常常很快地成為鹿港孩童模仿的對象。然而為後續跟進起見，我們著實需要發展出一個長期的英語教學計劃。求主呼召長期宣教士派駐鹿港，建立英語事工。

2009年3月，我的母親被診斷出肝癌，開始接受治療。當短宣隊在八月到達鹿港時，她的身體已很虛弱，但她仍堅持留在鹿港，服事短宣隊。她在聖誕節前的星期天，安詳地歸回主懷。她在世時打了一場漂亮的仗，願有一天，她的祈禱會蒙應許，使她關心的親友與鹿港居民，接受主耶穌基督為他們的救主。

我們教會的鹿港短宣隊得到許多弟兄姐妹們的支持與奉獻，其中包括黃思義牧師動員全家、盧洲國傳道、周文景傳道、科琳・惠勒、許志靖傳道、李穎霖長老、李萬居長老、林思正長老及他們的夫人們、謝瑋恩執事、思群、…、我的太太謝坤蒨及多位年輕的朋友們。願聖靈感動更多忠心的基督徒為鹿港短宣隊奉獻與禱告。

2009 "鹿港心鹿港情" 短宣隊合照於鹿東醫院，作者陳明敏（中）
"Hearts and Souls for LuKang" Mission Team at Lu-Tong Hospital. Author and team leader Michael Ming-Min Chen (mid)

Lu-Kang Mission

Michael Ming-Min Chen
Taiwanese American Christian Church in New York

My home town, Lu-Kang, has preserved its rich heritage of historic temples. Yet, it is a hard soil with strong resistance and indifference to the Gospel. In recent years, Lu-Kang had also become a popular tourist attraction under the push of government and civic organizations, making idol worshipping and historic temples the main source of income. But praise the Lord! Even though the percentage of Christians is small there, God has not forgotten them.

My parents were baptized in 2006 when they came to New York to visit me. Following their baptism, their desire to share the Gospel with the relatives back at home became the catalyst for our church's mission plan. In July 2007, our church, Taiwanese American Christian Church, launched its first mission called "Hearts and Souls for Lu-Kang." By God's grace, we continued our mission to Lu-Kang for three years.

In the past three years, our mission teams have not only shared Jesus Christ with hundreds of students in English camps but we also visited centers for the disabled, mental institutions, senior homes and remedial schools for delinquent youths. The theme of our English camp is called "Let American-Born Chinese (ABC) Teach Your Children ABC," which had a strong appeal to the children in Lu-Kang. The musical talents, manners, speech and faith of our youth missionaries quickly became examples to the children. However, we need to develop a long-term English teaching plan to continue follow-up work. May the Lord send long-term missionaries to Lu-Kang to build up its English ministry!

In March 2009, my mom was diagnosed with liver cancer and began her medical treatment. When the mission team arrived in August, she was very weak but still insisted on staying in Lu-Kang to serve the team. She passed away the Sunday before Christmas. She had fought a good fight. My prayer is that her prayers to see beloved family and friends in Lu-Kang come to know Jesus Christ as their Savior will be answered one day.

Many faithful Christians have supported the mission financially and in prayers. Pastor Frank Hwang mobilized his whole family for the first mission. Minister Caleb Loo, Minister Wen-Ching Chow humbly served the mission. Evangelist Colleen Wheeler shared the gospel in local temples. Minister Mathew Hsu, Elder John Lee, Elder Edward Lee, Elder David Lin and their spouses sacrificed their vocations to serve in the mission. In addition, our young missionaries exemplified their strong influences; Ruth Lee joined the mission twice, Brian Hu returned with his brother Morgan. Stephanie Shen joined again with her sister Jessalyn, and Karen Lin returned with her mom Jinny. Phoebe, Leslie, Cindy, Pauline, and Stephen all further strengthened the mission. My dear wife Christina and lovely son Ryan were a great help to the mission, too.

8/17-21/09 紐約台美教會的 "鹿港心鹿港情" 美語夏令營結業照於鹿港國小
"Hearts and Souls for LuKang" English Summer Camp at LuKang Elementary School by Taiwanese American Church in New York.

探親成為短宣
Family Visit Can Be a Short-term Mission

周神耀牧師
紐澤西台灣第一長老教會
台灣宣教基金會救難隊牧師
Rev. Philip Chou
First Presbyterian Church in New Jersey
Rescue Team Pastor of Taiwan Mission Foundation

探親成為短宣

周神耀牧師
紐澤西台灣第一長老教會
台灣宣教基金會救難隊牧師

2006年夏天，我回台灣探望九十五高齡的母親。在過去數年，我每年都回員林故鄉一次，除探視老母外，也應邀至我受洗的母會—員林和平長老教會或其他教會講道。

2006年，經由和平教會張文明牧師的安排，我成為高中學生的英文老師。我在晚上到教會教學生中級英文，前後上了十堂課，每堂課兩小時，結果三星期的探親成為一次很有意義的短宣。

台灣的夏天酷熱不堪，教會免費提供冷氣教室，因此不少學生都在放學後到教會自修。張文明牧師認為我能以教英文的方式傳佈福音，因此為我安排時間、教材與設備，招募了約二十名學生。

那些學生來自附近的社區，大部份未信主，大都有英文基礎，然而聽講能力較弱，而且因為習慣講台語，比較不易發出英語中的雙母音連接音(Diphony)。

我們因此作了不少英文發音練習，尤其強調雙母音連結音與英文特有的強弱音節型態演練。與此同時，我用國際版英文聖經(NIV)與他們一起查馬太福音第五章的〈山上寶訓〉及約翰福音的一些經節。我一邊唸，一邊講解，發現他們都認真地學習。

每天的上課由祈禱開始，然後唱一首短的英文讚美詩，再進入課程。上課時，我常從經節的解釋談到人生的意義與生活的目標，進而宣講福音。我們談家庭、社會或國際間發生的一些問題、甚至宇宙的迷思，然後我告訴他們：信靠主耶穌，可找到一切答案。

他們讀了〈山上寶訓〉後，十分驚嘆裡面提及的崇高道德標準。我則指出很多信徒依靠聖靈，心中充滿神的愛，因此能體驗較高的道德標準。在查經的過程中，我們也藉著耶穌的言行，解說一些基本的教義如創造、道成肉身、十字架、復活、救贖與恩典等等。

最後一堂課時，學生們送給我一張他們自製的大型卡片，裡面寫的話語十分感人。我在珍惜這些情誼之際，發現原本只是一個簡單的探親之旅，竟變成一次意義深長的短宣。而且在我離去之後，教會裡的弟兄姐妹們繼續不斷耕耘。不久前，在員林和平長老教會擔任長老的弟弟告訴我，好幾位學生都接受洗禮，榮耀歸主名！

我相信北美洲的基督徒都有回故鄉傳播福音的機會，每個人都有神賜的恩典，在宣教的禾場上必有一個為神作工的角落。因此，請大家熱忱地加入短宣。相信宣教的事工將帶給你無限的喜樂，並使主的莊稼收成百倍。

作者周神耀牧師與夫人
Author Rev. and Mrs. Philip Chou

Family Visit Can Be a Short-term Mission

Rev. Philip Chou
First Presbyterian Church in New Jersey
Rescue Team Pastor of Taiwan Mission Foundation

During the summer of 2006, I visited my ninety-five year-old mother in Yuan-lin, Changhua. Prior to 2006, each time I went home, I visited my mom and also preached at my home church and nearby churches. However, that year, through the arrangement of Pastor Chang of Ho-Ping Presbyterian Church, I became an English teacher to high school students. I taught intermediate English at church in the evenings. With ten two-hour sessions, my family visit trip turned into a meaningful mission trip.

With the unbearably hot summer weather, many students went to the church after school to study because the church had air-conditioning. Pastor Chang believed that I could use English teaching as a method for evangelism. Thus, he made arrangements for classroom schedules and facilities and recruited about twenty students for me to teach. Most of the students came from nearby communities. The majority of them were non-believers and had basic English skills, but they were weaker in conversational English because their native tongue, Taiwanese, had a different diphthong than that used in English.

We went through pronunciation drills, emphasizing diphthong sounding and typical stressing patterns of the English language. At the same time, we also used the New International Version Bibles, studied the Sermon on the Mount in Matthew, chapter five, and selected passages from the Gospel of John. I read the passage verse by verse, followed by an explanation, and I found that they listened very attentively.

We began each class with a short prayer, followed by a short praise song in English. In class, I often talked with them about the meaning and purpose of life, and the Gospel. We talked about family, society and international problems and issues from current events. We even talked about the existence of the universe, and from that, I told them that they can find these answers through trusting in Jesus Christ.

After reading the Sermon on the Mount, they were astonished by the high ethical standard in the passage. I told them it is only possible to attain that standard if one has God-given love through the work of the Holy Spirit. We had a chance to share the doctrines of creation, incarnation, crucifixion, salvation and resurrection.

At the last class, they presented me with a big handmade card. Many remarks touched and moved my heart. I found that a short visitation to my family in Taiwan turned out to be much more rewarding than I expected.

Only recently, I had a chance to talk to my brother, who is an elder in the church, and heard about the wonderfully surprising news that many of my former students were baptized. Glory be to God!

I believe God wants to give opportunities to Christians who are willing to make good use of any occasions to spread the Gospel. God has given each person the grace to serve in a special corner in the huge harvest field, where one can be the most joyful and fruitful missionary.

快樂的福音志工

The Happy Volunteer for the Gospel

謝吟雪
加州柑縣愛恩台福教會
Linda Y. Hsieh
Evangelical Formosan Church of Irvine in S. California

快樂的福音志工

謝吟雪
加州柑縣愛恩台福教會

十多年前，一位來自台灣的病友對我說：「許多優秀的人自美國回台灣服務，使當地人受益良多。」

這些話在我心裡萌芽，加上神的美意，使我在紐約哥倫比亞教學醫院服務達三十四年後，決定趁身體還健壯時提早退休，回台灣宣教。

2006年夏天，我在北美路加團契退修會上，認識了來自台灣的翁瑞亨醫師伉儷。翁醫師曾在嘉義基督教醫院擔任十多年院長，爾後到神學院深造，再回來擔任該院的院牧部代理主任。他與他的夫人皆態度謙卑又和藹可親。經他們的牽引與安排，我走上回台當福音志工的路。

我在美國擔任過許多年的化療師，有不少腫瘤護理的經驗。自2006年秋退休後，我三度回台，擔任福音志工，前後在嘉義基督教醫院、花蓮門諾醫院⋯等八家醫院服事，與不少台灣年輕的護理人員共事。由於百分之八十五的嘉基和百分之七十五的門諾醫院員工都還不認識神，大家對我這個從美國回來志工所分享的見證，都很感興趣。

同時，感謝主賜予我智慧與膽量，讓我能在不同場合與不同背景的人分享神的奇異恩典。我甚至得有機會參與門諾醫院的病房平安禮拜，在為病患、家屬及門診者所設的佈道聚會中，向等候看診的民眾分享見證。

此外，神還擴展我的境界，讓我到各地的教會、松年團契或學生團契，甚至非基督徒的團體去教導「戰勝癌症的最佳武器」。我由衷感謝神，賜給我如此美好的機會，讓我得以回故鄉，傳播祂珍貴美好的信息。

The Happy Volunteer for the Gospel

Linda Y. Hsieh
Evangelical Formosan Church of Irvine in S. California

Ten years ago, a patient said to me, "Many outstanding Taiwanese American immigrants come back to Taiwan to serve, bringing many benefits to the people." These words began to germinate like seeds in my heart. And according to God's beautiful plan, I retired from the New York Presbyterian Hospital Columbia Medical Center after thirty-four years and decided to go back to Taiwan for mission while my body was still healthy.

At the CCMM retreat in the summer of 2006, I met two missionaries from Taiwan, Dr. David Weng and his wife. After serving as the President of Chia-Yi Christian Hospital (CYCH) for more than 10 years, Dr. Weng went to seminary and is now serving as the Deputy Director of the Pastoral Care Department. Dr. Weng and his wife are very humble and friendly people. Through their connections and arrangements, I began the path of being a Gospel volunteer.

I was an oncologist for many years in the United States and had performed numerous cancer treatments. Ever since I retired in 2006, I visited Taiwan three times to serve as a Gospel volunteer. I served and worked with many young healthcare professionals in eight different hospitals, including CYCH and Menno Christian Hospital (MCH), where eighty-five and seventy-five percent of the medical staff respectively, did not know God, and they took great interest in my testimony.

At the same time, God gave me the wisdom and courage to share about God's amazing grace with different people in different places. I even had the opportunity to join MCH hospital service where we could evangelize and share

The Happy Volunteer for the Gospel

testimonies with patients, their families and people who were waiting to see the doctors.

Moreover, God extended my boundaries to many different churches, as well as senior and student fellowships. I also had the chance to reach out to non-Christian groups by giving a talk on "The Best Weapon of Fighting Cancer." I am very grateful for the wonderful God-given opportunity to return to my homeland to share His precious Good News.

10/19/2009 退休腫瘤護理專科化療師謝吟雪演講 「戰勝癌症的最佳武器」
Retired oncology nurse specialist, chemotherapy division, Linda Y. Hsieh giving speech on "The Best Weapon to Combat Cancer"

退休腫瘤護理專科化療師謝吟雪
Retired oncology nurse specialist, chemotherapy division, Linda Y. Hsieh

護理之家的宣教

Mission of the Nursing Home

李碧珣
大波士頓台灣基督長老教會
(大里)葡萄園護理之家創設人
Yana Lee
Taiwan Presbyterian Church of Greater Boston
Founder of (Tali) Vineyard Nursing Home

護理之家的宣教

李碧珣
大波士頓台灣基督長老教會
(大里)葡萄園護理之家創設人

我早年在彰化基督教醫院從事專業社區的護理工作時，即察覺隨著醫藥的進步，台灣老人的數目與年歲將不斷地增加，失能老人也會與日俱增。

十幾年前，台灣很少有私立的護理中心，不少老人住在沒有立案、也沒有專業護理的簡陋私營居所。我覺得那些老人很可憐，便於1997年在台中縣大里鄉開設一家能容納三十個床位的「葡萄園護理之家」。這是台中縣第一所立案的私立護理之家，在創立那年，還得過衛生署頒發的十大全台護理中心獎。

自「葡萄園護理之家」成立迄今，我們每年都舉辦宣傳福音的活動，也在平時結合當地教會的志工定期關懷，並為失能老人們禱告。

2009年，我們與潭子工業福音中心一起舉辦慶祝中秋節活動，為失能老人及家屬安排精彩的國樂演奏、詩歌讚美、見證分享、有獎徵答與摸彩等活動。雖然有一些失能老人無法言語，但從他們的眼神，我們可以感受到他們的確喜歡這樣的活動，他們的家屬也都很感激。雖然我們不確定他們何時會認耶穌為救主，但相信持之以恆，上帝的恩典必會降臨到他們身上。

十年來，除了有些老人在護理之家歸入主名外，也有好幾位工作人員受洗為基督徒。同時，不少老人的問題也透過禱告獲得改善，感謝主！

我於2004年移民美國波士頓，因此聘人管理經營。今(2009)年四月底，「台灣宣教基金會」會長楊宜宜訪問大波士頓台灣基督長老教會時，請我擔任該基金會的護理老人宣教事工組長，並鼓勵我寫下這段有關老人宣教的見證，與大家分享。

如今，因為我住美國，就決定將「葡萄園護理之家」讓予在台灣關心老人事工

的主內專業護理人員。求神帶領承辦者能繼續愛顧這些失能老人，點燃他們生命得救的火苗；也盼望更多人參與這樣的宣教事工，讓更多老人得到屬靈的生命。

【編註: 因著有愛心的牧師和基督徒願意定期至「葡萄園護理之家」關心老人，作者已決定不頂讓出售，而要將「護理之家」繼續保留下來，從事關懷老人的宣教事工。】

2009春作者李碧珣(右一)與同工在葡萄園護理之家分享福音
Spring 2009- Author Yana Lee (1st right) & coworkers sharing the Gospel with the elderly at Vineyard Nursing Home

Mission of the Nursing Home

Yana Lee
Taiwan Presbyterian Church of Greater Boston
Founder of (Tali) Vineyard Nursing Home

While working as a specialized community nurse at Chang-Hwa Christian Hospital, I had sensed that, with the advances in medicine, the average age of the elderly population would also rise, causing an increase in the number of disabled seniors. Ten years ago, there were very few private nursing care centers in Taiwan. Most seniors lived in non-registered private facilities without professional nurses. I felt deep compassion for these seniors, so I started a thirty bed capacity nursing facility called Vineyard Nursing Home. It became the first registered private nursing home in Tai-Chung County, which was awarded as the best nursing care facility by the Health Department.

Since the establishment of Vineyard Nursing Home, we have hosted evangelism and outreach events annually. We have also worked with volunteers from local churches to care and pray for the seniors. In 2009, we worked with Tanzu Industrial Mission in hosting a Mid-Autumn Moon Festival for disabled seniors and their families. The event included Chinese music performance, praise and worship, testimony sharing, raffles and games. Although some disabled elders were unable to communicate, the look from their eyes revealed how much they enjoyed the event. Even though we were uncertain when they would receive Jesus Savior, we were confident that, if we were faithful, God would pour out His grace. Not only did many seniors become God's children in the past ten years, but many staff members were also baptized. Moreover, many of the seniors also experienced the power of prayer to resolve their problems. Praise the Lord!

Mission of the Nursing Home

I immigrated to Boston in 2004 after arranging new management to take care of Vineyard Nursing Home. When Eileen Yi Yi Chang, President of the Taiwan Mission Foundation (TMF) visited our church, Taiwan Presbyterian Church of Greater Boston, in April 2009, she invited me to head the division of missions in nursing homes within TMF. She also encouraged me to share my experiences through writing.

I have decided to transfer management of Vineyard Nursing Home to healthcare professionals because I am in the United States. May God continue to lead these successors to care for disabled seniors and to kindle a fire of salvation in them. Moreover, I hope to see more people join hands in this ministry.

【Note: In light of a continuing effort by Taiwanese pastors and Christians to support Vineyard Nursing Home, the author has decided to continue to run the nursing home to serve the elderly.】

4/2009葡萄園護理之家的創立者/作者李碧珣(中穿藍衣)與同工合影
Spring 2009 - Yana Lee (mid in blue) - Author and Founder of Vineyard Nursing Home with mission team

育幼院的春天
Spring in the Children's Home

高天星
北加州台灣迦南教會
Caroline Kao
Canaan Taiwanese Christian Church in N. California

育幼院的春天

高天星
北加州台灣迦南教會

我在1996年拿到比較宗教學碩士後，誤打誤撞地進入科技公司，成為一名專案經理，雖然薪水不錯，心靈卻常感到孤單，因此向上帝呼喊：「主啊，求祢指示我一條道路！」

2004年四月起，我常夢到一系列相關的異象：總有一群小朋友在教室等我，或在路上跟隨我，告訴我說他們在等我，請我去教他們！

我想起出國前的教師生涯，覺得那是我一生中最愉快的時光，所以到了那年九月，我毅然辭掉科技公司的職務，在太陽谷市成立「展望教育中心」。此後，我和學生們陸續捐寄一些英文兒童書本，給台灣偏遠山地的國小和育幼院。在從事這些事工時，我逐漸明白回台灣傳福音是神要我走的路。

2008年十二月，我回到台灣，在西螺信義育幼院住了一星期。這是一個多家道壇支持的育幼院，我很感激他們給我學習的機會。清晨醒來，幼兒班的小小頭顱已出現在窗邊。從小就是孩子王的我與幼兒班的八位小朋友都玩得很開心。他們之中的幾位都來自破碎的家庭，有時會私下來找我。聖靈常給我啟示，讓我能溫暖他們的心。

一個溫暖的午後，我坐在長椅上享受陽光、閱讀書本。十歲的小俊坐到我旁邊來，我們相視微笑。我知道他小小的心靈曾受過傷，便對他說：「有時大人不知道自己在做什麼，你得學習原諒他們。」孩子睜著大眼睛，望了我一下，便走掉。幾分鐘後，他再回來，問道：「要如何原諒？」我告訴他耶穌被釘十字架的故事，以及祂在十字架上的話語：「父啊！赦免他們，因為他們所做的，他們不曉得。」然後對小俊說，這是一個非常困難的課程，但我們得盡量學習遠離黑暗，生活在光明中。我不知道他明白多少，但看見他的眼裡泛著淚光。

育幼院的春天

四歲半的小鐵蛋是我的麻吉小兄弟，常自願保護我的皮包，也要求我保護他的玩具。一到周末，總有一些善心人士到育幼院探訪，他常常跑到不同的客人面前，哀求道：「叔叔，請你帶我回家。」許多訪客都不知該如何回應。

我離開那天，怕孩子們會哭，便趁他們午睡時離去。然而一到停車場，卻發現十一歲的亞倫和另一個男孩已在那裡等候。他們送我到客運站搭車，讓我十分感動。回美國後，我有時想起信義育幼院的那五十名孩子，會不禁淚水盈眶。若非上帝選召我，我依舊是一個終日惶惶、心靈空虛的人。感謝主，允許我為祂作見證。

西螺信義育幼院因為建蓋在公園預定地上，2011年將面臨拆遷，求主保守。我則希望在來年的夏天，能多找幾個朋友，一起回台灣教英文，盼大家一起來做主的聖工。

【編註：2011年5月作者偕美籍夫婿搬回台灣，並計劃從事長期宣教】

2008作者高天星回台輔助西螺信義育幼院可憐無辜的孩子
2008- Caroline Kao served the children with a loving heart at Xin-Yi Orphanage

Spring in the Children's Home

Caroline Kao
Canaan Taiwanese Christian Church in N. California

After receiving my Master's degree in Comparative Religion in 1996, I was hired as a department manager at a hi-tech company. Although I had a very decent salary, my heart often felt very lonely. I cried out to the Lord, saying, "O Lord, please show me the way!"

Starting in April 2004, I often had dreams and visions, where I would see a group of children waiting for me in a classroom or walking beside me to tell me that they were waiting for me to teach them! As I continued to have these dreams, I would recall the good old days as a teacher in Taiwan. The memories led me to my resignation from the hi-tech company in order to establish an educational center in Sunnyvale, where we collected children's books in English and shipped them to schools and children's homes in rural Taiwan. Through this ministry, I gradually realized that the Lord had been leading me to Taiwan to share the Gospel.

In December 2008, I spent a week in Xin-Yi Orphanage in Shi-Lo, Taiwan. Although the orphanage was sponsored by Taoist temples, I was very grateful for the opportunity they provided for learning. In the morning when I woke up, I saw little kids pressing their heads against my windows. The kids and I really enjoyed playing together. Many of them came from broken families, and when they came to talk with me privately, the Holy Spirit often gave me words to warm their hearts.

One afternoon, as I was sitting on a bench reading, Jim, a ten-year old, came to sit next to me. Knowing that he had been hurt before, I said to him, "You have to learn to forgive adults because they do not always know what they are doing." The child gazed at me and then walked away. A few minutes later, he returned and asked me, "How do you forgive?" I shared with him what Jesus said when He was on the cross– "Father, forgive them, for they do not know what they are doing." I also explained that forgiveness was a very difficult lesson, but we must learn to walk in light and not in darkness. Although I did not know how much he understood, I saw his eyes tear up.

A four year-old boy named "Iron Egg," who often guarded my wallet and who I often helped to guard his toys, was like a "machi" brother to me. Every weekend, when visitors came to the orphanage, he went to different visitors and asked them to take him home. Most visitors did not know how to respond!

On the day of my departure, I left the orphanage during the afternoon naptime because I was afraid to see them cry. Yet, while I was still in the parking lot, an eleven year-old boy, Allen, and his friend were waiting for me to accompany me to the bus station. Oh, how it touched my heart!

After returning to the United States, tears would well up in my eyes whenever I thought about the children at Xin-Yi Orphanage. If the Lord had not chosen me to go back, I would still be living with the emptiness inside. Instead, I am grateful that He gave me the opportunity to witness for Him.

Because the orphanage was built on land designated for public park land, it will be relocating in 2011. May the Lord watch over them! My hope is to find more people to join me in this ministry!

[Note: The author and her husband returned to Taiwan in May 2011 as long-term missionaries.]

紐約長島豐盛生命教會
與台灣宣教
Long Island Abundant Life Church and Taiwan Mission

高林麗蒂
紐約長島豐盛生命教會普世宣教部長
Lydia Kao
Long Island Abundant Life Church
Chairman of World Missions Committee

紐約長島豐盛生命教會與台灣宣教

高林麗蒂
紐約長島豐盛生命教會
普世宣教部長

1999年9月21日，台灣發生百年來最嚴重的大地震，中部地區無數城鄉房塌人亡，數萬人流離失所，實為我們這一代在台灣長大的人有記憶以來最嚴重的一次天災。

「九二一」大地震發生後，紐約長島豐盛生命教會在短時間內即為之籌款，然後交由世界展望會，再轉給台灣世展會作賑災用。因此，台灣世界展望會在災後邀請我們參與他們在災區後續心靈重建的服事。

長島豐盛生命教會在此之前，沒有組織海外宣教的團隊經驗，只有個人參加宣教機構所組織的短宣隊或培訓工作。因此當教牧同工決定接受台灣世界展望會的邀請後，大家都戮力共襄盛舉，從組織到一切準備，均在短時間內成形。

2000年七月，我們首次的短宣隊正式出發，成員有教師、學員與一位來自香港、不諳普通話的教師。因為每位成員都為傳福音的緣故到台灣，神便將得救的人數天天加添給這個團隊。

羅馬書第十章第十五節說：「若沒有奉差遣，怎能傳道呢？如經上所記：報福音、傳喜信的人，他們的腳蹤何等佳美！」兩百年前，馬禮遜宣教師到中國傳道；一百多年前，馬偕醫生到台灣宣教，豈不都是「奉差遣」而來？

神用「九二一」大災難，教導長島豐盛生命教會不僅用金錢差傳，也要用行動差傳。普世宣教的功課很多，因為對台灣的宣教，使教會得到造就，也使許多人成為神的出口。

我們認為台灣是一塊安全又自由的傳福音之地，沒有宗教迫害的顧慮，只要有傳福音的心志，聽神的差遣與吩咐，到台灣宣教應是一項義不容辭的聖工。

Long Island Abundant Life Church and Taiwan Mission

Lydia Kao
Long Island Abundant Life Church
Chairman of World Missions Committee

On September 21, 1999, the most catastrophic earthquake in the history of Taiwan took place, causing many buildings in central Taiwan to collapse and many people to lose their homes. This event became one of the most devastating natural disasters that our generation would remember.

Following the earthquake, Long Island Abundant Life Church conducted fundraising events to raise money for the needy. Later through World Vision U.S. headquarters, the money was channeled to World Vision Taiwan to support earthquake relief efforts. Through the donation, World Vision Taiwan invited us to co-labor with them and participate in the post-disaster renewal work.

Long Island Abundant Life Church had no prior experience in organizing overseas missions, although individual members had worked with other mission organizations. When our pastor and the deacon board accepted this invitation from World Vision Taiwan, everyone was very excited and all of the work, from organizing the team to preparing the trip, was formed and shaped quickly.

In July of 2000, New York Long Island Abundant Life Church sent its first short-term mission team to Taiwan. The team consisted of our pastor, students and a teacher from Hong Kong who did not speak Mandarin. Since every team member went to Taiwan for the sake of the Gospel, God added to the number of people saved each day.

Romans 10:15 says, "How can they preach unless they are sent? As it is written, "How beautiful are the feet of those who bring good news!" Two hundred

Long Island Abundant Life Church and Taiwan Mission

years ago, Robert Morrison went to China as a missionary. One hundred years ago, Dr George MacKay went to Taiwan. Was it not because they were sent?

Through the catastrophe, God taught Long Island Abundant Life Church that mission is not only about sending money, but also about action. There are many lessons we need to learn in the world mission area. Through this particular short-term mission, the church was being equipped to become a channel through which God could work. We firmly believe Taiwan is a safe and free place for spreading the Gospel. Without a concern for religious persecution, a willing heart to preach the Gospel is all it takes to respond to God's call to send us to Taiwan for mission work.

長島豐盛生命教會短宣隊與桃園高城浸信會合辦暑期兒童營，作者高林麗蒂(二排右一)
Children's Camp by Long Island Abundant Life Church short-term mission team and Tao-Yuan Gao-Chan Baptist Church co-workers, Author Lydia Kao (2nd row 1st right)

短宣隊長用三福佈道法向兒童傳福音，作者(左立者)
Mission Team leaders used EE materials to spread the Gospel

紐約晨星教會赴台短宣

Morning Star New York – 2009 Missions Trip

David Miller 主任牧師
紐約晨星教會
Senior Pastor David Miller
Morning Star New York

Morning Star New York – 2009 Missions Trip

Senior Pastor David Miller
Morning Star New York

In July 2009, a team of eleven people from Morning Star New York (MSNY) journeyed to Taiwan. The team's main objective was to assist Taiwanese Pastor K.C. Liu with his gospel outreach efforts in Taiwan. Pastor Liu received Christ while studying as a graduate student at the University of North Carolina-Chapel Hill. He came to the Lord while attending King's Park International Church in Durham, NC in 1983, a church founded by MSNY's Senior Pastor, Ron Lewis.

In the 1980s, Pastor Liu and his wife, Shih Chia, received a call from God to minister in Mainland China. They spent many years planting underground churches in several major cities, only leaving when persecution from the Communist authorities made them fear for their safety. Their efforts in Mainland China were very fruitful, and they left many thriving churches behind. After spending some time on furlough, in 2008 Pastor Liu began to feel God's call to return to his native Taiwan to begin spreading the Gospel there. In early 2009, Pastor Liu founded Every Nation Taipei Church.

Located near the campus of National Taiwan University, ENTC's mission is to reach young Taiwanese leaders for Christ. Recognizing that 95% of all Christians come to Christ before the age of 25, the college campus is a key harvest field for souls in Taiwan. Furthermore, as NTU attracts the best and brightest young people from all over Taiwan, ENTC has the opportunity to reach and disciple the future leaders of their nation.

Morning Star New York is a non-denominational church comprised of individuals from over fifty different nations. Since the congregation is very diverse, the pastors at MSNY recognize that they have a call to reach many nations around the world. Pastor Lewis decided to focus MSNY's mission efforts on Taiwan for several reasons. First, he has a rich history of ministry with Pastor Liu, having mentored him in North Carolina. Second, the current state of Christianity in Taiwan, with only three percent (3%) of the nation professing Christ, created a sense of urgency to help reach that nation with the Gospel. Finally, Taiwan's strategic location in East Asia and the ongoing improvement in relations with mainland China suggest that Taiwan has a very strategic role to play in the Kingdom of God in years to come.

The MSNY team's evangelistic strategy focused on two main areas: the NTU campus, and the business community of Taiwan. On the NTU campus, the team focused primarily on relational evangelism. The team was composed primarily of young people about the same age as NTU's students; it was therefore easy for them to meet students who were interested in befriending Americans and practicing their English. As relationships formed, the MSNY team was able to share the Gospel with the students. By the grace of God, dozens of students came to Christ. In the business community, Pastor Lewis and his wife Lynette used an outreach strategy focused on corporate events. Lynette Lewis is a well-known speaker in corporate America, and a couple of events that featured her as the key speaker were well-attended by Taiwanese business leaders. In addition, several members of the MSNY team were also successful professionals in corporate America, and were also able to share their testimonies. Many good connections were made, and Lynette Lewis was even featured in the popular Taiwanese magazine, "Citta Bella."

All of the individuals reached by the team were referred to Pastor Liu and Every Nation Taipei Church for follow-up. Many of the young people from NTU who were reached by the team have since begun attending ENTC, and are being discipled in the foundations of the Christian faith. In addition to Senior Pastor Ron Lewis and his wife Lynette, members of the team included Associate Pastor Bruce Ho, David Tang, Bertina Hu, Maria Guinto, Isabel Lin, Connie Chen, Alana Yost, Sara Piali, and Lydia Velichkovski. The team from MSNY was blessed to have been used by God in the nation of Taiwan and plans to return again in the near future.

台灣之友
舒曼徹 Chuck 叔叔
Friend of Taiwan - Uncle Chuck

林青瑤
維吉尼亞州黑堡
Cindy Lin Dillard
Blacksburg, Virginia

台灣之友 ──舒曼徹(Chuck)叔叔

林青瑤
維吉尼亞州黑堡

這五、六年來，每年夏天，如果你在台灣南部的大埤、蒜頭、鳥松或長治等地方，可能會看到一個藍眼睛、高鼻子的美國人 ── 舒曼徹Chuck叔叔與一群當地的年輕人，穿梭在南台灣鄉下的學校、教會與街道中。

我在二十多年前還是維吉尼亞理工暨州立大學 (Virginia Tech) 研究生時，認識了舒曼徹(Chuck)叔叔。那時，我尚未信主，但到中文查經班查經、學習。舒曼徹(Chuck)叔叔與我們一起查經，他曾在台灣當過宣教士，與太太及三歲大的女兒在台灣住了兩年。

當時，我們中文查經班的成員大都是台灣來的留學生，說的是台灣國語，但曾就讀師大國語中心的舒曼徹(Chuck)叔叔則講著一口標準的國語。當他讀起中文聖經，會令我們為自己的國語汗顏。

舒曼徹(Chuck)叔叔在查經班裡很得人緣。他是個很會修車子的電腦工程師，不拘小節，又熱心、隨和、極富幽默感。留學生中，許多人都知道這個很會講北京話、又很熱心幫助人的美國人，有時還會邀請他在我們的春節晚會中表演相聲。二十多年來，我沒有搬離黑堡，但卻從留學生變成教師眷屬。我眼見維大的台灣留學生逐漸減少，但中國留學生卻直線上升。目前，台灣留學生人數大約只有中國留學生人數的十分之一，成為一個不被重視的宣教禾場。

舒曼徹(Chuck)叔叔也仍住在黑堡，也始終服事華人的宣教事工。多年來。他不僅協助成立華人主日聚會，也負責週六的長青團契。每年，我家玉米成熟，請台灣留學生來摘玉米、烤玉米時，舒曼徹(Chuck)叔叔都會偕太太前來，藉此認識新來的同學。

台灣之友 - 舒曼徹Chuck叔叔

2003年,台灣的陳文逸牧師到美國宣講台灣「鄉福」的事工,舒曼徹(Chuck)叔叔從中得到感動,此後每年夏天,都帶領一群不大會說國語的美語年輕人飛到台灣,短宣一個月。年紀已過半百的他與隊員們一起睡地舖、吃大鍋飯,毫無怨尤。曾有教會的姊妹見他如此服事,非常辛苦,心疼地問:「你年紀不小了,還這樣長途跋涉地到台灣短宣,怎麼受得了?」他卻只哈哈一笑,繼續樂此不疲地服事台灣的「鄉福」。

我們相信這是上帝的愛與恩典,使舒曼徹(Chuck)叔叔能年復一年,如鷹展翅般地飛到台灣,傳遞福音。台灣能有這樣的朋友,著實福氣!我們實在需要更多像這樣的好朋友,也希望更多的台灣人能夠認識主,得到救恩!

舒曼徹的暑期事工
Chuck Schumann's summer camp service

相片取自網路
Photos from internet

Friend of Taiwan — Uncle Chuck

Cindy Lin Dillard
Blacksburg, Virginia

In the past five or six years, if you were a child from the villages of southern Taiwan, you might have seen a blue-eyed, high-nosed American man called Uncle Chuck and a group of young people, traveling to various schools, churches and streets to evangelize.

I met Uncle Schumann when I was a graduate student at Virginia Tech more than 20 years ago. Although I was not a believer at the time, I attended a Chinese Bible Study led by Uncle Schumann, who had gone to Taiwan for two years as a missionary with his wife and their three year-old daughter. At the time, most members of the Chinese Bible Study were from Taiwan. Our spoken Mandarin had a heavy Taiwanese accent, but Uncle Schumann's Chinese was quite accurate. We often felt ashamed of our Chinese pronunciation when Chuck read the Bible in Chinese.

Uncle Schumann, a computer programmer, was very lively, humorous, easygoing, compassionate, and good at fixing cars. Many Taiwanese and Chinese students knew that this "foreigner" could speak Chinese very well and was always willing to help others. So he was often invited to do Chinese drama shows at Chinese New Year parties.

More than twenty years have passed. I have not left Blacksburg but my status has changed from a student to a Virginia Tech professor's wife. Throughout all these years, I have witnessed how the number of Taiwanese students at the church has dwindled from several hundred to no more than one tenth of the students from China. Perhaps there are several reasons to explain this phenomenon. However, it is a fact that the mission field of Taiwanese students has been neglected. Uncle Schumannhas not moved away from Blacksburg. He also has not stoppedserving Chinese people. In the past few years, he has helped establish the Chinese Fellowship and Evergreen Fellowship. Every year, when we invited Taiwanese students to harvest corn at our small farm, Uncle Schumann and his wife would also participate because it was an opportunity to get to know new Taiwanese students.

In 2003, when Pastor Wen-Yi Chen from Village Gospel Mission (VGM) came to share the vision of preaching the Gospel in the villages of Taiwan, Uncle Schumann was deeply touched. In response to this calling, he has led a group of youth on one month short-term mission trips to Taiwan every summer since 2004. Although he is in his 50s now, every year on short-term mission trips, he would sleep on the floor with his young teammates. An elderly sister, who understood that this kind of life could be quite tough for adults, said to him one time, 'Uncle Schumann, you are getting old. How many years do you think you can act like those young people to go abroad for short-term mission?" But he just laughed and continued serving Taiwan tirelessly.

I believe it is God's love and grace that inspires him to serve Taiwanese people without ceasing. It is a great blessing to have a friend like this. Taiwanese people need more friends like him.

舒曼徹的暑期青少年事工
Chuck Schumann summer youth service

鄉福宣教分享
Village Gospel Mission Experience

舒曼徹叔叔
黑堡基督徒團契 - 維吉尼亞州
Chuck Schumann
Blacksburg Christian Fellowship in Virginia

鄉福宣教分享

舒曼徹(Chuck)叔叔
黑堡BCF基督徒團契－維吉尼亞州

「我立了志向,不在基督的名被稱過的地方傳福音,免得建造在別人的根基上。就如經上所記:未曾聞知他信息的,將要看見;未曾聽過的,將要明白。」(羅馬書15:20-21)

我願意與大家分享,為何我們的教會在最近七年,每年夏天皆差派短宣隊到台灣的鄉村宣教。

這許多年來,我們看到很多人對到中國宣教感興趣,我們為此讚美神,但是,我們也看到其他宣教工場因此被取代了。據估計,在台灣,真正認識耶穌救主的人僅佔全人口的百分之三。至於在鄉間,基督徒更是少之又少。

然而,我們並不因此而絕望。每年暑假,許多北美教會皆與台灣的宣教機構如「鄉村福音」一起同工,在一些小學或國中舉辦英語營,對「鄉福」工作的社區展開服務。鄉福的工作區皆設在基督徒較少的地方。同工們透過課後輔導、成人教育與社區發展,使鄉福成為地方的光與鹽。

與很多教會一樣,我們剛開始只差派一小支由年輕人組成的短宣隊,幫忙英語營,給鄉福人力上的支援,也藉此與鄉福的同工及台灣的學童們分享主的愛。每個英語營為期一週,約有六十至一百名學生參加。我們與十五至二十名台灣青年基督徒一起服事。不少早期參加過英語營的孩子年年都會回來,其中有些已經成為基督徒,並且在暑假期間與我們同工。

由於鄉福長期服務社區,所以事先能與學校、學生取得聯繫,做好準備工作。我們去教英語,只是短期服事。在英語營結束後,鄉福同工繼續長期跟進。 因此,許多參加暑假英語營的孩子都與同工建立友誼,後來繼續參加教會所舉辦的課後輔導。

我們每年都面對超過我們能力與智慧所能解決的新挑戰，也學到如何謙卑地與同工及在地教會彼此相互服事。神常常讓我們看見我們的不足，因而體會在困難中仰賴主耶穌是多麼地有福！

我們與台灣的同工一起生活，並沒有享受任何特別的優待。當我們順服大使命，看到鄉村的學童得以認識主耶穌，鄉間的教會也因此更加堅固，就覺得十分欣慰。我相信到台灣宣教的事工，會給予就讀美國中學與大學的年輕人一個改變人生的機會。換句話說，我們在傳揚福音的過程中，也學到作基督門徒的寶貴屬靈功課。

舒曼徹的暑期事工
Chuck Schumann's summer service

【編註Editor's Notes】【悼念舒曼徹宣教師】連續八個夏季致力台灣宣教的舒曼徹Chuck叔叔，是極受台灣孩子歡迎的短宣勇士，也是本篇『鄉福宣教分享』的作者。10/21/2012，他突然蒙主恩召，未及見著本書的出版，但我們永不忘他對台灣的愛。- 編者註 -

【In loving memory of Chuck Schumann】Chuck was a beloved and devoted short term missionary to Taiwan for 8 years, also writer of "Village Gospel Mission Experience". Chuck died suddenly on October 21, 2012 before this book was published. His love for Taiwan and Taiwanese souls will forever be remembered. - by Editorial Board-

Village Gospel Mission Experience

Chuck Schumann
Blacksburg Christian Fellowship in Virginia

"… I make it my ambition to preach the gospel, not where Christ has already been named lest I build on someone else's foundation, but as it is written, 'Those who have never been told of him will see, and those who have never heard will understand.'" (Rom 15:20-21)

I would like to share with you why our church will be taking our seventh trip to Taiwan this coming summer, July 2010. For many years we have seen renewed interest in reaching Chinese people with the gospel. For this we praise God, but this seems to have come at the expense of other mission fields. It has been estimated that the total number of Christians in Taiwan is only approximately three percent. In rural towns, less than one percent of the people know the Savior.

But we are not without hope. Every summer several American churches team up with a Taiwanese church-planting organization, the Village Gospel Mission (VGM), to run summer English camps in public elementary and middle schools. This is done as a service to the communities where the VGM is working. The VGM focuses on communities where there is no meaningful Christian witness. Through after-school programs, adult education, and other community development efforts, VGM seeks to be salt and light in these dark places. Like other churches, we have begun sending a small team of young people every summer to partner with the VGM to help with the summer English camps. Together with the VGM we are able to love and serve Taiwanese children in the name of Christ.

As part of this effort, we will be working with fifteen to twenty Taiwanese believers to present a weeklong program in public schools. Each camp has between sixty to one hundred students attending, and most return year after year. Some have come to faith in Christ and are now serving with us as co-workers during the summer.

Because the VGM has committed full-time staff in each of these communities, they are able to prepare the way beforehand by working with the local school administration and students. Although we are there for only a short time, the VGM worker remains behind to continue building relationships and counseling students. Many of our English camp students begin to attend after-school programs because of the friendships that have been established during the summer.

Every year we face new challenges and need strength and wisdom which are beyond us. It is amazing how much we learn about humbly serving one another and our hosts. Many times we have seen God giving us what was lacking in ourselves. What a blessing to learn to lean on Christ in the difficult times.

We are equal partners with our Taiwanese co-workers, living and working alongside these brothers and sisters without special accommodations. We have learned that, by our obedience to the Great Commission, village children can learn of Christ's love for them and churches in rural towns are strengthened. This opportunity to serve Christ in Taiwan can be life-changing to an American young person. So, it could be said that we go to preach the gospel and in the process learn valuable spiritual lessons as disciples of Jesus.

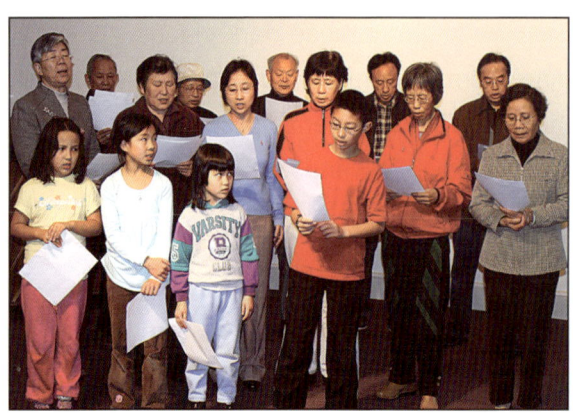

舒曼徹的事工
Chuck Schumann's mission work

此相片取自網路
photo from internet

第三篇
台美青年回台短宣篇
Short-Term ABT Taiwan Mission Teams

III. 台美青年回台短宣篇

籌訓「美語營」短宣隊

莊澤豐主任牧師
南加州柑縣台福基督教會

近年來，神奇妙地為北美及紐澳台福教會打開台灣宣教的大門，直接進入台灣的校園，向容易接受福音的國小、國中學生傳福音。最近這十年可說是以英文教學的青年及成人返台宣教的好時機。根據我過去多次帶團回台短宣的經驗，籌組一次成功的「美語營」短宣隊，大致需要下列幾項步驟：

一、計劃擬訂
1.短宣日期： 短宣的日期與地點宜在出發前的五、六個月內確定。青年通常利用在寒暑假組隊回台，成人則可選擇機票較便宜的季節回台灣。
2.地點選定： 首次參加短宣的人宜選擇到開拓性的鄉村教會或自己熟悉的教會，比較容易收到學習的成效。

二、短宣策略
1.青年短宣：
a.透過當地教會的連繫，在各學校舉辦為期一週的「雙語福音營」(或品格營、領袖訓練營、聖誕晚會)，以英文教學、唱詩歌、演話劇等方式介紹福音。由教授英語的青年，以愛心誠懇地與台灣的國中或國小學生交談、相處，並傳講耶穌、信主禱告，其後再由當地的教會作後續的栽培。
b.以到社區探訪、講道、發福音傳單、街頭或夜市佈道、探訪老人院、孤兒院、監獄等方式傳福音。
2.成人短宣
a.舉辦如保健、家庭、婚姻、親子、理財、科學等的專題講座。
b.舉辦如插花、胸花製作、摺彩色紙藝、教樂器等的手工藝班。
c.舉辦成人英文會話班、福音茶會或魔術、木偶戲表演，讓社區居民與教會自然接觸。

d.以個人談道、逐家探訪、心靈協談、城鄉走禱、街頭佈道、發福音單張等方式傳講福音。
3.成人青年混合短宣
a.成人可協助照顧青年隊員的生活、飲食、起居、財政，及與當地教會協調溝通，或擔任課堂上的助教等服務性質的工作。
b.帶領短宣隊的每日靈修，及負責攝影、寫日記、代禱等記錄或文書的工作。
c.帶領主日崇拜、敬拜詩歌、講道、見証分享、教主日學、領青少年團契，或開佈道會、培靈會、陪讀聖經、帶領查經班與從事課後輔導等服事。
4.教會詩班可組團返台，配合當地牧者赴監獄、學校、養老院…等地方，從事音樂佈道。譬如，加州橘郡的愛恩台福詩班最近三年都回台，先後在四十六所監獄從事短宣與佈道。

三、徵召隊員
1.暑期短宣隊宜在每年一至三月成立，冬季短宣隊宜在八至九月成立。由於鄉下教會的食宿與交通均受限制，每隊人數以六至十人為佳，青年佔三分之二的最適當。
2.隊員：可於半年前開始在週報或網站徵募志工，以十七歲以上重生得救、並有宣教使命之青年及成年基督徒為主。如有低於十七歲的青少年想參加，應有其父母陪同。
3.指定籌備組連絡人，報名時即應填妥報名表，繳交費用，以掌握資料。
4.經費預估：教材、集訓、在台食宿、交通費等的經費預估，每人每週約一百美金，另加返台之來回機票。費用可自行籌募，或各教會酌予補助。

四、準備與連繫

1.參加隊員及台宣同工每週定時舉行禱告會，並作事工計劃、討論。
2.隨時將短宣隊之籌備組訓經過、隊員名單〈年齡、恩賜、負擔〉傳給前往宣道之教會，彼此代禱。
3.請對方教會也將其安排計劃、一週活動時間表、學生報名人數或名單傳回〈以四至六年級及國中生為營會對象〉，彼此代禱。若有重要事宜，隨時以越洋電話或郵電與對方的牧師連絡。

4.如對宣教工場不熟悉，最好連絡人能於三個月前或營會一週前先行返台，接洽有關食、宿與營會細節等事宜。
5.每人必須繳交一篇三分鐘的「信主得救見證」，及「基要真理」簡述，並輪流上台見證、演練。
6.短宣隊員行前三個月需努力操練體能，方能勝任繁重的任務。
7.短宣隊需預備簡單的醫藥包，以應急需。

五、行前訓練
1.在出發前應妥為選定短宣隊之成人與青年領隊，掌握各項籌備細節，並對參與隊員實施密集之短宣訓練。
2.可協調各教會負責基督徒教育之長執，每年固定編排有關「宣教事工訓練」之主日學課程。
3.訓練課程：
a.宣道理念　b.個人談道　c.團隊事奉　d.探訪協談
e.屬靈爭戰　f.醫病趕鬼　g.基要真理　h.民間宗教
i.教學技巧　j.禱告操練　k.短宣注意事項及生活守則
4.青年英文教學教材編寫參考：
五天教學內容：a.神創造的愛、b.人的罪、c.耶穌救恩、d.你需要耶穌/呼召決志、e.教會生活。
5.冬季短宣：講聖誕節的由來，或介紹美國四大節期〈復活節、母親節、感恩節、聖誕節〉，再導入福音。
6.品格營可參考「真善美講座」，或自行編寫教材。
7.其他：審慎挑選短劇、美勞、遊戲與詩歌。

六、差遣典禮
出發前，由牧師、長老在主日聚會中召集所有短宣隊員，舉行差遣禮，讓全教會兄姊也以禱告參與。

七、現地集訓
1.營會前三天，在台灣集中訓練，讓外地加入之短宣隊員彼此認識、調整時差、了解宣道工場、研討教學策略、促進團隊精神。

2.營會前一天，進駐宣道工場，與地主教會同工互相認識，瞭解每日作習時間，規劃探訪分配表，或繞城禱告。

八、短宣代禱
1.每位隊員出發前，要請二十位有使命感的代禱勇士簽署，承諾每天為你的宣教行程、爭戰禱告。
2.營會期間，短宣隊書記須每天填寫宣教日記，並傳回母會，請禱告網及全教會共同為短宣隊代禱。

九、結束檢討
短宣結束後，召集全體隊員與宣道委員，舉行各項事工檢討、並作財務結算、決志名單之跟蹤輔導與照片資料之處理。

十、見證分享
教會應安排一次短宣見證主日，播放剪輯短片、隊員宣道心得分享、牧師短講，並呼召其他會友投入宣教禾場，遵行主的大使命。

結論：
主對保羅說：「我差你到他們那裡去，要叫他們的眼睛得開，從黑暗中歸向光明，從撒但權下歸向神。」〈使徒行傳26：18〉讓我們同心宣揚福音，為主圖謀大事。

作者莊澤豐牧師與夫人
Author Pastor Tse-Feng Chuang and his wife

Part 3: Short-term ABT Taiwan Mission Teams

How to Recruit and Train a Short-term Mission Team

Pastor Tse-Feng Chuang
Evangelical Formosan Church of Irvine in S. California

Introduction:
In recent years, God has opened a door of wonderful opportunities for the EFC churches in North America and New Zealand to do missions in Taiwan by serving as English teachers in Taiwan elementary and junior high schools, where learning English has become an emphasis over the past 10 years. The following is a step-by-step plan for organizing a successful English Camp short-term mission trip, based on my experience:

I.   Initial Planning
a. Set the Dates: Decide the dates for the mission trip at least 5 to 6 months prior to the trip. Summer and winter vacation times are usually more suitable for young people. Adults may prefer times with cheaper airfare.
b. Select Location(s): I recommend choosing start-up churches in the rural areas or churches that one is familiar with (for first-timers).
II.   Strategizing
a. For youth teams:
i. The local church should help contact local schools to set up a one week camp (e.g. Bilingual Gospel Camp, Character Camp, Leadership Training Camp, Christmas Celebration Event, etc.) that uses English teaching, songs, drama, and other methods to build relationships and to introduce the Gospel message. It is important to ask the local church to continue with follow-up work after the mission has ended.
ii. Other options are to work in the communities, on the streets or in the markets, or visit senior homes, orphanages, or prisons.

b. For adult teams:

i. Teams can host topical workshops (e.g. health, family and marriage, parenting, personal financial management, science and religion).

ii. Teams can also host arts & crafts classes (e.g. floral, corsage-making, origami-folding, music instrument classes).

iii. Teams can host English classes for adults, tea time or alternative events (e.g. magic shows, puppet shows) to help the local church build a closer relationship with the community.

iv. Teams can also do personal evangelism, family visitation, counseling, prayer walks, street evangelism, and Gospel tract distribution to share the Gospel.

c. For combined adult and youth teams:

i. Adults can assist youths in taking care of basic living arrangements, financial management, and getting involved with local churches. They may also serve as teaching assistants in classes.

ii. Adults can help lead daily devotional times; take photos and do other secretarial-related tasks (e.g. prayer letters and daily journals).

iii. Adults can be involved in leading Sunday worship services through sermons, testimonies, worship, Sunday school, youth group, or through evangelistic meetings, retreats, Bible study/reading classes, after school classes for youths, etc.

d. For church choir teams:

i. The church choir can form a team for music ministry in local prisons, schools, senior centers, military bases, or community centers (e.g. EFC of Irvine's choir has visited 46 prisons in Taiwan in the past three years and led approximately 5000 prisoners to Christ).

III. Recruiting

a. Summer mission recruiting should take place in January-March. Winter mission recruiting should take place in August-September. Each team should consist of 6 to 10 people (approximately 2/3 youths). The number of people should be limited to accommodate the limited living space in rural areas.

b. Qualification for team members:

i. 17 years and older (exception: if someone less than 17 years old has a calling for mission and a parents are willing to accompany them).
ii. Born-again Christians.
iii. Must be called to mission and to winning people to Christ.
c. Select a person to be in charge of all communications and registrations.
d. The cost estimate should include teaching materials, training, boarding, transportation (approximately $100/week), and roundtrip airfare. Please consider personal fundraising or church financial aid support.

IV. Preparation and Contact

a. Participants and the mission board should meet at least once a week for prayer, ministry planning, and discussion.
b. Frequently update local churches in Taiwan about team recruitment (ages, gifts, and callings of team members), planning, and training so each can keep the other in prayer.
c. Ask local churches in Taiwan to help plan out the week's schedule, take care of student registration and promote the mission activities. Constantly keep each other in prayer. Use e-mail or telephone to communicate with local church pastors.
d. If the team is unfamiliar with Taiwan, it is best that the contact person visit at least three months prior to the trip, or else arrive at least one week prior to the camp, to make arrangements for boarding, food and other details.
e. Team members must prepare a three-minute Personal Testimony about how he/she came to Christ and know how to share the Gospel message. Team members should be required to share their testimony and give a gospel presentation during the training.
f. It is also recommended that team members begin physical training at least three months prior to the trip, as the mission trip will be physically demanding.
g. Each team should also prepare a basic first-aid kit.

V. Training

a. Before leaving, each team needs to have an adult and a youth team leader who can be in charge of all the details of the trip and stay in close contact with team members. The team leaders should be heavily involved in the training process.

b. It is recommended that the church work with the Christian's Education department prepare a Sunday school curriculum related to missions at least once a year.

c. Training Content:

i. What is mission?

ii. Personal evangelism

iii. Team ministry

iv. Family visitation

v. Spiritual warfare

vi. Healing and exorcism

vii. Basics of Christianity

viii. Folk religion

ix. Teaching techniques

x. Prayer

xi. Important reminders and basic rules for mission trip

d. Suggested Content for English Teaching Material:

i. 5-day teaching material: 1) God's love, 2) Man's sin, 3) Jesus and salvation, 4) Why you need Jesus? (include invitation to accept Christ), 5) Basics of Christian growth

ii. Winter mission: The origin of Christmas or introduce the major Christian holidays (Easter, Thanksgiving, Christmas) and bridge into the Gospel message

iii. Character camp: may consult Character First's materials on character development, etc.

iv. Others: drama/skit, crafts, games, songs, etc.

VI. Commissioning

a. Before leaving for the mission trip, it is important to have the pastor and the elders of the church commission and pray for the mission teams in a send-off ceremony.

VII. On-site Training

a. Commit three days on-site in Taiwan to training prior to beginning the actual mission. The on-site training allows team members from different places to meet, bond, build the team, and adjust for jet-lag. It also provides a head start in understanding the culture and further discussing and planning the mission.

b. Arrive one day prior to the start of the camp to meet the local church co-workers, familiarize yourselves with the living conditions, do a prayer walk, and finalize the schedule.

VIII. Prayer

a. Team members must gather at least 20 prayer warriors who are committed to praying for them daily.

b. During the mission trip, each team must have at least one secretary who records daily journal entries and prayer requests to update the sending church back home.

IX. Debriefing

a. After the mission trip, the team members will gather for debriefing to evaluate the trip and to finish all remaining financial-related matters, follow-up work, and picture updates, etc.

X. Testimony Sharing

a. Ask the church to schedule a mission testimony Sunday Service for team members to share their testimony and show a brief video presentation of the mission trip to encourage brothers and sisters to join the mission work in obedience to the Great Commission.

Conclusion:

The Lord said to Paul: "I am sending you to them to open their eyes and turn them from darkness to light and from the power of Satan to God, so that they may receive forgiveness of sins and a place among those who are sanctified by faith in me" (Acts 26:17b-18). Let us proclaim the Gospel with one heart! Join the Lord in the great work of saving souls!

聖達教會台東短宣隊

Hacienda Heights Summer Short-term Mission Team

王桂美牧師
南加州聖達台福教會
Pastor Kay Kuei-Mei Wang
Evangelical Formosan Church of Hacienda Heights in S. California

聖達教會台東短宣隊

王桂美牧師
南加州聖達台福教會

2007年正月,在第一次長執會議中,連國卿執事提供台東教育局正籌劃邀請台美青年至台東舉辦暑期美語營活動的消息,長執會即成立特別委員會,收集資訊並研議與台東教育局合作的可行性。在國殤日靈修會期間,經謝建國主任牧師與師母的鼓勵,共有十二個人接受呼召。

七月十二日營會開始。連續三梯次的美語營。每梯次三天,每天三班,每班三位老師,每天早上八點半上課,下午四點下課,中間只有一個星期日休息。

美國生長的短宣隊小老師們十分熱情賣力,除了整天教學外,也與學生們打球、談話,時常忙到下午六點才精疲力竭地回到住處休息。雖然如此,我們仍持續每天早、晚的靈修與分享。這種熱情實在感動了許多家長。

短宣隊也與當地的長老教會配合,晚上分三隊到學生家裡探訪、贈送聖經、並為家庭禱告。這種家庭訪問的目的是希望教會以後能做跟進工作。因此在營會結束前一晚,我們在台東長老教會舉行一個成果晚會,讓學生表演在英語營所學的豐富內容。教會的長執也出面邀請家長們帶小孩參加往後的主日學和主日聚會。隨後有一個家庭受洗,榮耀歸主名!

美語營裡一位學生家長名叫「幽為」老師,是台東教育廣播電台的主持人。她因為被我們感動,特別邀請我們到電台接受訪問,分兩個時段播出。這是一個意想不到的收穫,使我們能向收音機前的聽眾傳播福音,感謝神!

雖然台東短宣十分辛苦,我們卻受到當地鄉親的熱情接待與鼓勵。譬如台東縣政府教育局安排住宿、連國卿執事親人提供台灣美食、學生家長自動供應冰

水、教育局多位同事家庭招待郊遊與泡溫泉等等，都帶給短宣隊極大的鼓勵。感謝神一路帶領，讓我們有一個溫馨平安的台東之旅。雖然天氣熱，隊員們汗流浹背，但個個身心健康，每天都有足夠的體力完成神所交付的任務。

我認為短宣隊除了順利完成神所託付的撒種工作外，也使這群在美國出生長大的青年藉此認識他們的根，激發他們愛故鄉的心，實是一項很有意義的事工。

台東三仙台八拱橋
The Taitung Sansiantai Island Eight Arch Bridge

相片取自網路
Photos from internet

Hacienda Heights Summer Short-term Mission Team

Rev. Kay Kuei-Mei Wang
Evangelical Formosan Church of Hacienda Heights in S. California

On January of 2007, during the EFC Hacienda Heights (EFCHH) Board meeting, Deacon Lien Kuo-Qing presented an invitation from the Taitung County Education Department urging Taiwanese American college students to establish English camps in Taitung. During the Memorial Day Weekend retreat, through the encouragements of Senior Pastor Chien-Kuo Shieh and his wife Ingrid, twelve church members responded to this calling.

July 12th was the English Camp's opening day. The Camp was designed as a three-day program in three tiers, and in every class, three teachers. Instruction began at 8:30 AM and ended at 4:00 PM for six days of the week, and the team rested on Sunday.

The young teachers taught passionately and diligently. To establish stronger friendships with the locals, the Team played basketball, outdoor games, and conducted regular meet-ups. A typical day would end at 6:00 PM or so, and after sharing about the highlights of the day, the praises and the prayers, the Team headed off to bed, tired—it was energy well spent for the Lord. Many campers' parents were moved by the dedication of the team and received them with great hospitality.

During a few of the evenings, the team partnered with the Taitung Presbyterian Church to reach out to the students' families through prayer, sharing, and giving out Bibles as gifts. The purpose for the home visits was to connect the local church to the families. A special night service was held at the Taitung Presbyterian Church to bring the English Camp to a conclusion and to give the students a chance to present the English and Biblical teaching they had received at Camp. The local Church staff was introduced, and they invited the families to attend Sunday Church service. Praise the Lord, an entire family was baptized soon thereafter.

Several team leaders were also invited by the host of the Taitung Educational Radio Station (who was a parent of one of the Camp students) to be interviewed about their English program. God opened this unexpected door for them to share the gospel over the airwaves.

Though the short-term mission trip was very challenging, the team members received much encouragement and generous reception from the Taitung locals. Deacon Lien's family in Taitung and the camp students' parents kept the team well-fed and hydrated with local delicacies and chilled beverages.

The representatives from the Education Department also took the team to must-see sites to explore the unique textures and smells of the land, and treated them to enjoy the revitalizing Taitung hot springs. In tense heat and through the hectic work, the Lord strengthened each team member and watched over each of them as they traveled back home.

This was a worthwhile trip for the mission team and the team members came out as the greater beneficiaries through the experience of discovering their own Taiwanese roots. This experience also grew their love and spiritual burden for their home country.

Year 2007 EFC Hacienda Heights Summer Short-term Mission Team: Rev. Kay Liu, Elder Andrew Yu, Secretary Hilary Chang, David & Andrew Shieh, Neilsen Yu, Jessica Chen, Elise Chen, Eric Chen.

一個ABT的台灣宣教之旅
My Summer Missions Trip to Taiwan

汪思涵
紐約 Redeemer 長老教會
Su Han Wang
Redeemer Presbyterian Church in New York

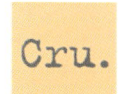

My Summer Missions Trip to Taiwan

Su Han Wang
Redeemer Presbyterian Church in New York

It was the year of 1995 when I went to Taiwan for a 10-week summer mission trip. I was finishing college and heading to medical school. I was part of the Baptist Student Union, and when I interviewed for the mission trip, they were excited when I told them my parents were from Taiwan and I spoke the language. The Southern Baptist Convention had many missionaries in Taiwan, and it was a perfect match for me to serve with them.

The mission board had organized the summer mission trip so that I would rotate between different missionaries around the island. I helped out with the campus ministry at the local Universities in Chiayi and Hsinchu. We worked with both Campus Crusades for Christ and the Navigators. The missionaries hosted many events on campus and opened their homes to students.

There was a fervency in the student fellowships to reach their nonbeliever classmates that I had rarely seen on my own campus. I found myself learning from the boldness of new believers who shared their testimonies as we talked with students in the cafeteria and dorm rooms. Though we didn't know these students, we approached them as friends, and I was encouraged by how positive their responses were to us. When I shared my own story with the students, I think they enjoyed hearing what it was like to grow up as an ABT (American Born Taiwanese). I enjoyed hearing their stories too since many of the students grew up in families that were Buddhist. For them, becoming a Christian was a difficult decision because it meant facing disapproval and ostracism.

My Summer Missions Trip to Taiwan

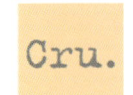

In Tainan, I worked with missionaries that were helping to set up a church. These missionaries in the south spoke Taiwanese, not just Mandarin, which I thought was a real commitment to reach the locals. They shared with me many stories of how they were ministering to broken families. Divorces were becoming more common, and people were suffering from depression, anxiety and a sense of hopelessness. We did a prayer walk around a temple where they felt Satan had a stronghold, and we prayed that it would be broken. It was eye opening for me to see spiritual warfare more vividly than anything I had experienced in the U.S.

In Taichung and Tienmu, I helped out with Vacation Bible Schools (VBS). One was at Morrison Academy, and it was for the missionary children at the annual retreat for the Southern Baptist Missionaries in Taiwan. In Tienmu, I worked with a Taiwanese pastor of a house church that was hosting a VBS for the neighborhood children.

I've often heard that short-term mission trips are humbling because you feel like you've gain more than what you've contributed, and I certainly felt this way. I was blessed to work closely with missionaries in so many different cities in my short time there. Through them, I was able to see God's redemptive work in Taiwan. Even after 15 years, I still keep in touch with one of the missionary families and am continually amazed at how God is using them in Taiwan.

← Lost Way
God's Way →

改變生命的經歷
A Life-Changing Experience

杜立欣
紐約聖教會
Li-hsin Tu
Queens Taiwanese Evangelical Church in New York

改變生命的經歷

杜立欣
紐約聖教會

2002年夏天，我隨加州的「萬國之心」回台短宣六星期，是一次名符其實的「改變生命的經歷」之旅。

那年暑假，我剛完成大二的學業。想家的我為了說服爸媽讓我回台灣一趟，我上網報名「萬國之心」在台灣的短宣活動，結果得到家人的支持與經濟上的協助，讓歸心似箭的我雀躍不已。

我為此準備了完整的得救見證，但在出發前卻因為膽怯而退縮。從小內向害羞的我實在無法想像自己能與全然陌生的同工同住六星期，更別提在眾人面前表演戲劇、帶動唱跳、教小朋友學英語等恐怖的事了。

我因此迫切地禱告，求神能看出我是如何地不適合加入「短宣隊」，而讓我「全身而退」。可是神卻給我馬可福音裡的一個窮寡婦奉獻兩個小錢的故事的回應：主耶穌對門徒們說：「這窮寡婦所投的比眾人還多。因為眾人都是自己有餘，拿出來投在捐項裡；但這寡婦是自己不足，把她一切養生的都投上了。」(路加福音21:1-4)。

那天，神透過這段經文，教我一個重要的功課：「不論我的信心、個性與才藝是如何地不足，只要我願意獻上，神必看重我卑微的奉獻，重用我所投入的，來祝福祂所愛的人。」那個領受讓我有信心地踏出自己熟悉的範圍，加入充滿活力的短宣團隊。

在台灣短宣的那六星期，無論體力、心力或靈命，對我都是極大的試煉。我好像一再地被徹底解體，再重新組裝。除了仰望神外，我也依賴團隊裡的其他肢體，學習與大家相愛。我頭一次將自己倒空，允許神以我想像不到的方式差遣

我。從帶團體遊戲、在講台上分享見證、戲劇表演，到為講員與隊友翻譯、教兒童英語等等，我完成了許多從前自以為「不可能」的任務。更奇妙的是，我在服事英語教學上，感受一種無法言喻的快樂與成就感，以致在教育這塊舞台上，找到了自己的熱忱。

在加入短宣隊前，主修企業管理的我每談到未來，總把自己想像成一個安份守己的上班族。但經過台灣短宣的洗禮後，我恍然發現教育才是我真正的興趣，因此回美國後，便開始追修「應用語言學」，全心走向以教育為專業的道路。

當我的夢想與神的計劃連接時，奇妙的事情便接二連三地發生。我如破繭而出的蝶，開始在教會活躍起來。我教兒童主日學，也在講台上作翻譯。此外，成績一向不特別出色的我竟在大學畢業前，同時收到日本教育局的雇用函與哥倫比亞大學教育學院的錄取通知！

如今，我已是個備受祝福、在紐約曼哈頓執教的中學教師。我時常回想，若當年我因害怕而沒加入陌生的短宣隊，很可能就錯過了神寶貴的呼召與祝福。

在七年多後的今天，我回顧當年的情況，仍能堅定的說：「神在我回到故鄉台灣傳講福音的那年，向我啟示了人生的方向。」透過當時的經歷，愛我的天父帶領我走向那超過我所冀求卻充滿祝福的旅途。

我祈禱您也能像當年的我一樣，在神的話語中找到希望與力量，當祂叩門時，適時地回應祂，跳脫自己預畫的界線，走向榮神益人的道路。

A Life-Changing Experience

Li-hsin Tu
Queens Taiwanese Evangelical Church in New York

My short-term mission trip with a California-based organization called "Heart for the Nations" in the summer of 2002 was a "life-changing experience," and I mean that literally.

That summer, I had just finished my sophomore year in college, and wanted very much to visit Taiwan, a place called "home" that I missed very dearly. In order to convince my parents that I had a meaningful trip planned out, I signed up to be in a six-week missions team with a group that I had worked with in an English language camp a few years back. All seemed to go very well and my application went through smoothly.

I had my personal testimony typed out for the first time in my life and got the financial support of my family and I was excited about the trip. However, a week before the mission trip, I got cold feet. All my life I had been known to be a girl who was extremely quiet and painfully shy. The idea of having to live and serve alongside strangers was scary enough, not to mention performing skits, sharing and speaking in front of people, and the most terrifying of all things, teaching little kids.

In one of my quiet sessions with God, I prayed and pleaded for a way out, hoping God would see how unfit I was to be serving like that and what a bad idea it was for me to be on the team. God's answer to me was the familiar story of the widow's offering in Mark 12:41-44. He taught me very gently that I didn't have to be very capable to serve Him or bless the people He loves. What pleased Him was that I came to Him just as was, and offer Him my all. With that gentle assurance, I decided to trust the Lord as I stepped out of my comfort zone, and joined the very dynamic team of colorful individuals from different backgrounds.

During the six-week mission trip, my strength, both physical and spiritual, was tested, stretched, and expanded. I felt as if I was broken and then built anew many times over. I learned to rely on God and His body (the team) that I was made a part of. I learned to open up to my teammates and to allow God to use me in ways I had never envisioned for myself. Beyond my wildest dreams, I was leading games, sharing testimony to large groups, dancing, performing skits, interpreting for keynote speakers, and teaching English to students young and old. Most wonderfully and miraculously, I found unspeakable joy in teaching, and discovered a new passion I had never experienced outside a classroom.

Being a business major, I had always envisioned myself as a quiet, comfortable office worker. After that summer in Taiwan, I knew I wanted to be a teacher. I added applied linguistics as my second major, and set to pursue a career in education. It's amazing what life can become when your dreams finally align with God's dreams for you. I stepped out of my quiet cocoon, and became a Sunday school teacher at my church, and a regular interpreter for Sunday services. And having been just a little bit above average all my life in my second-tier schools, I was astonished when I was offered a teaching position in Japan through the well-known JET program and acceptance to a master's program at Columbia University's Teacher College at the same time before graduation.

Today, I am a very blessed 6th grade teacher at a public school in lower Manhattan. I often look back to that summer of 2002 and wonder where I would be if I had given in to my own fears by not joining the team. I would have missed God's calling for my life!

I pray that you too will find strength in His words, and respond to His calling when God asks you to step out of your comfort zone to bring Him glory.

台灣短宣記

Short-term Mission in Taiwan

陳以理
紐澤西普林斯頓華人教會
Daniel Chen
Princeton Christian Church in New Jersey

台灣短宣記

陳以理
紐澤西普林斯頓華人教會

我生長在美國，從小認為美國是我的國家，覺得台灣不過是我父母來自的地方，於我並不具特別的意義。

但是2003年的一次回台探親，徹底改變我的想法。我那時已經很久沒到台灣，起初覺得這不過是一次探親之旅。但在台灣的兩星期裡，我逐漸喜愛那地方的人與種種特質，包括鄉土小吃與文化，然後開始覺得台灣不只是我父母生長的地方，同時也是我的根。

此後，我開始認同我是一個台美人，但這樣的認同卻也讓我面對新的挑戰。當我發現台灣的基督徒僅佔全島人口的百分之三時，我憂心地問自己：如果我是個真正的台美人，我願意讓我的骨肉之親不認識耶穌基督的救恩嗎？如果他們正走向滅亡之路，我能無動於衷嗎？

也因此在2007年，當我聽到回台短宣的機會時，便立刻報名。那年暑假，我回台灣一個月，到桃園的元智大學附屬小學教英文。事實上，我們不僅教學生們英文，也向他們講聖經故事，要他們學習耶穌和祂的應許。當我看到他們聽聖經故事時臉上流露的敬畏神情，心裡充滿了歡喜。

2009夏，我再度回台灣，到彰化從事教英文的短宣。這些美好的經歷都使我期待2010年暑假能再度回台灣，到不同的地區宣教。

雖然這些孩子的年紀都還小，到營會的目的也不過是想學英文，但我們卻因而有機會在他們小小的心田播下福音的種子。我祈求這些種子在他們之中萌芽、成長，使台灣基督徒的比例逐漸升高。

Short-term Mission in Taiwan

Daniel Chen
Princeton Christian Church in New Jersey

I've wonder what Taiwan meant to me. Was it just a small country across the world that rarely posed significance in my life other than it being the place of my parents' birth? Being born and raised in America, I constantly felt this way when I was young. In my mind, the place of importance was here in the present. Little did I care about my past ancestry or where I was from.

All that changed when I went back over my winter break in 2003. It was a simple family visit and it was my first time back in many years. I remember that it was difficult to understand the idea that there was such a place where everyone looked at me differently and all around me was the language spoken only at home. During the two weeks I was there, I gradually grew a liking to Taiwan. Its culture, food, people and unexplainable character made me fall in love with it. Taiwan was no longer simply a country where my parents were from, but more of a country where I was from. Soon, I was dead set on the notion that I was not just an American, but a Taiwanese American.

This decision was soon put to the test when I learned a startling statistic: only 3% of the entire population of Taiwan was considered to be Christian. If I was truly a Taiwanese American, would I let my own people live without knowing the salvation of Jesus? In a sense, I was letting my own people walk to their demise. Surely, I couldn't consider myself Taiwanese if I was so passive as to not share the good news in the place which gave me identity.

This was why when I first heard of an opportunity to return to Taiwan on a mission trip in the year 2007, I couldn't help but volunteer. In the summer of 2007, I returned to Taiwan for one month, teaching English to elementary school children at Yuanzhi University in Taoyuan. Along with teaching English language and vocabulary, we used Bible stories and shared the love of Jesus to the students, and they quickly grasped not only the academic reason we were there, but also the spiritual reason, learning about Jesus and His promises. It was a joy for me to see their faces widen with awe as we taught them about the Bible, and in the summer of 2009, I again returned to Taiwan with the same agenda as my previous trip, except I served in Changhua.

This is why, after these experiences, I look forward to return again in the summer of 2010. I believe that though the children are young and probably have the simple goal of learning English in these camps, it is important to sow the seeds of the gospel in their hearts. I pray and trust these seeds we plant will, in time, grow in the future, and that the statistic mentioned earlier will also begin to grow.

臺灣歌仔戲班劇團 - 福音歌仔戲十周年紀念
Performance: Taiwan Traditional Opera Troupe - 10th Anniversary of Taiwan Gospel Opera

上帝的差傳
God's Mission

曹仲恆傳道
紐澤西台美團契長老教會
Minister Samson Tso
Taiwanese American Fellowship Presbyterian Church in New Jersey

上帝的差傳

曹仲恆傳道
紐澤西台美團契長老教會

有一次,在退修會中,一位講員對我們提出挑戰:「差傳到底是我們的差傳?還是上帝的差傳?」這個問題使我們對「差傳」作了一番深入的探討。最後,這位講員的答案是:「上帝的差傳,我們的社群,我的回應」。

他要傳達的信息是上帝的心中有一個奇妙的使命,經由耶穌基督的救贖與福音的大能來完成。當我們被呼召、前往社區服務時,上帝就給了我們服事的機會,讓每個人都能自由地回應。這個過程,看似簡單,卻是建立在「我們是誰?被呼召作甚麼?去哪裡?及誰掌管這一切?」的信仰認知上。

2007年暑假,我很榮幸地參加了『我愛台灣』的短宣營。這是我第一次到台灣,有如異鄉中的一位陌生人。我的中文還不足以和當地人溝通的程度,不知道這一趟短宣會有甚麼效果?但是我還是和紐澤西台美團契長老教會的幾位青少年同行。

我不確定上帝要我在這兩星期裡作甚麼,只知道我將在英語營裡輔導約七十位原住民的小朋友。我每天教他們唱英語詩歌、玩遊戲、讀聖經故事。奇妙的是,經過這次短宣,使我對「上帝的差傳,我們的社群,我的回應」有了新的體驗。

上帝讓我看到參與這項事工的不是我們,而是上帝本身。我們到台灣短宣,不論我們被差遣到何處,上帝必先我們而到,也必和我們同工。上帝甚至呼召我們到最想不到的地方去傳揚祂的信息。

當我們與孩子們一起歡唱嬉戲時，福音的種子就播種在他們的心中。上帝提供孩子們好的土壤、水和養份，使福音的種子成長、開花和結果。

我祈禱有一天，孩子們能成為上帝國的子民，信仰成長茁壯。因為耶穌基督說：「讓小孩子到我這裡來，不要阻止他們，因為天國的子民正是像他們這樣的人。」（路加福音18：16）

無論上帝呼召我們到那裡，祂都會賜予我們特別的恩賜去服事。在信仰的國度裡，願我們每個人都能回應上帝的呼召，服事社區，完成上帝對人類的期望。感謝上帝！

God's Mission

Minister Samson Tso
Taiwanese American Fellowship Presbyterian
Church in New Jersey

One time when I was attending a retreat, the speaker challenged us by asking, "Whose mission is it anyway? Is it ours or God's?" It wasn't meant to be a rhetorical question. We thought long and hard. The speaker went on to claim that it is after all, "God's Mission, Our Community, but it's My Call." What the speaker meant was that God has a wonderful mission in mind through the saving work of Christ and the powerful message of the gospel.

God gives us the context of our ministry through the community in which we are called, and we respond individually and freely through God's calling in our lives. This may sound like a simple process, but it lays out the proper foundation for our beliefs of who we are, what we are called to do, where we are to go, and who is ultimately in control.

During the summer of 2007, I had the privilege of participating in the I Love Taiwan program. This was my first time visiting Taiwan. I had no idea of what to expect out of this "mission" trip experience. I was a stranger in a strange land. My Mandarin was not good enough to allow me to carry on a meaningful conversation with people. Nevertheless I went along with a few of the youths from Taiwanese American Fellowship Presbyterian Church (TAFPC). I had no idea what to expect or what God had planned for us to do during those two weeks. All I knew was that I would be helping to lead a Vacation Bible School style English camp with close to 70 aboriginal kids. Each day we would teach them bible songs in English, play games with them, and teach them Bible stories. Little did I know that through this experience, God would give me a whole new perspective of what "God's mission, Our Community and My Calling" was all about.

Through this experience, God has shown me that He is ultimately at work in the lives of these children and not us. We were just sent there as agents of His love. No matter where we go on the face of this earth, God was there before us and He will be there with us. God may call us into communities where we might be least expected to share His message. We planted the seeds among the children with whom we shared our laughter and cheers; God will supply the good soil, water and nourishments in order for these seeds to grow and blossom into maturity. It is my prayer that someday I will be able to visit and see some of these children as they grow and mature in their faith. Even if I don't, I have the confidence that they are in God's hands and are part of God's Kingdom. For Christ declared, "Let the little children come to me, and do not hinder them, for the kingdom of God belongs to such as these." (Luke 18:16)

Each one of us bears special gifts from God, no matter where God might call us to serve. The most important thing that we must remember is that God does call us, individually and collectively as a community of faith. God calls us to go into our community to fulfill God's mission for humanity. Thanks be to God.

我的台灣宣教

My Mission in Taiwan

羅秀慧
Atascadero 聖經教會 – 加州
Jessica Chan
Atascadero Bible Church in California

我的台灣宣教

羅秀慧
Atascadero 聖經教會 - 加州

這是我的第一次宣教之旅。決定之後，我有些焦慮，但也使我與神更加接近。神為這事預備我的心。

當我在機場候機時，鄰座的女孩問我要去哪裡？我說我要到台灣短宣，她立刻興奮地說她回台灣的一個目的就是要向家人傳福音，她和我都驚訝神差我來鼓勵她。

我們在台灣的短宣一共三星期。第一星期，短宣隊到台南。從星期一到星期五，我們每天早上教大約六十位初中生，下午教大約四十位小學生。有時，學生不太聽話，但神賜予我愛心與耐心。奇妙的是，每當我講起聖經故事、福音或我個人的見證時，他們便聽得很專注，讓我不禁想起耶穌說：「讓小孩子到我這裡來，不要禁止他們；因為在天國的，正是這樣的人。」（馬太福音19：14）

他們問很多問題，也真心誠實地分享他們的想法。我知道他們多數來自破碎的家庭，因此盡心和他們建立關係，希望他們從愛裡看到耶穌。當第一個禮拜結束，竟然全部的學員都願意信耶穌！感謝神，祂作的工真奇妙。

第二星期，我們到新竹。這地方到處是極具挑戰的偶像廟宇。我們的工作是上午教約一百二十位初中生，下午教約六十位小學生英語。孩子們大都能敞開心門，接納神的話語。其中有一位比較剛強，然在聽到耶穌受試探與被釘死之後，他在討論福音時就變得開朗些。我知道聖靈在他身上作了工。

第三星期，我到豐原加入另外一個團隊。我在第一天就累到隨時隨地都可以睡著，但神賜我力氣與耐心撐下去。我的工作是教十二位幼稚園至一年級的小朋友。剛開始，我擔心無法讓這些躁動的孩童安靜，但神要我信靠祂，接受挑

戰,好讓祂用我作大事。第一天的情況很糟糕,他們又吵又不聽話。但很奇妙地,第二天,他們就變得很規矩,肯聽我的分享。最後決志時,竟然全數接受耶穌!

最後那星期,我們到廟宇前唱詩歌。這是我不曾有過的經歷,感覺像是向神表白我們不以傳福音為恥。廟宇門口的守衛不但沒有叫我們離開,還歡迎我們再來,甚至告訴我們甚麼時候來最好!

我看到台灣傳福音的門大開,願神差遣更多的工人到台灣播種。我看到台灣的人心靈空虛,得不到滿足。從他們眼中,我看出他們需要愛。我們要讓他們知道真愛來自耶穌基督。祂因我們的罪被釘死十字架,過去如此,現在如此,未來亦如此。

「這天國的福音要傳遍天下,對萬民做見證,然後末期才來到。」 (馬太福音 24:14)

作者教導豐原幼稚園及一年級小朋友
Jessica teaching kindergarten to 1st graders in Feng-Yuan

My Mission in Taiwan

Jessica Chan
Atascadero Bible Church in California

This journey marks my first mission trip. I wanted to obey God and step out of my comfort zone. I also wanted to encourage and help, in any way I could, the churches of Taiwan to share the gospel. I was very anxious after making the decision to go; however, worrying just seemed to draw me closer to God, and He helped prepare my heart for this mission.

Traveling to the mission destination was amazing in itself. While waiting for the flight at the airport, a girl sitting next to me asked me where I was going. I discovered that one of her purposes for visiting Taiwan was to share the gospel with her family. She was amazed, as I was, that God sent me to encourage her! God uses us in the most common life situations and with seemingly little preparation for such events. We should always be alert to divine appointments as they present themselves.

For the first week in Taiwan, my team taught junior high school students (about 60 students) in the morning and elementary school students (about 40 students) in the afternoon from Monday to Friday. Even though at times they didn't really listen to me during class, God gave me patience and love for these kids. Amazingly, every time I shared Bible stories, the gospel, or my testimony, they listened intently. I remembered Jesus said, "Let the little children come to me, and do not hinder them, for the kingdom of heaven belongs to such as these." (Matthew 19:14) Sometimes they would ask mature, even seminary-level questions, and share their honest, heart-felt opinions. I did my best to build up relationships with the students because I knew that most of them were from broken families, and I really wanted to show them love so they would see Christ. By the end of the week, when I made the alter call, ALL of them committed their lives to Christ! I was really amazed by God's work.

For the second week, the mission team moved to Hsinchu. This place was challenging because there were idols and temples just about everywhere. Our mission was to teach junior high school students (7th to 8th grade), of which there were about 120 of them. In the afternoon, we hosted a summer English program. There were about 60 kids from 1st to 6th grade. All of these kids were open to God's Word and responded affirmatively. There was one student who was adamant about not believing in Jesus Christ; however, after hearing the story of Christ's trial and death, he became more open to discussing the gospel. I realized that the Holy Spirit was working in his heart.

In the third and final week, I moved to Fengyuan and joined a different team. The first day I was so exhausted that I could fall asleep at any moment in any place. However, God gave me strength and patience to make it through the whole week. My mission in Fengyuan was to teach 12 kids (kindergarten to 1st grade). When I was first assigned this position, I was concerned that I might not be able to handle the young kids' rowdiness, but I decided to step out of my comfort zone again and try. I knew it was a mission from God, and He wanted me to trust Him and take up this challenge so He could do great things through me. The first day was tough because they were very noisy and didn't want to listen, but amazingly on the second day, they became very well-behaved and started listening to what I was sharing with them. When I did the alter again, ALL of them committed to Christ!

During the final week, the team went to a temple to sing gospel songs. I had never done anything like this before and felt it was an opportunity to show God that I am not ashamed of the gospel! There was a security guard sitting in front of the temple. However, instead of asking us to leave, he welcomed us to come back to sing more songs, and even recommended the best schedule for us to come back!

I can see the door for the gospel is wide open in Taiwan and this is the best time to send out missionaries. May God continue to raise more workers to join the harvest in Taiwan. What I saw in Taiwan is that people's hearts are very empty and they want to find something to fill their hearts. They put their hearts in materialism and idols, which will never satisfy them. They need the gospel of Jesus Christ. I can see from their eyes that they need love, and I want them to know that true love is from Jesus Christ, the One who died on the cross for our sins past, present, and future.

Matthew 24:14 "This gospel of the kingdom will be preached in the whole world as a testimony to all nations, and then the end will come."

作者教導幼稚園小朋友
Jessica teaching kindergarten Children

作者羅秀慧教導新竹國中生
Author Jessica teaching junior high students in Hsinchu

我的第一次宣教
My First Mission Trip

馮傑利
亞特蘭大台灣基督長老教會 — 喬治亞州
Jerry Feng
Atlanta Taiwanese Presbyterian Church in Georgia

我的第一次宣教

馮傑利
亞特蘭大台灣基督長老教會 – 喬治亞州

台灣宣教基金會長楊宜宜於2008年，十月到亞特蘭大台灣基督長老教會傳遞「上帝的呼召，故鄉的需要」的異象。咱教會牧長與兒童主日學同工，遂興起與台灣的小朋友分享我們的暑期聖經學校的念頭。

於是六位年輕的同工加上五位青少年在2009年7月，帶著五、六箱教材、T恤、糖果及佈置的道具，飛到台中縣霧峰鄉，與霧峰長老教會合作，展開「鱷魚碼頭」美語營，這是我們第一次回台宣教。

一切榮耀都得歸主。此次宣教從開始的聯絡、計畫、招募同工，到募款、宣傳、課程安排、場地佈置、與當地同工的搭配、排練歌唱與舞蹈動作，乃至每日課程的進行、各種突發狀況的應變…等等，處處都充滿了上帝豐盛的恩典。

這次營會一共有近百名小朋友與四十位同工參與。我們期盼藉著這五天半的美語營，讓霧峰教會在這群小朋友身上，播下福音的種子。

我們誠然不知果子何時會成熟，然而在營會開始前兩天，Ted、Michelle與周維駿等三位曾在亞特蘭大就讀短期語文學校的同學，自動自發地從台北趕來，與大家一起佈置場地，讓我們充滿了士氣。

這三位同學在亞特蘭大期間，曾是本教會佳樂團契關懷的對象，返台後，在各自的領域求發展。感謝上帝，他們在返台半年後，竟願意與我們在宣教的事工同盡一分心力，足見上帝的應許必不落空。

聖經記載：「 我告訴你們，舉目向田觀看，莊稼已經熟了，可以收割了。收割的人得工價，積蓄五穀到永生，叫撒種的和收割的一同快樂。 俗語說，那人撒種，這人收割，這話可見是真的。 」(約翰福音書4：35-37)

我的第一次宣教　　221

2009年霧峰短宣是咱教會第一次組團回台宣教。我們的團員包括林玉惠、張祐哲、蕭以苓、蕭以理、張幼齡、馮傑利、Grace Liang、Jasmine Hwa、Christy Chang、Clair Chang 與 Justin Wang 等十一人。我們所做的僅是讓霧峰的小朋友們，經由暑期聖經學校接觸福音，然而在上帝的計劃裡，相信必有奇妙的安排，讓這些福音的種子萌芽、結果與收成。

7/6/09 "樂活一夏"兒童夏令雙語營所有參與學員，教會同工及ATPC短宣隊員於台灣霧峰長老教會
7/6/09- Taiwan Mission in Wufong TPC- all participating children, Wufong church coworkers & ATPC mission team members

My First Mission Trip

Jerry Feng
Atlanta Taiwanese Presbyterian Church in Georgia

It all started back in December of 2008 when Taiwan Mission Foundation's founding President, Eileen YiYi Chang, came to the Atlanta Taiwanese Presbyterian Church to share her vision of "God's calling, Homeland's Needs." Thanks to her, our pastor, elders and Sunday school volunteers had this idea of, "Why not let children in Taiwan have the opportunity to participate in our Vacation Bible School(VBS)? Thus, those of us young adults who were not kids anymore, in addition to five youths, carried five to six boxes of VBS material, T-shirt, candies and props. In July 2009, we flew to the town of Wufeng in Taichung to collaborate with Wufeng Presbyterian Church with the theme: Crocodile Dock English language camp. This was also our first mission trip back to Taiwan.

All glory belongs to God. From the starting correspondence, planning, volunteer training, fundraising and publicity activities, classroom arrangement, location usage/planning/decoration, and the training and cooperation with the volunteers in Taiwan, to the singing rehearsals and dancing moves, daily lessons progression, in addition to unexpected occurrences, the whole walk was filled with abundant grace of God.

Nearly one hundred children and forty workers participated in this camp which lasted five and a half days . We saw that Wufeng church sowed seeds of the gospel among these kids. We also saw that in the midst of the summer school bustle, the children started to hear the gospel. We didn't know when the fruit of the gospel would ripen, but from a small testimony, we knew that God's promise is always kept: two days before the camp started, we saw three people who used to study in Atlanta's English as a Second Language school: Ted, Michelle and Engin Chou, rush from Taipei on their own initiatives to encourage us.

They rolled up their sleeves to decorate the place with everyone. During their time in Atlanta, we really cared for these three students. When they went back to Taiwan, they worked hard in their own respective lines of work. Thank God, half a year after they went back to Taiwan, they were willing to contribute their instead of, with hearts and strength in this work.

Like John 4: 35-37 said, "I tell you, open your eyes, and look at the fields. They are ripe for harvest. Even now the reaper draws his wages, even now he harvests the crop for eternal life, so that the sower and the reaper may be glad together. Thus the saying "One sows and another reaps" is true."

Yes, 2009 Wufeng short-term mission was our church's first mission trip back to Taiwan. What we did was merely to let Wufeng children get in touch with the gospel through Vacation Bible School. However, in God's plan, it would have wonderful arrangements, so that the seeds of the gospel would sprout, bear fruits and be harvested.

The team members this time included Yuhui Lin, Jason Chang, Yi-Ling Hsiao, Yilee Hsiao, Yio Ling Chang, Jerry Feng, Grace Liang, Jasmine Hwa, Christy Chang, Clair Chang, Justin Wang.

鱷魚碼頭美語營的學生
students of Crocodile Dock English language camp

台中宣教經驗

Taichung Mission Experience

黃孝一
紐約新城歸正教會
James Huang
Reformed Church of Newtown in New York

台中宣教經驗

黃孝一
紐約新城歸正教會

2009年暑假，我到台灣宣教的經驗，使我得以透視屬靈的信心，以及神對我們宣教事工的眷顧。

早在一年多前，林天祥長老即開始籌劃咱教會的宣教之旅。起初，我們擔心參加的人數不夠。但在神的奇妙安排下，報名快截止時，竟有二十個願意放棄寶貴暑假的大學生報名參加！

我們都是台裔美國青年，很多人不曾住過台灣，有的即使住過，也是在很小的年紀就出國，對台灣的記憶始終停留在孩提的年代，因此我們在行前都參加密集的訓練。從訓練課程裡，我們知道台灣人十分勤勞，但僅有百分之三的人信主。由於我們的人數多到足以分成兩隊，因此一隊前往雲林縣，在一所小學和一間教會傳福音。另一隊到台中，在兩所公立高中及一間教會引人歸主。

我被分派到台中這一隊。我們這個團隊的課程主要分成三部分：加強台灣學生對美國文化的瞭解、改進學生們的英語能力、以及栽種上帝國的種子。我們講述美國節日包括復活節、獨立紀念日、感恩節和聖誕節的歷史與傳統，也教唱與節日有關的民謠、聖歌。我們對在公立學校教宗教課，感到有點緊張。

第一星期，我們都在台中縣的霧峰農工短宣。我教感恩節的部份，主要在傳達「感恩」的意義。學生們都同意感恩，但更重要的是我們要向著天上的父神感恩。

剛開始時，學生們不太發言，但到最後一天，每個人都搶著要說話。有人說中文，有人說英語，都說上帝有改變人的能力。他們學到復活節的意義在於耶穌的復活，而不在巧克力兔子或彩色蛋。他們也學到宗教不僅在美國建國時扮演重要的角色，而且也是美國的立國精神。在亞洲，聖誕節被叫作「冬假日」，一般人逛街、買禮物。他們還說我們是他們這個暑假的最好禮物，他們從沒想到暑假會如此充滿歡樂與文化，但更重要的是認識了上帝。

第二星期，我們到南投縣的草屯商工短宣。那裡的學生比較活潑，但對上帝的信息卻沒那麼熱衷。我們不巧遇到莫拉克颱風來襲，不得不提前一天離去。後來我在學生的部落格裡讀到，他們十分惋惜沒機會和我們說再見，也沒能在課程上好好作個結束。

他們還在給我們的電子信上寫道：「因著你們，我們學習，也明白耶穌對我們生命的重要。祂讓我們對未來充滿希望。還有，那些耶穌的歌真好聽呢。」讓我們十分感動。我相信上帝確有超越我們能力的方式與他們溝通。

2009夏紐約新城教會短宣隊在國立霧峰農工，作者黃孝一（二排中穿淺藍青年），隊長林天祥長老(前拿麥克風)
2009- Newtown Reformed Church Mission team at National Wufeng Technical School- Team Leader Tien Hsiang Lin (front holding microphone), Author James Huang (2nd row light blue T-shirt)

Taichung Mission Experience

James Huang
Reformed Church of Newtown in New York

This past summer's mission experience in Taiwan opened my eyes to new perspectives of spiritual faith and allowed me to see God's providence in every facet of our mission work. Our trip did not begin in July 2009, but instead it began almost a year ago, with countless nights of planning by Elder Tien-hsiang Lin. Our initial fear was that not enough people would sign up. However, as the deadline approached, more than twenty willing hearts signed up to give up their otherwise leisurely summers to participate. This was a harbinger of amazing things that God began to do for the team.

We had enough team members to split into two teams and serve two high-need areas: one team in rural Yunlin, and the other in Taichung. The Yunlin (South) team took the message of the Lord to an elementary school and a local parish. The Taichung (Central) team evangelized to two public high schools and a church. Many of us were of Taiwanese or Chinese descent, but had never lived in Taiwan or had been away from the island so long that our memory of Taiwanese culture was frozen in our childhood memories. During our training sessions, we learned that people in Taiwan today were hardworking and studious, but that Christians comprised only 3% of the population.

I was assigned to the Taichung team. Our team developed a curriculum that aimed to enrich students' understanding of American culture, improve their English language skills, and sow seeds of God's Good News in their hearts. Our lessons taught about the history and traditions of American holidays, including Easter, the Fourth of July, Thanksgiving, and Christmas. We also taught a music class, during which we taught folk songs and hymns that were sung during American holidays. Our team was nervous about our lesson plans because we knew we were teaching religious content in public schools.

We spent the first week at National Wufeng Technical Senior High School. I taught the Thanksgiving section, and many students agreed that it was more than appropriate that a day be set aside so everyone could count his blessings. Most importantly, students came to understand that "thanksgiving" was a "directional" word from which our Thanksgiving must go somewhere, and that somewhere was up, to our God in Heaven.

Although our students were very hesitant to speak when we first arrived, everyone wanted to speak on our last day.. Some spoke in Chinese, others spoke in English, but all spoke of how God was a transformative force. Many learned that it was the empty tomb of Jesus that made Easter significant, not chocolate rabbits or colored eggs. Many also learned how crucial religion is to America's founding and that it has sustained America throughout her long history. Students also commented how commercialized Christmas has become; noting that it is simply called "Winter Holiday" in Asia and shopping for gifts is the norm. Many called us the greatest gift of their summer, for they hardly expected that their summer session could be so fun-filled, culture-filled, and, above all, God-filled.

We spent our second week at Nantou County's Tsaotun Vocational Senior High School. Although our students were more lively here, they were sometimes less receptive to God's message. Unfortunately, our stay was cut short by a day due to the arrival of Typhoon Morakot. Many students, on their blogs, expressed tremendous disappointment that they did not have a chance to say goodbye or have a real, solid conclusion to their summer session. They did, however, write us messages of thanks via email: "Because of you, we learned … and we also know Jesus is an important part of our lives. He gives us unlimited hopes to our futures. By the way, the songs about Jesus are great." We were not sure whether or not our message would reach the students, but I believe God has His way of communicating that far surpasses anything we plan.

豐原小學短宣記
Fong Yuan Elementary School

陳家林
矽谷基督徒聚會 - 加州
Jojo Chen
Silicon Valley Christian Assembly in California

豐原小學短宣記

陳家林
矽谷基督徒聚會－加州

我們九個人擠在一部七人座的車子裡，一個坐前座，八個擠後座，還有一個同工坐在後車廂，開往正在安裝冷氣、地板與牆壁都還在施工中的校園營地。

當我們的座車抵達時，已有二十幾個孩子在校門口等我們了。那些孩子們望著我們狠狠地自車裡爬出，再引我們到活動的地方。我們發現一個特殊的規矩：在這裡，進教室前，得先脫鞋。

等一切安置好，我們先自我介紹，再帶大家唱《美妙的旋律》與《平安如江河》等詩歌。小朋友們都很害羞，聲音微弱，動作也小。我們一再地請他們大聲唱，可是聲音仍然喑喑嗡嗡。敬拜歌曲結束後，我們演短劇，我扮演「落跑女孩」的角色。我們起初不太明白究竟該講多少英文，後來發現雙語參雜即可溝通。短劇結束後，我們有一小段的問與答，發現我們的信息皆能傳達。接著，我們將小朋友們每25到30人分成一班，開始上英語課。

在簡單測試學生後，我發現他們的程度參差不齊。有的孩子認識的英文單字很有限，有的孩子卻已能閱讀。小朋友們都很害羞、安靜，對我們這群精力充沛、活潑好動的老師都有點害怕。之後，我們一起做「我是誰」的美勞，大家都很認真地把作品做得很漂亮。

我們盡量使用中文，偶而參雜英文。我們講得口沫橫飛，他們卻光聽不答。我們教導他們認識自己較多，較少和他們談起神。第一天的營會結束後，孩子們害羞地跟我們道再見。回程，我們又擠進七人座的車裡，一路談著這日教學的種種。回到住處後，我們又與其他營區的老師們分享這一天的經歷，然後就寢。

數日後，我們九個人擠進一部五人的座車，兩人坐前座，五人擠後座，另外兩人坐後車廂。我們的車子似乎越來越小，但在校門口迎接我們的孩子們並未減少。他們一看到我們到達，都大聲喊「老師來了！」，然後簇擁著我們走進活動中心，再各自就位。

孩子們看起來都很興奮，期待著要看我們為他們安排的活動，也想繼續看我們表演的短劇。我們以教唱《大金剛》與《雲上太陽》作開場。每個孩子都歡喜地跳著《大金剛》的舞，也認真地學著比畫《雲上太陽》的動作。

他們以從未曾有的大聲，很有信心地唱著。當我們表演短劇時，他們笑得很開心，也專注地想知道結局是什麼。這是最後的一次上課，我們把一些未完成的作品做好。孩子們圍繞著我們，想多認識這些與從前的老師不同的我們。當我們問問題時，他們都爭先恐後地舉手回答。

營會的結業式開始。我們最後一次帶孩子們走進活動中心，然後各班的孩子輪流作成果表演。他們在台上唱著他們在營會學的新歌，如《美妙的旋律》、《平靜如江河》、《大金剛》、《Deep Down Down》與《舉目向山》等等。他們的表演自信又精采，不但動作很大，而且個個面帶笑容。

當所有表演結束後，老師們開始演《我心之王》的短劇。起初，孩子們笑著，以為這又是一齣逗趣的笑劇，但很快地，他們便明白這齣劇的真意。表演結束後，我們的同工Irene為孩子們講解劇情的涵意，然後進行呼召。所有的孩子們都誠心地低頭禱告，幾乎所有的孩子都決志信主！

我們最後放映一段這次營會的錄影作為結束。小朋友們都熱情地與我們擁抱，有的笑，有的哭，是個很感傷的時刻。大家都依依不捨地互道再見，但我們心裡明白，他們正將展開另一個全新的生命。

Fong Yuan Elementary School

Jojo Chen
Silicon Valley Christian Assembly in California

All nine of us teachers crammed into a seven passenger car; two in the back, one in the front shotgun seat, three in the passenger's seat, two in the back and one in the trunk. We pulled into the school, which was still remodeling for the New Year. They were installing the air conditioning, new paint, floors, and walls. There were about 20 or so kids already there standing at the front of the school waiting for our arrival.

The kids watched us as we all tumbled out of the car, tired after its heavy load. We herded the kids into the rally room, finding out that this was a school that took off their shoes before entering most classrooms.

When everyone was settled, we began introductions. We sang Making Melodies and Peace like a River. The kids were all shy and their voices muted. Their hand motions were small, inches away from their body. We kept on asking them to scream louder, but the volume stayed the same. After the worship was the skit. I was the runner girl. There was a lot of confusion over how much English we should use, but that problem was soon solved by talking in Chinglish. The skit part one came to a close and the kids were questioned to make sure that the point was clearly conveyed. It was. We then broke up into our "small" classes of 25 to 30 students.

The teachers met their students personally and the real teaching began. We tried their English level to see how much they knew. Some had only basic skills while others already knew how to read. The kids were shy, timid and a little afraid of the teachers who were all wild and energetic. We did the All About Me craft. They were all very careful to make it all pretty and nice. We spoke mostly Chinese and a little English. We talked a lot and they talked little. We taught them a lot about themselves but not a lot about God. We ended the day with shy goodbyes and raced out the doors.

Inside the car, cramped once again, we talked about the cute chubby kids and the lady like girls. There were a lot of "Oh Yeahs!" and "I think I saw him or her!" in the car. We talked about all of the kids, schools, and what we taught. At home, we compared the day with those who went to other schools, planned for the next day, and went to bed.

We now squeezed into a five passenger car, two in the trunk, five in the back, and two in the front shotgun seat. It seemed like the longer we taught, the smaller the car got! Still, the crowd that greeted us before school never changed. There were always kids that shouted "Laoshi lai le!" (Teachers here!) When our car pulled up, the children followed us into the rally room and found their seat on the ground.

They bubbled with excitement and anticipation over what we would plan for them each day, and what the last part of the skit was going to be. We started out with a simple worship of "Da Jingang" and "Yunshang Taiyang." The kids were all dancing and laughing to "Da Jingang" and were all listening attentively while they learned the hand motions to "Yunshang Taiyang."

They sang loudly and confidently, something that they did not do before. They were all laughing at the skit and waiting to see what was going to happen next. The classes were split, and it was class time for the last time. We all finished up any loose ends that needed to be finished, whether it was their passport, games, or they just needed to practice their class presentation. The children were always surrounding the teacher, wanting to know more about us, and what made us different than any other teacher they ever had.

A question asked by the teacher would always be followed by a sea of raised hands or shout out of answers yells. Afterwards, emails were given out, and it was time for our final rally. The kids were led into the rally room for the last time, and the classes began their presentation. The kids presented by class, and the songs sung were "Peace like a River," "Making Melodies," "Da Jingang," "Deep Down Down," and "Ju Mu Xiang Shan." The kids sang with confidence and without a flaw.

They were doing the hand motions perfectly, and smiles were plastered onto their faces. With that all done, it was time for the King of Hearts presentation. The kids were laughing at first, thinking it was another comedy skit, but soon, they began to see the real message. After the drama, Irene explained the meaning even deeper, and did an altar call. All the kids bowed their heads and almost all accepted Jesus into their hearts.

Afterwards, there was a slide show reviewing our whole week. Then, there were the goodbyes. The students all surrounded each teacher and gave them each a hug. Some were laughing and some were crying. Either way, they were sad that the week had ended, but as we all know, their new life had just started.

我的見證
My Testimony

劉開尹
生命河靈糧堂 – 加州
Benjamin Sunny Liu
River of Life Christian Church in California

我的見證

劉開尹
生命河靈糧堂 – 加州

寂靜的教室裡，老師與學生們正低頭禱告。從外面往裡看的人，也許不明白他們在做什麼？我在2009暑假參加了ADVENT（Americans Dedicated for Voluntary English Teaching in Taiwan），回台從事英語教學與短宣，真正見證了上帝救贖的恩典降臨在台灣的學生身上。

當我們進行呼召時，誠然有些學生沒有敞開胸懷接納主。遇到這些時候，我們覺得無助，僅能禱告，祈求救主耶穌很快地進入他們的心中。上帝的救贖十分奇妙，有時經過幾天、幾月、甚至幾年都似無動靜，但是上帝永不放棄，仍然繼續澆灌這些種子。當我們想要退縮時，令人驚奇的事卻發生。

我在彰化從事短宣，即目擊這種事情發生在一位學生身上。當呼召進行時，我們看到她選擇拒絕耶穌，因為她已有其他的宗教。可是我們在短宣中所傳遞的信息，使她想要到教堂看看這位愛世人、願為世人而死的耶穌究竟是誰？

數星期後，我收到她的電子信，她說她已接受耶穌進入她的心與生命！這是何其地喜樂！！ 她又寫道：「謝謝你給我一個認識耶穌的機會。」多麼美妙！想想看，假如所有愛耶穌的人都能給身邊的人一個機會，讓他們進入上帝的國度，這個世界將會是怎樣美好的一個世界！

我們著實倚賴上帝去行事，因為我們所做的不過是給予這位學生一個認識耶穌的機會。我們播種，上帝澆灌，使種子發芽，讓花盛開在台灣學生的心中。這一切都是上帝親手做成的。

My Testimony

Benjamin Sunny Liu
River of Life Christian Church in California

In the stillness of the classroom, the teachers and the students are gathered together. People standing from the outside looking in might wonder what they are doing. They are praying for their own salvation and for the salvation of those around them. In my 2009 experience in the ADVENT (Americans Dedicated for Voluntary English Teaching in Taiwan) Organization, I have seen things that truly testified to God's power as He worked through us. It was neither miracles nor wondrous signs that I saw, but the act of Christ's saving grace falling upon the students in Taiwan that got to me. The sight of souls being saved was awe-inspiring.

Unfortunately, there were some students who did not invite Jesus Christ into their lives during altar call. It was heartbreaking to see them step aside and reject the perfect love Christ had for them. At these times, all that the ADVENT teachers could do was pray—hoping and praying that these students would come to accept Christ into their hearts in the near future. How these teachers hoped that one day they would see their brothers and sisters in heaven! God has instilled within us a passion to serve Him—for us, it was by leading these students into Christ's open and outstretched arms.

Some of us would be quite amazed to know how far God is willing to go to bring someone into His family. Even if several days, weeks, months, or years go by and nothing happens, God is still watering that seed. In these times, we often feel like backing out, but that is when we have to persevere. Our God never gives up.

This is true for one of my students in Changhua, Taiwan. During the altar call, she chose not to accept Christ under the premises that she had been in other "religions" before. As heartrending as that was, there was nothing my teaching partner nor I, as human vessels, could do to change her heart, or the hearts of some of her classmates for that matter. It was all in God's hands from there on out.

However, there was one thing that was left in their hearts when we departed, and that was the knowledge that Jesus Christ loved them despite their shortcomings and He died for them so that they could live with Him forever in heaven. Before we left, that student decided that she would go to church to see what this Christ was like. Out of curiosity, right?

A few weeks later, I received an email from her stating that she had received Jesus into her heart and her life. What a marvelous letter it was! I could almost hear it then—the heavens rejoicing—and it was a beautiful sound!

The thing that I got from this was that she wrote, "Thank you [for giving] me a chance to know Jesus." A chance. Imagine what kind of world it would be if all the Christ-lovers in this world took that chance to plant that seed. What if we, as believers in Jesus, gave the people around us that chance to be accepted into God's family?

It is amazing how often we try to rely on our own strength to get things done when what we really need to rely on is God. In truth, all we actually did was to give her "a chance." We planted a seed, and God watered it. In Taiwan, He made those seeds sprout and those flowers bloom in the hearts of those students. It was truly by God's hands that these things were done.

「我愛台灣」宣教之旅

"I Love Taiwan" Mission Trip

吳宏恩
台美團契長老教會 - 紐澤西
Michael Wu
Taiwanese American Fellowship Presbyterian Church in New Jersey

「我愛台灣」宣教之旅

吳宏恩
台美團契長老教會 - 紐澤西

2009年是我第二度參加「我愛台灣」宣教之旅。我們的團員很多，分別來自韓國、印度、德國、泰國、英國、美國等國，雖然在語言上，大家必須靠翻譯成英語才能互相溝通，但我們仍都很喜歡這項活動。

台灣的志工們很認真地策劃一些如「洗腳儀式」等創意的節目。他們謙卑地為「我愛台灣」的團員們洗腳，如同耶穌為門徒洗腳一般。他們還將我們混合分組，再以表演短劇的方式展現各國的文化。我參與的那組一共有三個德國人、兩個美國人和三個廣東人。我們用自己的語言禱告主禱文。看到各國的人用不同的語言一起低頭禱告、並用歌舞讚美主的感覺十分奇妙。那情景讓我想起羅馬書14章11節，「主說：我憑著我的永生起誓，萬膝必向我跪拜，萬口必向我承認。」而祈禱全世界的人，認識上帝的日子會很快地降臨。

隨後，我們到排灣族的部落進行短宣。我們到村裡的一所教會，見證到村民如何用歌舞敬拜上帝。他們都有很好的歌喉，唱著「Mali Mali」的歌：
感謝讚美主耶穌
感謝讚美主耶穌
萬族萬民齊來敬拜
萬族萬民齊來敬拜
Hai ya na i yui in
Hai ya na i yui in （新聖詩311首）

歌曲儘管簡單重複，但他們就像開搖滾音樂會般地唱著讚美詩與跳舞，讓我們覺得我們唱讚美詩時像座雕像。真希望我們也能像他們那般熱情，為主自由自在地歌舞。

我第一次到台灣短宣時，曾帶了一個足球，結果那足球成為我與小朋友們親近的切入點。這回，我與德國來的法蘭克，在短宣正式開始前，環繞村落，看到

個籃球場,便輪流地投球入籃,很快地便吸引了一些小朋友的圍觀。我們邀他們一起玩球。大約十分鐘後,又有一些較大的孩子們加入,大家都玩得很開心。上帝藉著運動,讓我們與語言不同的人打成一片,再傳揚祂的信息。所以宣教能與玩樂並行嗎?「耶穌看著他們,說:在人是不能,在神卻不然,因為神凡事都能。」(馬可福音10章27節)

我住在山裡的村落時,學會謙卑。在美國,我們視淨水、冷氣與安全為當然。然在那貧苦、晚間外出都可能撞上醉漢的村子裡,孩子們仍然有笑容,村人視教會為全村的指標與交誼的場所。在美國的我們常以為教會是一個認罪悔改的地方,卻忘了它也是一個互相扶持、鼓勵與赦免的聖所。

台灣是一個百分之九十六的人民皆非基督徒的國家,然而藉著這次宣教,我見證到即使在這個基督教不普及的地方,上帝仍然是一位又真又活的神。祂賜給我機會與信心,讓我能夠帶領崇拜、分享見證及回答許多問題。這趟宣教之旅重燃我服務台灣人民的熱情,並且讓其他國家的團員看到台灣是上帝所眷顧的地方。

2009 紐澤西台美團契長老教會短宣隊在排灣族部落的「我愛台灣」短宣
2009 - Taiwanese American Fellowship of Presbyterian Church, NJ attending "I Love Taiwan" Mission in Aboriginal Paiwan Tribe

"I Love Taiwan" Mission Trip

Michael Wu
Taiwanese American Fellowship Presbyterian Church in New Jersey

In 2009, I went on my second "I Love Taiwan" (ILT) mission trip, but I was still surprised by the amount of people coming to Taiwan to participate in this program. I met people from all different nations such as Korea, India, Germany, Thailand, Wales, and of course the US. Even though there was still a language barrier and it was inconvenient to hear Mandarin first, and then have it translated into English, we all enjoyed this program.

The Taiwanese volunteers went through a lot of effort to think of creative activities that we could all participate in. For instance, there was the foot washing ceremony, where the volunteers humbled themselves and washed the feet of the ILT missionaries. There was another activity where we were randomly mixed without volunteers and performed short skits about our cultures. My group consisted of 3 Germans, 2 Americans, and 3 Cantonese. We made up actions that went along with the Lord's Prayer, which had every other verse in English, German, and Cantonese. It was an amazing sight to see people of all nations bowing down in prayer and singing and dancing songs of praise for our awesome and mighty God. As I saw this, this verse popped into my head: Romans 14:11 (New Living Translation), 11 For the Scriptures say, "As surely as I live,' says the LORD, 'every knee will bend to me, and every tongue will confess and give praise to God." It gives me hope that the day when all will know God will come soon.

One afternoon, we visited the church and saw how they praised God and it was amazing. Even though the songs were very simple and repetitive, they were all singing and dancing as if it were a rock concert. When I was there, it truly felt that I broke out of the chains of sin and was truly free. In the Paiwan tribe and in many of the aboriginal tribes, singing and dancing is an important part of the culture and they all have amazing voices. Bin-Bin, one of our guides there, taught us the

Mali Mali dance. It goes like this,

Mali mali ti ye su cemas

Mali mali ti ye su cemas

Sa ta ka na ma te vet te ve

Sa ta ka na ma te vet te ve

Hai yo i oh yi

Hai yo i oh yi

Ee ay yo hai ya

I wish that we could have the same passion that they do over here. I remember Albert Liu describing us as the "Frozen Chosen," since we seem like statues when we sing praises. I pray for the day where we would dance undignified for the Lord.

As some of you know, I brought a football with me last time to Taiwan as a way to reach out to the kids over there and it was a great success. I wondered if the Paiwan Tribe would have the same reaction to this sport that they have never seen before. It was just the same. A few days before we officially started to participate in the program, Frank, my German friend, and I went to explore the village. We came across a basketball court under a gigantic roof and started throwing a ball around. Soon enough, some of the little kids watched us with curious stares and we used this opportunity to play with them and get to know them. After 10 minutes or so, some of the older kids started to play with us too and we had a lot of fun. God showed me that we can use sports as a way to minister our faith and reach out to a people whose language we can't speak. Is it possible to have spread God's Love and have fun at the same time? Read Mark 10:27. "Jesus looked at them and said, "With man this is impossible, but not with God; all things are possible with God."

Living in this village has humbled me so much. In the U.S., we're so used to getting free clean water and having air conditioning. Not only that, we take security at night for granted. For us, walking out in the dark alone was scary since you

"I Love Taiwan" Mission Trip

never know when you would run into drunken people. We actually ran into three of them in broad daylight. Another thing that still surprises me is how the Paiwan children still find a way to smile even though they live in poverty. The church over there serves as a beacon for community and friendship. Many times we think of church as a place where people feel guilty for their sins. However, they fail to forget that the church is a sanctuary of support, encouragement, and forgiveness.

I feel that what God wanted to show me during this mission trip was how He was still active in countries where Christianity is not spread out. Taiwan is 96 percent non-Christian, yet there are still churches scattered around. I felt that He provided me opportunities to lead and be a witness to what He has in store for the people of Taiwan as well as the missionaries from other countries. During devotions, I felt frustrated that no one wanted to spend time reading the scripture, but all of us enjoyed singing songs of praise. God gave me an opportunity to take the initiative and lead worship even though I had no lyrics or guitar. During this time, I was so thankful for this trial since I struggled with having confidence leading worship, especially at church. God also gave me the opportunity to share my testimony with my team leaders and answer many of the questions they had, but which they felt they couldn't ask at church. I do not believe that this mission trip was a waste of my time, but another experience for me to undergo and a place to renew my passion to serve the Taiwanese people as well as let other missionaries see Taiwan as a place that God is trying to reach.

2009 紐澤西台美團契長老教會短宣隊在排灣族部落的「我愛台灣」短宣

2009 - Taiwanese American Fellowship of Presbyterian Church, NJ attending "I Love Taiwan" Mission in Aboriginal Paiwan Tribe

2009年的台灣短宣
My 2009 Mission Trip

楊詩恩
紐約台灣教會
Stephanie Yang
Taiwan Union Christian Church in New York

2009年的台灣短宣

楊詩恩
紐約台灣教會

2009年夏天,我到台灣參加了「我愛台灣宣教營」。我們的短宣隊員先受訓,上了一些台灣歷史和台灣宣教史的課。之後,我們的小組受派到台東阿美族的長光教會,在那裡參加了一堂阿美族語的禮拜。

短宣時,我們早上先教孩子們唱歌,由簡單的「I am a C, I am a C-H…」的英語福音歌曲開始,然後講聖經故事。接著,我們用玩具鈔票教他們如何賺錢、花錢與省錢。我們設置了可以買飲料、玩遊戲、買糖果的站,讓他們學著用錢。偶爾,他們也得要付自己的午餐!若是要賺錢,他們就得製作手工藝品或抹桌子、掃地、洗碗。他們還要學會如何在銀行存錢、領錢。這些,全得用英文說才可以。

晚間活動後,我們要預備明天的課程、活動、教材、教具等。洗澡洗衣後,通常已過了凌晨兩、三點。隔天一早,我們就被迫不及待的小朋友叫醒。天天如此,雖然疲憊不堪,但到別離的日子,我們都流下了不捨的眼淚。

短宣結束後,我們回到新竹聖經學院。每個小組要做地方教會工作簡報,也要提交一張照片參與競賽。我交了一張我跟第一位遇到的小朋友道別的照片,獲得第二名。我也認識了一群從世界各地回台短宣的新朋友,令人難忘。當大家道別時,真的需要強烈噙住眼眶的淚水。我在此要感謝我的媽媽,讓我參加宣教營,也強烈推薦這個短宣營給大家。

這次宣教營改變了我的生命。我再也不會過奢侈的日子。這些兒童生活在山區,前不著村、後不著店。最近的便利商店騎摩托車也要20分鐘。整個地區大概只有5台電腦,包括教堂的2台。他們的父母多在城裏工作,不在身邊。然而,這些孩子們是那樣的無憂無慮和獨立,操場就是他們的世界。這個我所見

過最美麗的地方，坐落在太平洋和山脈之間。我能在那裡生活一個半星期是莫大的榮幸。我可能被孩子們遺忘，但我希望他們記得我們說的故事，或因我們的短宣而更愛上帝。

2009夏作者楊詩恩(中穿黃衣)於台東阿美族長光教會宣教
2009- Stephanie (mid with yellow shirt) in Taitung

作者楊詩恩(前左一)等「我愛台灣」短宣隊員差遣禮後(2009於淡水)
Stephanie (1st left) and team after the sending ceremony in Tansui

My 2009 Mission Trip

Stephanie Yang
Taiwan Union Christian Church in New York

In the summer of 2009, I joined a mission trip in Taiwan. There, we were lectured to about history: both the history of Taiwan and the history of Christianity in Taiwan. Then my church group left for Ciwkangan Church, a church of the Amis tribe of the Taiwanese aborigines, and attended their church service.

In the mornings, we taught the aboriginal kids simple English Christian songs like "I am a C. I am a C-H…" Then we would tell a Bible story. After that, we had them practice saving, spending, and earning toy money. To spend money, there was a station to buy drinks, play animal games, and buy candy. Occasionally they also had to pay for their lunch! To earn money, they make crafts, clean tables, sweep, or wash dishes. They also had to save and withdraw money from a bank, but they had to do all these tasks in English. Then in the evening, we would have some activity for the kids, when they were all showered and asleep, the teachers would plan the lessons and stories for the next day until usually about 2 or 3 in the morning, do laundry and shower. Then we'd get woken up by the kids at the crack of dawn the next day. Repeat. Although the kids tired us all out, we all broke down into tears when it was time to leave (fine, just me). It broke my heart to think that there was a very good chance that I would never again see the children that I had grown to love so much, and there were definitely a load of good times that were left behind in Ciwkangan.

We left the church at midnight on Sunday for an eight hour train ride to Hsinchu. Over the next few days, we met up with the old friends we made during orientation, and a few new ones. A photograph from each church was submitted to be judged, and a picture of me with one of the first kids I met holding hands to say goodbye was submitted, and it won second place. Leaving at the end of the four days, uncertain if any of us would see each other again, was one of the hardest experiences I have ever gone through. I made some incredible friends, had unforgettable times, and I am absolutely grateful to my mom for making me go on this mission trip. I strongly recommend it to everyone.

This mission changed my life that I will never again take for granted the luxuries that I enjoy every day living in America. These children live in the mountains in the middle of nowhere. The nearest convenience store is a 20 minute motorbike drive away. They have probably about five computers in the entire area, including two in the church. They have no parents; they're mostly working in the cities. Yet these children are so carefree and independent. They take care of themselves. Their playground is the entire town, one of the most beautiful places I have ever seen, right between the Pacific Ocean and the mountains, and they are happy. They are satisfied. It was a great honor to live their way of life for a week and a half, and to see the beautiful Taiwan. It makes me sad to know that I will most likely be forgotten by them by the end of the year. But part of me hopes that they will still remember their crafts teacher, remember the stories that we told them, and come to love God because of our work in Ciwkangan.

台東長光基督長老教會
Taitung Ciwkangan of Presbyterian Church

台灣短宣日誌

My Mission Trip in Taiwan

郭詩娜
紐約台灣基督教會
Johanna Go
Taiwan Union Christian Church in New York

台灣短宣日誌

郭詩娜
紐約台灣基督教會

2009年暑假，我到台灣參加「我愛台灣」短宣訓練營，在台灣度過充滿溫馨回憶的二十天。以下是我回台短宣的日誌：

6月28日
學校一放暑假，我便隨姨婆自紐約搭飛機到台灣。在機場，我遇到一位從前認識的朋友麥可，發現他竟也要和我搭同一班飛機，到台灣參加「我愛台灣」短宣訓練營，彼此都很興奮。飛行的時間很長，但當我看到台灣的美麗後，都頓時忘卻疲勞。

6月30日至7月3日
台灣的夏天又熱又潮濕。六月三十日早上九點左右，我到淡水的真理大學報到。註完冊、在房間放好行李後，我便與其他的團員外出逛街、買珍珠奶茶。

開幕典禮在下午才舉行，大約有六十名學員來自世界各國，其中一半來自美國。我們玩遊戲、互相認識。接下來的課程是學習台灣的歷史，並準備宣教的工作。星期四晚上，我們到淡水鎮上騎腳踏車、逛夜市。

星期五(7月3日)上午，我們結訓，準備到各地方教會實習。大家一起照了很多相，互道再見。我參加的那組要到屏東市的迦南教會。Janet、Ching、Polly、Eric、Kevin、Gary和我等七名團員搭了約五小時的火車，在晚上九點左右抵達屏東的迦南教會。隨後，牧師安排我與Janet、Ching三人住同一個房間。

7月4日至7月5日
睡醒時發現午餐已經上桌。牧師與所有團員及營地義工一起開會討論這次夏令營的教材、詩歌與要演的話劇。討論結束後，大家一起去逛夜市。待回宿舍後，我很快地進入夢鄉。

禮拜天，我們參加教會的主日崇拜。牧師介紹我們給會友們認識，並宣佈夏令營將開始。禮拜後，我們結伴到墾丁公園玩。

7月6日至7月10日
夏令營的第一天從自我介紹開始。一共有六十個小孩，自一年級到六年級都有。老師們在自我介紹後，和小朋友們玩遊戲，隨後教唱一首英文歌，唸一段聖經章節，如此大家輪流地教。吃了點心後，我們便分成小組，排演話劇。

每日課程結束後，牧師便和大家討論當天節目進行的情形。如此連續五天，在星期五的結業典禮上，學生們都活潑地唱著英文歌、表演英文話劇，家長們都看得笑呵呵。

7月11日至7月12日
我們到一座文化公園看表演，也參加教會的主日崇拜。牧師在會堂裡宣佈美語營辦得非常成功。禮拜結束後，我和其他的女孩到高雄的市區逛街。

7月13日至7月17日
我們向迦南教會道再見，搭車到新竹聖經學院。在那裏，大家分享短宣的經驗。我和同組的團員共同製作一捲錄影帶，放映給大家看。十六日晚的「文化之夜」，各國團員都表演節目。美國來的學員分成美東與加州兩組，美東組表演舞蹈，加州組表演唱歌。我們也一起玩許多遊戲，「黑手黨」是其中最受歡迎的遊戲之一。

禮拜五上午，團員們含淚互相擁抱告別。當我與姨婆搭計程車離去時，我依依不捨地向這個帶給我許多回憶的地方道再見。

My Mission Trip in Taiwan

Johanna Go
Taiwan Union Christian Church in New York

Sunday June 28th
The school year had just ended and I was about to fly to Taiwan for a mission trip. My grandaunt and I were sitting in the waiting area when I met an old friend, Michael. It turned out he was also going on the mission trip. The flight was a long one, but when we arrived, the beauty of Taiwan was an inspiration for us.

Tuesday June 30th - Friday July 3rd
The air was hot and sticky as we met others who also journeyed to Taiwan as part of our mission trip. We rode a bus to Alethia University in Taipei, signed in, and took our suitcases up to our rooms. It was about 9:00 AM and the program started in the afternoon, so we had time to kill. A bunch of the foreigners, myself included, wandered around looking at shops and buying bubble tea. As time passed, more people arrived and the program finally started. There were about 60 foreigners and half were from the USA. We had ice breakers, played a couple games, and got to know each other better. We learned about the history of Taiwan and prepared to be missionaries over the next three days. On Thursday night, everyone went on a trip to get to know Taiwan better.

My group went biking in Tamsui and checked out their night market. Friday was the last day everyone was together before we were off to our local churches. We took a lot of pictures and said our goodbyes. My group was traveling to Chianan church in Pingtung. The train ride took five hours. My group consisted of seven people: Janet, Ching, Polly, Eric, Kevin, Gary, and me. We finally arrived at 9:00 PM. We met the pastor and her kids. Two other foreigners, Janet and Ching, and I were taken to a room that we would share.

Saturday July 4th - Sunday July 5th
We slept in and woke up to lunch that was already cooked in the church. The pastor and the local volunteers all had a meeting with us. We discussed what we would be teaching in the summer camp that would take place over the next week. We talked about skits and music. After the discussion, everyone in my group went out to explore the night markets. Night fell as we crawled into our beds. Sunday morning came and we all attended service. We were introduced as foreigners and the summer camp was announced. After service, my group went to the beach in Kenting.

Monday July 6th - Friday July 10th
The first day of camp started with introductions. There were about 60 kids from grades 1-6. We teachers introduced ourselves and played games with the students. We would teach the kids a song in English, read one line of Scripture, and get a break for half an hour while the kids learned from the other teachers. Snack time would come and afterwards, we would get into little groups and work on our skits. After the kids left, the pastor would hold a meeting and we would talk about our progress for that day. Friday was the last day of camp. We presented our skits to the parents. The kids showed off their knowledge of songs and the parents wore smiles on their faces.

Saturday July 11th - Sunday July 12th
We all decided to go to a theme park to learn about Taiwan's culture. We saw a wonderful performance and had the time of our lives. Afterwards, we visited a church and ate hot and cold shaved ice. Sunday came and we attended service again. An announcement was made that the camp was a success. After service, the girls and I went to Kaohsiung and shopped around.

My Mission Trip in Taiwan   255

Monday July 13th - Friday July 17th.
We said our goodbyes and headed back to the train. This time our destination was the Bible College of Hsinchu. Everyone met and talked about their experiences. We roomed with the people in our group. We made a video and presented it. There was culture night and since the USA group had too many people, we split into two groups: USA East and California. We East-siders performed a little dance and the Californians sang a song.

Every night groups of people gathering and played games. Our favorite game was Mafia. Friday morning came and everyone said their goodbyes with tearful hugs. I looked back one more time at the place so many memories were born as the taxi that carried my grandaunt and me pulled out of the parking lot.

作者郭詩娜(二排左一白T恤)2009夏與各短宣隊出發前於車站
Mission team members at the train station heading towards different mission fields. Johanna Go (1st left in white shirt)

I ♥ 台灣

「我愛台灣」短宣訓練營

"I Love Taiwan" Short-term Mission Training Camp

鄭清妍
紐約台灣基督教會
Ching-yen Cheng
Taiwan Union Christian Church in New York

「我愛台灣」短宣訓練營

鄭清妍
紐約台灣基督教會

感謝上帝，讓我有機會參加今(2009)年6月30日至7月17日，台灣長老教會主辦的「我愛台灣」短宣訓練營。因為比較高齡，我獲准當旁聽生，觀察年輕人的活動。

6月30日
我們抵達台北縣淡水鎮的真理大學。報到後的隔日，我參加開訓典禮暨「台灣基督教會青年團契」六十週年慶祝紀念會。兩天的專題演講包括神學反思、族群文化探討與認識台灣基督長老教會… 等等，內容十分豐富。

淡水有馬偕博士與他的兒子創辦的淡水教會、淡江中學、純德女中、淡水工商專校、馬偕醫館和馬偕墓園等等，都深具歷史意義。馬偕博士早年創辦的牛津學堂就在真理大學附近，是我年輕時就讀的學校，教室與宿舍迄今都還保存得很好。

「我愛台灣」短宣訓練營共有64位來自世界各國的學員參加。其中，34位來自美國，13位來自德國，其餘的分別來自加拿大、泰國、香港、印度…等國。他們經過兩天集訓後，將被分發到二十四所地方教會短宣，因此每個接受短宣學員的教會，亦派二至五個青年前來參加，然後在集訓後，帶隊前往各自的教會。

7月3日
大家在隆重的差遣典禮後，出發到各地的教會，展開為期一星期的短宣。我參加由吳樂昌長老夫婦帶領的台北縣土城教會青年短宣隊，前往台南縣關仔嶺下游的白水溪教會和屏東市的迦南教會。

7月7日

我們沿著曲折的山路上關仔嶺，但見路旁種滿了果樹與花草。關仔嶺的白水溪教會為英國宣教師甘為霖牧師所創設。甘牧師一生熱愛台灣，不顧生命的危險，跋山涉水到此建立教會，宣揚福音。教會前有一個紀念碑，記載紀念甘為霖牧師因宣教受難的事蹟。

白水溪因溪水中帶石灰質呈白色而得名，教會週遭的環境非常優美。自山坡俯瞰，但見遠方的蓄水池碧綠，近處有無數或棲息或飛翔的白鶴，旁邊的樹林還可見到美麗的台灣國寶鳥──「朱麗鳥」，確是遠離吵雜城市的靈修好地方。

此地因為年輕人皆出外謀生，大多數的村民為祖孫輩，所以盧瑩惠傳道計劃將廚房倉庫改建成多功能的建築，使之成為傳教、靈修與服務村民的會所。

7月8日
我們離開白水溪教會，前往屏東市的迦南教會。教會在市區內，有許多間主日學教室與客房，我們受到熱情招待，並且住得很舒適。

迦南教會每年都辦暑期活動，今年則舉辦為期五天的英語營，由我們的學員教孩子們英語、詩歌、聖經章節、並演英語話劇，結果約有八十名當地的學生參加。最後一晚，教會邀請家長與會友們一起觀賞學生的成果表演，吸引了很多居民前來。由於節目生動，氣氛非常熱烈。

7月13日
「我愛台灣」短宣訓練營的學員再度集合於新竹聖經學院，舉行檢討會與分組報告。今年是宗教改革家加爾文牧師誕生五百週年紀念，聖經學院特別推出一系列靈修祈禱活動，紀念這位宗教改革者。

7月15日
今晚是短宣訓練營的最後一夜，由來自各國的學員在「文化之夜」上表演各地的文化節目，真是多采多姿。

我愛台灣 短宣訓練營　　**259**

7月16日

上午舉行閉會禮拜，大家在離情依依的氣氛中，互道再見。

我雖已七十五歲，但今年蒙主恩，得以參加這項成果豐碩又深具意義的「我愛台灣」短宣訓練營，內心很受感動。我要鄭重推薦這個訓練營，鼓勵年輕人多接受這種裝備，以便將來作傳福音與教會的接棒人。

2009夏作者75歲鄭清妍長老(左一穿粉紅格子襯衫)於屏東迦南教會短宣
2009 Summer- Author 75 year-old Elder Ching Yen Cheng (left)- joined a mission at Pintung Chia-nan Presbyterian Church

短宣隊長們
Mission team members

"I Love Taiwan" Short-term Mission Training Camp

Ching-yen Cheng
Taiwan Union Christian Church in New York

Praise the Lord for giving me the opportunity to attend the "I Love Taiwan" Short-term Mission Training Camp held by the Taiwan Presbyterian Church in the summer of 2009. Because of my age (I was 75!), I was there to audit, mainly to observe the youth participants and their activities at the camp.

On June 30th, I arrived at Aletheia University in Tamsui. On July 1st, we had a ceremony celebrating the 60th anniversary of the youth Christian fellowship of Taiwan (or "TKC," short for its Taiwanese name, Tai-oan Ki-tok Tiun-lo Kau-hoe Chheng-lian Thoan-khe) as well as the opening session for the training camp. We had feature speakers and workshops on theology, Taiwan's ethnic and cultural diversity, and the history of the Taiwan Presbyterian Church.

Our venue was Tamsui, a historically significant location in northern Taiwan. It was in this place that Dr. Mackay and his son established Tamkang Middle School, Chun-te Girl's Middle School, and Oxford College. It was also where I went to school back in the days. All the historical buildings were very well-maintained and located near our event venue.

The event had a total of 64 attendees from Germany, Thailand, Hong Kong, India, Canada, and the U.S.. There were 24 participating local churches, and each church sent two to five of their youth members to train with the overseas attendees.

On July 3rd, we had a special missions "send-off" Sunday service, and after that, the participants were sent on missions to different local churches to serve. After we were dismissed from the camp, I continued my journey to Peh-chui-khoe Church and Chia-Nan Church to serve as a short-term missionary.

July 7, my first stop was Peh-chui-khoe Church located near the mouth of Guanziling River. My teammates were the youth group members from Tu-Cheng Church of Taipei County, led by Elder Lok Chang Wu and his wife.

Peh-chui-khoe Church was established by a British missionary, William Campbell, who was also known as Rev. Kan Weilin in Taiwanese. It was located in the mountains and surrounded by beautiful flowers and trees. It was a great place for retreat. Rev. Kan loved Taiwan and invested his life in establishing and nourishing this church, and spreading the good news to the local people. In front of the church was a monument documenting the persecutions Rev. Kam endured in his missions. From the mountains, we could see a beautiful pond where thousands of endangered species of cvanes lived freely. Peh-chui River is known for the minerals its water carries. We could see beautiful and precious birds of many kinds in the woods. The current pastor of the church plans to turn the kitchen and the storage room into a multi-purpose community center to better serve the local people and make it into a retreat facility for other churches.

July 8, we went to Chia-Nan Presbyterian Church in Pingtung. The church was located in downtown Pingtung City, and held vacation bible school every summer. This time around, they had a five-day bilingual drama summer camp, attracting eighty local children. We taught them English, songs, and Bible verses, and performed skits in English. On the final night of the camp, the church invited the parents and many local people to watch the kids perform. It was a lively and joyous event with a great crowd. The church was also a great host that provided us with very good accommodations. I had a great time there.

On 7/13, after the training, the teams reconvened at Presbyterian Bible College in Hsinchu to debrief. That day was also the 500th year anniversary of the birth of Reverend John Calvin, the pioneer church reformer. The college provided us with spiritual readings for us to commemorate this devout and humble servant of God.

On July 15th, we had a "Culture Night" where participants from every country performed something unique to their culture. On July 16th, we had closing ceremony and were dismissed. This event was very meaningful and fruitful. I was deeply touched by the youth participants, who took the time to attend this event, to be trained, and to learn valuable life and leadership skills. They are the future of Taiwan missions, and the ones to take the baton. I highly recommend the "I Love Taiwan" Missions Training Camp.

I praise the Lord for his special blessings to use an old lady like me. I'd like to take this opportunity to encourage young people to be equipped and get trained while they are young, so they can become good church leaders and servants once the baton is passed to them.

關仔嶺的白水溪教會
Peh-chui-khoe Church

甘為霖牧師紀念碑
Rev. Missionary William Campbell Monument

短宣─我們仍在學習中

Short-term Mission -
We Are Still Learning

陳耀生牧師
迦南基督教會 - 紐約長島
Pastor Mark Chen
Kalam Christian Church in Long Island

短宣—我們仍在學習中

陳耀生牧師
迦南基督教會 - 紐約長島

2006年暑假，紐約迦南教會三位社會青年在聖靈感動下，參加了亞利桑那州那瓦荷（Navajo）印地安原住民保留區為期十二天的短期宣道。當他們回到教會後，他們的宣道分享與生活見證感動了許多人。這是聖靈教導咱教會走上短宣的第一步。

兩年後，台灣基督長老教會總會舉辦「我愛台灣」宣教營。消息傳來，咱教會執事會經過禱告，認為咱教會在各方面都還在學習中，若鼓勵青少年回台參加「我愛台灣」宣教營，將比自己籌組短宣隊回台更具效果。

因此，我們提出補助計劃，引導青少年產生回台宣教的意願。感謝主，咱教會的T.J. Lin、 Daniel Chiu 與Michael Chen等三位青少年接受呼召，參加了「我愛台灣」宣教營。

他們回台後，經過台灣基督長老教會青年部的訓練，隨後被分派到不同的地區與教會實習。其中有一位前往嘉義朴子，一位前往屏東車埕，還有一位到蘭嶼。他們都是父母的寶貝兒子，若不是信靠上帝，領受使命，以及天父莫大的恩典，他們也不會獨自到那麼遙遠陌生的地方去。

兩星期的短宣結束後，他們發覺不僅在自己生命裡，有過那麼一次「愛人如己」的實際行動，也在信仰裡看見天父的愛不僅及於美國、台灣，也遍及全世界。感謝主賜給我們許多愛主的兄弟姊妹，使我們同心合意地成就祂在咱教會所作的美好事工。

身為教會的牧師，我學習到天父尋找的，其實只是我們一顆炙熱的心。咱教會青年的回台短宣從籌備到完成，都是天父在做工，我們只是祂的同工而已。我們或有許多不足，但在天父的國度裡，凡事皆能。藉著這次的經歷，我們再一次體驗到「祂必興旺，我必衰微」的真理。

Short-term Mission - We Are Still Learning

Pastor Mark Chen
Kalam Christian Church in Long Island

Having felt the touch of the Holy Spirit in the summer of 2006, three young adults from the Kalam Church of New York attended a short mission trip to the Navajo Indian Reserve in Arizona for 12 days. When they returned home to their church to share their experience and personal testimonies, many people were moved. Here was an example of learning by doing. Their testimony was the first step of how the Holy Spirit guided our church into missionary work.

Two years later, the Taiwan Presbyterian Church (TPC) youth ministry hosted the "I Love Taiwan" mission camp. When we heard about this mission, knowing the challenges we were facing in areas like manpower, experience, organization, and teamwork, we knew we were facing a steep learning curve. After we prayed, the deacons unanimously agreed to encourage our youth to attend the "I Love Taiwan" mission. It was more practical than setting up our own short-term mission program.

We also provided grants to encourage our youth to participate in missions to Taiwan in the hope that they would develop a better understanding of Taiwan and of the love of God at the same time. We hoped they would develop hearts for the spiritual needs of Taiwanese people. Thanks to the Lord we had three youths from our church that attended the mission: T. J. Lin, Daniel Chiu, and Michael Chen. After their training at TPC, they were sent to local Taiwanese churches, one went to Puzi, one to Checheng of Pingtung, one went even further to the island of Lanyu. These three young adults are their parents' precious sons. If not for their faith in God, their willingness to accept the mission, and the grace from our Heavenly Father, they would not have had this challenging opportunity. The two week mission passed quickly.

Short-term Mission - We Are Still Learning

Not only did they experience the act of loving others as themselves, but they also had the opportunity to see the love of God spread throughout the world outside the U.S. and Taiwan. Perhaps it was the most profound experience that they ever received, putting the Bible's teachings to practical use. We thank God for the many loving brothers and sisters who were united together and accomplished this work in our church.

As the pastor of the church, I have learned a few things. In order for a short-term mission team to succeed, the minister himself must provide support. When God is calling, we must be willing to hear and accept. From preparation to completion, the mission is all the work of God - we are only His coworkers. More importantly, we cannot extinguish the moving touch of the Holy Spirit that helps us to focus our faith in Him and not to focus on our own circumstances. We know we have many shortcomings, but everything is possible in God. When we are able to see and be moved by the Holy Spirit, our submission to God becomes the eternal blessing. From this I have been taught once again to experience God who is true and alive. It also helps to teach our church the truth of "God must be prosperous, we must diminish."

攝於11/21/2009
「關懷留學生餐會」，作者長島迦南教會陳耀生牧師(站立者)帶領教會社會青年關懷紐約區15位台灣留學生並邀請來參加感恩節晚餐。

11/21/2009 Author Pastor Mark Chen from Kalam Church in Long Island led church young adults to express care and love by inviting 15 overseas Taiwanese students for Thanksgiving dinner.

1884年，巴克禮牧師創設「聚珍堂」，為台灣第一家西式印刷所，即今日的「台灣教會公報社」，而1885年7月（清光緒11年6月）便發行了台灣的第一份報紙《台灣府城教會報》，即今日的《台灣教會公報》，創刊至今已有126年歷史。

為了讓當時的信徒容易閱讀與了解，巴克禮牧師認為，採用容易學、容易寫、容易讀的白話字來書寫，會比只有知識分子才認識的「孔子字」（漢字）更好。而當年的報紙內容，除了發布教會消息，也將聖詩的詞曲刊登出來，讓信徒在家就可以吟唱；此外，還利用圖片來解釋聖經、介紹西方知識與教會信仰生活。

遇挫愈堅強
Finding Strength in Trials

陳昭容
北澤西(佳壇)台灣長老教會
Terry Su
Taiwanese Presbyterian Church of Northern Jersey

遇挫愈堅強

陳昭容
北澤西(佳壇)台灣長老教會

我們全家在1980年移民美國時，大女兒蘇代千年方十二歲。她後來在紐約完成中學，然後進哥倫比亞大學附屬女校巴納學院主修教育。大四那年，她轉進宗教系，畢業後，進協和神學院繼續進修。

協和神學院是間超教派的神學院，代千雖全心向學，卻越來越對信仰感到迷惑，便想休學或轉唸別校。這時正逢〈台灣教會公報社〉徵求台美青年回台參與英文版的事工，啟發代千回台服事的心。

後來，經郭恩仁牧師的推薦，代千成為美國聯合基督教會(UCC)海外事工部的宣教師，並且在1993年5月16日，由UCC海外事工部亞洲區負責人蕭清芬牧師，在紐約恩惠歸正教會主持差遣禮，宣佈代千為美國聯合基督教會世界教會事工部海外宣教師，將在台灣基督長老教會的教會公報社，擔任翻譯暨英文版編輯。我們都非常感動，也深為代千感到驕傲。

代千初回台灣時，常常覺得天氣很熱很潮濕，不時要與蚊子、蟑螂搏鬥，更大的挑戰是觀念不同，為人處事的方式不一樣，有時覺得困惑。幸好，她每禮拜日在東寧教會英語部司琴，東寧教會的會友大都是外國宣教師，藉著他們的鼓勵與分享，代千得到勇氣，繼續向前。

她在台灣工作三年期滿後，回美國訪問差傳大會，並作報告，然後再回台就任第二任的宣教師。這時的她，工作已較勝任愉快，並且較習慣台灣的生活，能與同事打成一片，經常一起結伴參加各項活動。

然而有一次，她騎摩托車外出，在台南市東豐街口，不幸被一部快速衝來的警車撞倒，被送到成大醫院急救。等到醒來後，她才打電話通知在台灣的親人。

遇挫愈堅強　**269**

我們在一個禮拜後才接到消息，非常地擔憂。其時，正好有一位英國青年宣教師在屏東因車禍身亡，他的父母自英國趕去參加葬禮，還原諒了肇事主。我那時經常在想：假如這事發生在代千身上，我真不知該作何處理。

雖然如此，代千仍繼續她在台灣的奉獻。她在完成第二任宣教師職責後，回到美國，專修「TESOL教英文當作第二語言」的課程，然後又回台灣，將所學的奉獻給台南神學院、長榮中學與長榮女中。

她在回美國期間，也曾在法拉盛的金鷹學院教書。她愛她的學生，用心教導他們，遇到有特殊需求的學生，更義不容辭地幫忙。

她有兩個願望，一是當老師，二是回神學院進修。願神保守她、祝福她！

台灣教會公報社
Taiwan Church News

臺灣教會公報創辦人巴克禮牧師
Fonder of Taiwan Church News
Thomas Barclay

Finding Strength in Trials

Terry Su
Taiwanese Presbyterian Church of Northern Jersey

In 1980, when our daughter Vivian Su was twelve, our family immigrated to the United States. Upon entering college, she initially studied education at Barnard but changed her major to religion her senior year. After graduation, she went on to attend Union Theological Seminary, a member of the Interdenominational Evangelic Society.

Even though she studied and worked diligently, Vivian often seemed frustrated and confused spiritually. Perhaps this was due to her inexperience or young age. As a result she considered taking a leave of absence or transferring to another school. Coincidentally, the Taiwan Church News was looking for a second generation Taiwanese to return to Taiwan to work for their English department. The combination of some disillusionment and the appearance of an interesting opportunity piqued her interest and she applied for the position.

The application process was a long and difficult one, but finally Vivian was able to receive the opportunity to go to Taiwan as a missionary on May 16, 1993, Winfield Reformed Church in New York held a Thanksgiving service that also served to officially commission missionaries from the church. Pastor Ching-fen Hsiao conducted the commission service saying, "Today in God's name, Vivian Su has been called to be an oversea missionary with the United Church of Christ. Her work will be as a translator and editor for a publication distributed by the Taiwanese Presbyterian Church. She will be primarily translating news received overseas from English into Chinese. She will also be responsible for reporting the activities of the Taiwanese Presbyterian Church to the world while also establishing and maintaining contacts all around the world." Pastor Huang

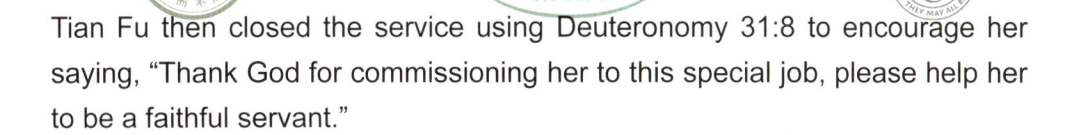

Tian Fu then closed the service using Deuteronomy 31:8 to encourage her saying, "Thank God for commissioning her to this special job, please help her to be a faithful servant."

Upon arriving in Taiwan, Vivian took over the work of missionary Gary Hoff. The first three years was a difficult period of adjustment. Vivian found it hard to adjust to the weather, environment, interpersonal relationships, and cultural and societal differences. She also found it difficult to adapt to the hot and humid weather, and the constant mosquitoes and cockroaches. In dealing with different people, she found it hard to openly express her opinions, leaving her feeling very confused, frustrated and often misunderstood. On the other hand, she also didn't get the respect that other "foreign" missionaries received. Fortunately, she was part of Dong Ning Church's English service serving as their piano accompanist. Most who attended the service were foreign missionaries, and through sharing and encouragement, Vivian found the strength and courage to keep going.

After serving there for three years, she came back to visit the U.S. to share her experiences. Afterwards, upon her return to Taiwan, she realized that she had become accustomed to living there and was clearly a lot happier. Even at work, she participated in many activities and got along well with her co-workers. Once, while at Dong Feng intersection, a speeding police car inadvertently struck her while she was riding her scooter and she was sent to the emergency room. Her relatives were contacted once she woke up, but her elder brother only notified me a week later. At the same time Vivian had her accident, another missionary from England also had an accident and passed away. His parents flew from England for his funeral, while also forgiving the man who struck their son. Had it been me, I'm not sure what I would have done.

Nevertheless, Vivian continued her life in Taiwan until her contract expired. Upon returning to the U.S., she went back to school for her degree in TESOL.

Finding Strength in Trials

Now, she has again returned to Taiwan using what she has learned to serve at Tainan Seminary, Chang-Jung Middle School and Chang-Jung Middle School for Girls. When she returns to the US, she will sometimes help teach classes at the Golden Eagle Institute in Flushing. She cares a lot for her students, especially when working with special needs students, with whom she makes an even bigger effort to take care of.

These days, she has two wishes: one, to become a teacher and two, to return to seminary. She continues to diligently pray that God will continue to bless and guide her future.

長榮女中
Chang-Jung Middle School for Girls

長榮中學
Chang-Jung Middle School

台灣第一所大學 - 今台南神學院，
為巴克禮牧師創立
Taiwan's First University - Tainan Seminary, was established by Rev. Thomas Barclay

復興台灣正是現在

Time for Gospel Revival in Taiwan

彭榮仁牧師
紐澤西第一長老教會
Pastor David Peng
First Presbyterian Church in New Jersey

復興台灣正是現在

彭榮仁牧師
紐澤西第一長老教會

四年前,廖明發長老到大紐約地區巡迴佈道,提到台灣在接受福音一百五十年後,基督徒的比例仍然只佔全部人口的百分之三左右,而南韓的基督徒卻在過去三十年間從百分之三增至百分之二十五。

廖長老同時提到台灣的基督徒以原住民比率最高,外省族群次之,閩南人和客家人分別只有千分之七與千分之三信主。若以現今的宣教學分類,台灣仍是最需要傳福音的未得之地!

那天晚上,我輾轉難眠,心想進步的台灣卻被歸類為福音未得之地,真是情何以堪!我因此不斷地禱告,同時思索海外的台灣人教會與基督徒該如何幫忙故鄉的宣教呢?

感謝主,終於讓我們有機會帶領海外的青年回台,以教英文的方式播撒福音的種子。自2006年起,咱教會與台灣數所教會締結姊妹教會,每年暑期都回台短宣,既可服務故鄉,也藉此培養咱教會青少年宣教的經驗與心志。

過去四年,由於神的祝福,大家所經歷的聖靈、感動與見證,真是數說不盡!我們目睹所撒的種子在短短的四年便有收割,那份喜樂與興奮讓我們覺得短宣所面臨的挑戰包括財務負擔、身體疲倦、炎熱天氣、時差調整、語言文化差異等等都值得,因此年年都再回去。

回憶2006年第一次回台辦兒童英文福音營時,我們根本不知該從何做起。當我們連說三次「哈囉」時,都沒有一個孩子回答。但是主憐憫我們,以後短短的一星期,小朋友由逐漸回應,到非常投入。第四天,我們在台上向小朋友們呼召:願意接受耶穌基督為救主的,請站到台上來。結果數到第三下,小朋友們都蜂擁而上,老師及短宣的隊員只好站到台下去,在場的許多大人都被這一幕感動得流下眼淚。

赤峰街的蔡牧師頻頻說：「這真是太奇妙了，我從沒看過小朋友如此熱情回應過。」當時站在台下的我激動不已，心中聽到主對我說：「不是你們能做什麼，乃是靠著我凡事都能！」

在此特別感謝台北赤峰街長老教會的蔡鴻銘牧師與林怜利校長、台北南港長老教會的許榮豐牧師與賴國揚校長、桃園龍潭長老教會的彭榮道牧師，以及台南自由教會的陳坤生牧師與梁祐欽傳道。我也要在此誠懇呼籲關心台灣兩千三百萬靈魂的兄姐們，請把握機會，到台灣宣教，因為台灣復興的契機正在此時！阿們！

紐澤西第一長老教會於2006年7月30日首次返台短宣，和台北赤峰街教會假宜蘭頭城YWCA舉辦兒童英文福音營
7/30/06- New Jersey FTPC's first short-term Taiwan mission for the Children's Gospel Camp in Yilan YWCA

8/6/2006 紐澤西第一長老教會在宜蘭頭城的兒童英文福音營
2006 - English Gospel Camp by New Jersey FTPC at Toucheng YWCA in Yilan

Time for Gospel Revival in Taiwan

Pastor David Peng
First Presbyterian Church in New Jersey

Four years ago, Elder Paul Liao, an executive of Scripture Union in Taiwan, came to the greater New York area for evangelical tours. He compared the percentage of Christians in Taiwan and South Korea after 150 years of missionary work. There were only 3-5% of Christians in Taiwan. Under similar cultural and popular local folk religion backgrounds, the Christian population in South Korea grew from 3-5% to 25% in the past 30 years. The aboriginal and mainlander population in Taiwan represent the highest portion of the Christians in Taiwan. The Minnan and Hakka populations were less than one percent of the Christian population (0.007 and 0.003 respectively). Taiwanese people were the unsaved people; our land was still the unsaved land under the present missions classification.

After hearing that, I could not sleep that night wondering about my beloved homeland, Taiwan. Taiwan had flourished in so many ways yet it was still being classified as an unsaved land like other remote lands that had never heard of the Gospel.

I could not help but pray. "What can we do as overseas Taiwanese Christians and churches?" I thank God for giving me the inspiration to bring our young people from overseas back to Taiwan to teach English and spread the seeds of the Gospel in the hearts of the next generation. With the cooperation of local churches in Taiwan, we were able to provide the experience of missions and give purpose in our overseas young people.

We have established sisterhood with many local churches to carry on the mission. In the past four years, we have experienced the blessing of the Holy Spirit working among us through so many different camps. There have been endless testimonies about God's grace. The greatest joy was being able to harvest what was planted. With God's blessing, we were able to see results in a short time frame. The joy and excitement helped us to overcome the difficult situations that we faced, including financial worries, physical fatigue, unbearable hot weather, time difference, and language and cultural clashes.

At the first children's Gospel Camp in 2006, we were not sure how to begin. Not one child responded to our initial three greetings of "Hello." With God's mercy and wonderful work among us, however, children started to respond and actively got involved after one week. On the fourth day when we invited the children to come and accept Jesus as their Savior on the count of three, all of the children came rushing to the front. There was no room for the teachers and mission group members on stage. Everyone was so touched by the eagerness shown by the children. Rev. Tsai from Chifeng Street Presbyterian Church kept saying, "This is marvelous. I have never seen such enthusiastic response from the children." I was so moved standing at the bottom of the stage and I heard my Lord saying, "Everything is possible through me. No matter where you are, what program you are running, who your teammates are, call to me in faith and all children will be saved." God will save Taiwan through the children, the new generation, and none will be left behind. This is the will of God.

I would like to call on all who care about the twenty two million souls in Taiwan to grab this opportunity and work on missions in Taiwan. This is the time. Amen.

彭榮仁牧師
紐澤西第一長老教會
Pastor David Peng
First Presbyterian Church in New Jersey

第四篇 海外宣教篇
IV. Taiwan Missions Overseas

第四篇 海外宣教篇

巴西六家族的故事

莊守平口述　劉慈媛整理
巴西慕義教會

巴西慕義教會係由六個在1963年移民巴西的家庭開始的。他們原本是台灣彰化縣種稻的農民，其中陳振昌、紀慶誠、莊永得和陳恩勤四個家庭來自原斗教會，王首寶與陳榮華兩個家庭來自溪州教會。六個家庭裡的大人和小孩加起來一共三十二人，從台灣搭五十天的船到巴西。

在船上，他們每日作禮拜，由六位家長輪流主理。當時同船還有另外一戶台灣人基督徒家庭，來自雲林縣虎尾鎮，戶長是簡榮鴻長老，長子是簡建堂博士。所以那艘船一共有七戶台灣人家庭，總計三十九人。

1963年十月初，六家族在巴西的聖多斯港口上岸，稍後能夠暫時住在慕義的楊毓奇博士家的農場。抵達巴西後的第一個禮拜天，六家族的長輩們到聖保羅市的教會做禮拜。但在主日崇拜後，沒趕上最後一班公車，只好步行回家。返回慕義的家後，已是晚上十點鐘。

由於慕義市離聖保羅市很遠，小孩無法一起去做禮拜。所以自第二個星期日(十月的第三個禮拜天)開始，六家族在楊博士的農場做禮拜，慕義教會的設教紀念日，也因此訂為1963年十月的第三個禮拜天。最初，教會的聚會由六家族的家長輪流主理，後來聘請到曾天來傳道，成為六家族信仰上很好的同伴。

有一天，紀長老與莊長老外出拜訪吳煥良先生。經吳先生的介紹，兩人靠信心決定替大家買一塊地，就是後來六家族的安身之處。這塊地的地點很好，面積大約六甲，總價四千美金，相較於當時台灣農地一甲約需四千美金要便宜許多。

同日，吳嘉明先生則帶另外四位家長去看他的農場。吳先生想邀六家族到伊瓜培，和他一起種稻，但紀長老不為所動。紀長老深信買這塊地是神的帶領，若另外四位家長要去種稻，不參與買這塊地，他和莊長老還是一起要買。經過一番商議，六家族中的四家決定留下，兩家搬到伊瓜培。買了土地後，該如何劃分？因為每家的經濟情況不一樣，有的比較充裕，有的連吃飯都有問題。結果紀長老說：「方便的人先拿出來付，不方便的人以後再付。」

當時因為有兩家要搬走，剩下四個家庭，照理說，土地應該分成四份，可是紀長老說：「不行，還是要分成六份。萬一這兩戶去種稻不順利，要回來，在我們之中還是有一份土地。」結果，大家用抽籤的方式分土地。在人人自身難保的移民初期，六家族的長輩們能有這樣的愛心與胸懷，實在令人敬佩。

那塊土地原是一片茂密的樹林，四個家庭搬進後，便開始開墾、蓋房子。大人們砍樹、放火燒掉，再挖樹頭。然後，爸爸們當師傅，孩子們當小工，媽媽們煮飯和點心，開始蓋房子。大家先蓋家人住的三間屋。房子蓋得很簡單，只有四面牆和屋頂，所以一星期就蓋好一間。等到蓋房子的經驗較多、技術也較純熟時，大家就在那塊土地的最好地點上蓋第一間禮拜堂。

那年十二月二十五日，搬到伊瓜培的兩個家庭回來過聖誕節，也參與建蓋禮拜堂的工作。這兩個家庭在伊瓜培住了九個月，因為種稻不順遂，又搬回來，六個家族於是團圓在一起。

1964年四月五日，首座自建的教堂終於完工，舉行獻堂禮拜，命名「慕德如露基督教會」。慕義地區的生產業主要是種菜與養雞。當時種洋菇的人很少，一般人通常只從事一種行業，但我們一開始就從事三種生產業。起初因為人生地不熟，加上語言不通，實在困難重重。但是神為我們預備了很好的幫助，使我們得到吳煥良先生和王雄飛先生的關心與鄰近日本人的照顧，我們的生活遂逐漸上軌道。詩篇 30章第 5 節說：「一夜雖然有哭泣，早晨便必歡呼。」 萬事起頭難，我們雖吃盡苦頭，終究也有成功的果實。

新移民家庭的大大小小都得工作，沒有一個人吃閒飯。孩子從七、八歲就開始參與家庭的生產業，每天放學回家，就幫忙工作，直到日落。詩篇 129 篇第 2

至3節說：「從我幼年以來，敵人屢次苦害我，卻沒有勝了我。如同扶犁的在我背上扶犁而耕，耕的犁溝甚長。」

我那時覺得自己很可憐，現在才知道那段日子其實也很幸福。有汗流浹背的辛苦，也有抓小鳥、抓青蛙的樂趣；有工作的孤單，也有信徒交融的快樂。在四十六年後的今天，我回頭看，惟有感謝地說：「一切都是神的恩典，祂的慈愛永遠長存。」

六家族因為親歷新移民的艱苦，因此很能體貼同樣剛移民的人。即使不相識的來求助，他們都準備房子給人家住，甚至提供自己的菇舍讓他們種菇，還指導他們，幫助初移民渡過難關。六家族的愛心使得慕義地區百分之九十的新移民都到教會做禮拜，接受福音。「有愛才有羊」，我們的父母雖是卑微的農民，但在信仰上卻看見神處處彰顯祂的權能。

過了一段時日，自台灣屏東教會退休的許有才牧師移民巴西，成為慕義教會的第一任牧師。我們得到許有才牧師的牧養，不僅在信仰上獲得美好的造就，並且通力合作，使教會更加堅固。許牧師實在是一位很有恩賜又有經驗的牧師，講道深具感動力。神豐盛的生命通過許牧師，滋潤我們的心靈。每當我們遭遇困難，覺得灰心疲倦時，常從禮拜天的證道中，得到安慰和激勵。

紀長老很愛教會，計劃在第五年就要再蓋新的禮拜堂。許牧師從神得到智慧，具有遠大的眼光，計劃將教會遷到慕義市區。當時有部分人難以接受，認為慕義市區沒有會友，土地貴、路途又遠（離六家庄七公里）。然而現在回首，就很清楚地知道這是神的旨意。教會後來聘請許有才牧師的兒子許輝世牧師繼續他父親的聖工。許輝世牧師到任不久，就開始在市區找地方、買土地，蓋第二間禮拜堂和牧師宿舍。第二間禮拜堂大約可以容納一百二十人。1972年，教會遷移到慕義市區，同時易名為「慕義基督長老教會」。

七十年代台灣移民巴西的人很多，所以兩、三年後，第二間禮拜堂就容納不下全部會眾，教會開始計劃蓋第三間禮拜堂，也就是目前這一間。當時，一般信徒的事業與經濟都還不穩定，教會的存款不多，因此計劃先蓋樓下的交誼廳兼

餐廳，作為暫時聚會的場所。我們蓋禮拜堂的原則是讓神感動人奉獻。神會自己預備聖工，有多少錢，就作多少事工。就這樣，憑著信心，開始定根紮基。感謝神，交誼廳很快地完工，教會人數繼續增加，主日崇拜從第二間禮拜堂遷到新蓋好的交誼廳來。

教會的弟兄姐妹這時都主張不要停工。就這樣，樓下禮拜聚會，樓上的工程繼續進行下去。從開工到完工，不到兩年的時間，工程從沒停過。1978年一月一日，我們在設教的第十五週年，舉辦隆重的獻堂感恩禮拜。

工程完成後，剩下的錢竟然比剛開工時還要多。神的恩典果真超過我們所求所想，也讓我們經歷到亞伯拉罕在摩利亞山所經歷的「耶和華以勒」。金錢的增加，並不全然是最好的，信徒信心的增長，才是真正的可貴。蓋聖殿期間，從年初到年終，弟兄姊妹們的事業都得到神的眷顧與賜福。無論雞蛋或洋菇，都大豐收，價格也很好。所以有人說，這間聖殿是用白色的雞蛋和洋菇，如同白色的嗎哪蓋起來的。可見聖工若合乎神的旨意，必蒙神的賜福。

如今，六家族的家長已有五位安息主懷，只有陳榮華執事尚健在。他們一生美好的見證，永遠活在我們的心中。教會的第四代如今已漸長成，精通葡文的青少年已占教會將近一半的人數。長執們也看到向當地人傳福音的異象，現已設立三間佈道所，關心貧民區的兒童事工，聘請巴西的傳道人牧養，同時差派幾位長執和青年志工去協助事工。

近來，鑑於不少廣東人移居慕義市，所以自今年開始，我們每個月都分組探訪他們的店面，分發福音傳單、雜誌與光碟，並舉辦廣東同鄉聯誼會，邀請精通粵語的牧者傳講信息。感謝神，我們得到粵語聖約瑟華傳福音中心的傳道者與同工一起推展粵語事工。

教會的歷史故事很長，神的恩典滿滿，我簡述這些，唯有盼望神的榮耀能持續不斷地在我們當中發光，也盼望年輕的一代更加委身，一同建造，使巴西慕義教會成為一所更完全、更能榮耀神的教會！

IV. 海外宣教篇 巴西六家族的故事　　283

作者莊守平劉慈媛夫婦全家福
Author's family- Chuang Shou Phing & Liou Tsyr Yuan (wife), Eliseu (son) & Eunice (daughter)

到巴西前在船上每日靈修
1963- Daily devotions on the ship to Brazil

4/5/1964六家族與孩子們自建的第一個小教會""慕德如露教會"
The first church in Brazil, "Botojuro Christian Church" built by the 6 Families including their children and dedicated on 4/5/1964

Part 4: Taiwan Missions Overseas

Six Pioneer Families in Brazil

Dictated by Chuang Shou Phing, Transcribed by Liou Tsyr Yuan
Mogi Church in Brazil

The Mogi Church in Brazil was founded in 1963 by six immigrant farmer families from Chang-Hoa County, Taiwan. Four families came from Yuan Tou Church: Chen Chin Chang, Chi Chhing Cheng, Chuang Yung Ter, and Chen Ern Chhin. Two families came from Si Cho Church: Wang Shou Pau and Chen Jong Hoa. Altogether 32 people, young and old, boarded a ship in Taiwan and arrived in Brazil after traveling for 50 days. On board the ship, the families, which were led by the six patriarchs, worshipped together daily. Traveling separately, a family from Hu Woe, Elder Chian Jong Hong and his family, also joined in worship. Altogether, there were seven Christian families from Taiwan on board, totaling 39 people.

In early October of 1963, the ship arrived in Port Santos, and the six families temporarily stayed at Dr. Yang Yu Chi's farm in the city of Mogi. The first Sunday after their arrival in Brazil, all of the adults went to São Paulo for church but missed the last bus to go home. They ended up having to walk and did not get home until ten o'clock at night.

São Paulo is far from Mogi and the trip was too far to travel for little children. Accordingly, on the second Sunday – the third Sunday of October– they established worship service at Dr. Yang's farm. The Mogi Church was founded on the third Sunday of October 1963. The six patriarchs took turns leading worship until the church hired Evangelist Tseng Tien Lai, who became a great companion for these 6 families in faith.

With the help of Mr. Wu Huan Lian, Elders Chi and Chuang relied on faith to buy a piece of land in Mogi for the six families. This became known as the "Six Family Land." The land purchased was in a good location, measuring six "chia" (one "chia"- a Taiwanese way of measuring land is equal to about 10,000 square meters). At the time, it had costed $4000.00USD, which was the same as the price of one "chia" farmland in Taiwan.

At the same time, Mr. Wu Chia Ming invited the other four families to see his farm in Iguaçu (a coastal city about 200 km south of São Paulo) hoping the families would join him in rice farming. Elder Chi firmly believed that it was God's will for them to purchase the land. So if the other 4 families decided to do rice farming with Mr. Wu, he and Elder Chuang would still purchase the land themselves. In the end, only two families decided to move to Iguaçu.

The four families that stayed in Mogi now had another dilemma, how should the land be divided? They all had different financial situations, some were rich and some were very poor. Elder Chi said, "Those who have money pay now; those who don't, pay later."

Besides figuring out financial issues, the four families also had to decide on how to divide the land. Initially they thought it should be divided into four parts, one for each of the families that stayed. However, Elder Chi said, "No, we have to divide the land into six parts so the other two families can each have a share in case they decide to come back." So the land was divided into six equal parts by casting lots. In the midst of instability in those early days of immigration, this spirit of generosity and love was truly admirable.

The land purchased in Mogi was originally a dense forest. The four families moved there and started developing the land. We cut down the trees, burned the tree trunks, and dug out the tree roots. It was indeed arduous labor! Soon, we learned to build houses. Children helped out. Fathers directed the work. Mothers prepared meals.

We started by building one house per week, keeping it simple - only a roof and four walls. As we gained experience, we began to build the first church building in the best location on the plot of land.

On December 25, 1963, the two families who moved to Iguaçu came back to visit and participated in building the church. Nine months later, these two families moved back to stay with us because the rice farming in Iguaçu did not go very well. The six families finally were reunited again. On April 5, 1964, we dedicated the first sanctuary and named it "Botojuru Christian Church."

The Mogi das Cruzes region was known for its chicken farms and vegetable tending. Very few people grew mushrooms at that time. Usually, people focused on one kind of business, but we started with all three. In the beginning, with language barrier and cultural adjustment issues, we faced many difficulties. But God had mercy on us. Mr. Wu and Mr. Wang mentored and looked after us. Our Japanese neighbors were also very helpful. "Weeping may stay for the night, but rejoicing comes in the morning" (Ps. 30:5b NIV).

In the immigrant family, everyone had to work and contribute. Even seven and eight year-olds had to work after school until sundown as the Psalmist 129:2-3 (NIV) said, "They have greatly oppressed me from my youth, but they have not gained the victory over me. Plowmen have plowed my back and made their furrows long."

At the time, I often felt sorry for myself become of the hard labor. Now, I realize it was a blessed life. On the one hand, there was sweaty toil, on the other hand, it was great fun catching birds and frogs. The loneliness of work was accompanied by the joy of Christian fellowship. As I recall what happened 46 years ago, I am filled with thanksgiving: "It was all God's grace. His steadfast love is everlasting. "

As new immigrant families arrived in Mogi das Cruzes, the six families provided assistance and shelter. The six families understood the hardships of immigration and helped these strangers by guiding them through confusing times. These six families provided education and assistance to other Taiwanese immigrants on mushroom cultivation, and created a safe haven for new immigrants to overcome adversity.

As a result of their spirit of love and sacrifice, the six families drew about 90% of all Taiwanese immigrants to the church, and they later became Christians. "Where there is love, there are sheep." Our parents, though modest farmers, had faith in a sovereign God who acted among them.

Later, with God's providence, Rev. Hsu Iu Chai, from the Pin-Tung Church, became our first pastor. We were blessed to have Rev. Hsu as our pastor. He equipped us spiritually so that we worked together well and the church became stronger.

Rev. Hsu was gifted and experienced in preaching. Through him, God's abundant life nurtured our hearts. Whenever we faced difficulties or felt discouraged, we were comforted and encouraged during Sunday service.

Elder Chi loved the church and planned to build a new sanctuary on the fifth anniversary. With God-given wisdom, Rev. Hsu had a vision to relocate the church to downtown Mogi. Some people had a hard time accepting this change, because at the time, no members lived downtown, and it was seven kilometers away from the "Six Family Land." Land was also expensive. Yet today as we look back, we realize it was all God's leading!

Rev. Hsu's son, Rev. Hsu Hui Se, became our second pastor. Soon after his arrival, we began searching for land in downtown to build the second sanctuary and a parsonage for the pastor. The second church building was able to seat 120 people. In 1972, we moved into this new sanctuary in Mogi das Cruzes and changed the name of the church into Mogi Christian Presbyterian Church.

Many people immigrated to Brazil in the 1970s. Soon, the second sanctuary was overcrowded. During that time, we began planning for a third sanctuary, the one we currently use today, even though many members' financial situation was not stable. The church had very little savings at the time, so we planned to build the first floor fellowship hall and dining hall first, which could be used for worship on a temporary basis.

Our principle of sanctuary building was trusting God's provision. God would move people to contribute. With such faith, we began the construction. The fellowship hall was soon completed. Church membership continued to grow and we started using the fellowship hall for worship.

While we had the worship in the fellowship hall, the construction work upstairs did not cease. In less than two years, the sanctuary was completed. On January 1, 1978 – the 15th anniversary of the church, we dedicated the third sanctuary.

When we finished the third sanctuary, we discovered that we actually had more money than when we had started. God's providence was beyond our imagination and we experienced what Abraham experienced on Mount Moriah: "Jehovah Jireh (The Lord will provide)" (Gen. 22: 14a NIV). The growth of our faith was far more treasured than the surplus of money.

From the beginning to the end of the year during the sanctuary construction, God richly blessed everyone's business. The prices of mushrooms and eggs were good all year round. Some people claimed the sanctuary was built on white eggs and mushrooms like white manna. If our work is in God's will, God will definitely bless us.

Now, only Deacon Chen survives among all six patriarchs. Yet, their amazing testimonies remain. The fourth generation has come of age. Almost 50% of our members are youth, with Portuguese as their mother tongue. The leader-

分享阿根廷短宣的經歷

卓邦宏牧師
迦南基督教會 – 紐約長島

「來跟從我,我要叫你們得人如得魚一樣。」(馬太福音書4:19)
「你們往普天下去,傳福音給萬民聽。」(馬可福音書16:15)

六十多年前,我在少年的主日學裡,學到這兩句主耶穌對使徒及世人呼召的金句,便銘記在心。從小學到中學,我都處在民間宗教濃厚的環境裡。身為孤單的基督徒,我時常被同學冷嘲熱諷。譬如,他們會說:「我們廟裡有許多神明。你的神在哪裡?搬出來給我看!」

我就讀花蓮師範時,有一次試著對一些大我三、四歲的同學們傳福音,但抵不過他們的無理強辯,突然放聲大哭。我不是認輸,而是為對方頑固不信而難過!

1985年,我在傳道大半生後,因主奇妙的帶領,舉家移民阿根廷。到阿根廷後,首都布宜諾已有三間華人教會與台灣人教會。我原先只想以個人佈道和家庭訪問的方式,引領鄉親支援教會,但一路發展下來,竟與四位長執一起開拓了一所福音教會。在這五年間,我們從第一次的五十八人聚會,發展到受洗與堅信禮者達一百三十人之多。其中三分之一來自許久不上教會的老信徒,三分之二由篤信佛教或其他宗教的人轉來歸向主。

兩年半前,內人退休,我們決定到台北和中國做兩個月的短宣。內人在台灣一共有十二個兄弟姐妹,早先只有她是基督徒,於是我們一有機會,便向他們傳福音。但傳統的信仰根深蒂固,大家又安於安逸的生活,至今才有一個妹妹在臨終前,在馬偕醫院受洗信主。另有兩、三位已逐漸打開心門,嘗試做慕道友。我們真恨不得其餘的人能早日信主,同蒙救恩。

分享阿根廷短宣的經歷

今年五至七月期間，我又回台灣，除了參加鄭學仁牧師的短宣隊做為期一個月的短宣外，還向內人娘家的姐妹與近親友加強個別傳道，帶領好幾位決志信主。同時，我專程回花蓮鳳林，向中、小學的同學傳道，贈送拙著與自製的福音傳單，勸他們早日信靠救主耶穌，成為個人、家庭與子孫的福氣。

布宜諾斯艾利斯之花噴水池雕塑
Flor de Buenos Aires Fountain sculpture

布宜諾斯艾利斯博卡區
La Boca in Buenos Aires

維基共享圖片
Photos from Wikipedia

Sharing My Personal Short-term Mission Experience in Argentina

Rev. Philip Cho
Kalam Christian Church on Long Island

Matthew 4:19 "Follow me, and I will make you fishers of men."
Mark 16:15 "Go ye into all the world, and preach the gospel to every creature."

About sixty years ago, I learned these two verses while attending children's Sunday school. Growing up in Taiwan, I was surrounded by a Buddhist culture full of superstition. Starting in elementary school, I often had to defend myself from my classmates for my beliefs. Classmates would taunt me by saying, "We have many gods in the temple. Where is your god? Show us!" At Hualien Normal College, I tried sharing the gospel with some upperclassmen. Their close-mindedness caused me to cry in frustration! But this did not deter me. Once while I was attending Hualien Normal College, I tried to preach the Gospels to older schoolmates. I couldn't stand their reasoning and burst into tears, not because I felt defeated, but sorry for their stubborn unbelief!

In 1985, after ministering for half of my life, my whole family immigrated to Argentina under God's amazing guidance. When we arrived, we found that there were already three Chinese churches and one Taiwanese Church in the capital, Buenos Aires. My original intention was to support the growth of these established churches through personal evangelism and home visits. To my surprise, I was instead called by God to establish a new church with four elders.

Within a five year period, the congregation grew from 58 members to more than 130 members. One-third of the members were new Christians, and the rest converted from Buddhism or some other religious backgrounds.

Sharing My Personal Short-term Mission Experience in Argentina

After my wife retired two and a half years ago (in 2009), we decided to go on a two month short-term missions trip to Taipei and Mainland China. My wife is one of 12 children, but until recently, she had been the only Christian in her family. We have always tried to share the gospel with the rest of her siblings, but because of deep-rooted traditional beliefs and a relatively easy life, no one cared much about what we had to say. One sister was baptized at the Mackay Memorial Hospital just before she passed away. Recently, two or three siblings have expressed interest in learning about the Christian faith. We cannot wait for the rest of her brothers and sisters to receive Jesus as their personal Savior.

I returned to Taiwan from May through July this past year (2010). Besides joining Pastor Hsueh-Jen Cheng's short-term mission team for one month, we spent time preaching the gospel to my wife's sisters, relatives and friends. Many of them have decided to accept Jesus as their Lord and Savior. We also went to Fenglin, Hualien to spread the gospel to elementary and high school students, distributing a book I had written and some gospel tracts. I urged them to depend on our Savior and Lord Jesus Christ sooner than later, so they could receive blessings for themselves, their families and even their children.

阿根廷玫瑰宮
La casa Rosada in Argentina

維基共享圖片
Photos from Wikipedia

織就一張愛的網
哥斯達黎加短宣
A Tapestry of Love
- Costa Rica Mission Trip -

翁蕭幸美傳道
德州達拉斯
Hsin-Mei Weng
Dallas, Texas

織就一張愛的網
― 哥斯達黎加短宣 ―

翁蕭幸美傳道
德州達拉斯

2005年，在加州牧會遇到瓶頸，牧會二十七年來，我第一次感到如此沮喪，幾乎無法再向前走。我向上帝禱告，求祂用笑臉接待我，不要離棄我。有一天，我在靈修時，讀到馬太福音28章18-20節，「耶穌進前來，對他們說：『天上地下所有的權柄，都賜給我了。所以，你們要去，使萬民作我的門徒，奉父、子、聖靈的名給他們施洗。凡我所吩咐你們的，都教訓他們遵守。』」這段經文給我莫大的鼓勵。我在這時感到神調整我的眼光，將國度的帳幕擴大。不久，我聽到哥斯達黎加的呼聲，到中南美洲作為期三個月的短宣。

哥斯達黎加是一個很開朗熱情的國家。臺灣移民在那裡建立了三間教會，其中有一間缺乏全職的傳道人，我於是到這間教會幫忙。教會對內有主日學、祈禱會、成人靈修會、青少年靈修會、敬拜讚美團等培養與造就信徒的工作，對外有提供鄉親的各種免費課程，如烹飪課、音樂班、英文班、心理講座等，藉以和臺灣鄉親分享福音。

哥斯達黎加的第一代臺灣移民與他們的兒女，都還保持著傳統的臺灣文化，兩代之間沒有語言的障礙。他們的青少年都很有語言的恩賜，能講台語、北京話、英語、西語或德語等多種語言。他們很喜愛音樂，常常邊唱邊跳，非常融入，尤其在退修會的晚上更是徹夜唱歌，直到天亮。

在哥斯達黎加短宣期間，會友渴慕真理的心讓我得到很大的激勵。有位姐妹非常愛神的言語，以兩年的時間，用手抄聖經一遍，將許多聖經的章節寫在白板上，貼在冰箱與牆上，所以她家觸目所及，都是聖經的金句。有些會友每次都得開單程三個半小時的車程來教會。他們在隔天回家的路上，一遍遍地聆聽牧長講道的錄音。這些都令人感動萬分。

我在短宣結束回到加州後，每想起這些沒有牧者的羊群，便非常不捨。所以隔年復活節，我又回到哥斯達黎加，參加那所教會每年舉辦的復活節退修會。自2007年起，我發現個人的力量有限，便開始組團隊前往服事，迄今已連續三年。 我們的團隊每年都有新的團員加入，每次出發前，都定期為每一位參加者代禱，並準備節目，使之富有變化與趣味性。

我們的節目內容相當多元，包括戲劇、歌唱、舞蹈、壁報、背經、分組討論、分享、廣告插播、大地遊戲、變魔術…等等，當然最重要的是介紹主耶穌給他們。參加那教會復活節退修會的青少年人數年年增加。有些家長遇到我時，會向我反應說，他們的孩子們自從參加退修會後，心靈有很大的成長。也有的家長在臺灣，只有孩子在哥國唸書。那些孩子們說，他們的父母對他們參加教會的活動，都覺得放心，認為到教會的孩子不會變壞。

退修會最後一晚的獻心會是我們最感動的時刻。當牧長邀請青少年決志時，聖靈都會大大地在每一位年輕人身上作工。孩子們一個個地走到臺前，向神獻上感恩。看他們淚流滿面，有的甚至跪在台前向神懺悔，輔導老師們都會走出去，一齊為他們迫切禱告。他們的父母也都會過去擁抱他們，有時媽媽哭泣，孩子也陪媽媽跪下，向神仰望祈求。看了那些情景，令人永遠難忘。

最後一堂課，大家傳遞各種不同顏色的毛線，分享每個人的所得。分享越多的，就得到越多顏色的毛線。然後，大家用這些毛線織成一張彩色的網，網住彼此間的友誼，更網住上帝給我們的愛。每當我回想這些短宣經歷，心中便無限感動。所以每年我都會一再地組隊前往哥斯達黎加，也殷切地期待下一年復活節的到來。

哥斯達黎加地圖
Map of Costa Rica

A Tapestry of Love
- Costa Rica Mission Trip -

Minister Hsin-Mei Weng
Dallas, Texas

In 2005, I felt depressed and could not move forward. There was much difficulty in my church in California, and for the first time in my 27 years in ministry, I was at a loss. I prayed to God for help, and He answered my prayers.

One day, during my quiet time, I came upon Matthew 28:18-20 (NIV), which says: "Then Jesus came to them and said, 'All authority in heaven and on earth has been given to me. Therefore go and make disciples of all nations, baptizing them in the name of the Father and of the Son and of the Holy Spirit, and teaching them to obey everything I have commanded you. And surely I am with you always, to the very end of the age.'"

This passage gave me great encouragement. I felt that God was telling me to readjust my attitude and expand my vision of God's kingdom. Soon, I responded to a call for a three-month mission trip to Costa Rica.

Costa Ricans are known for being open-minded and passionate. Taiwanese immigrants in Costa Rica have built three churches. However, one of the churches has never had a full-time pastor, so I went to support them. My responsibility at the church consisted of giving Sunday sermons, teaching Sunday school, leading prayer meetings, and making home visitations. Inside the church, work with the believers involved Bible study, prayer meeting, adult and youth devotions, and inspirational worship. To the community, we offered free classes in cooking, music, English, and family counseling. The church also officiated wedding ceremonies and funeral services.

The first generation immigrants had maintained their traditional language and cultural values and instilled those values in their children, thus there was no language barrier between the generations. The youths were gifted in languages. They spoke many languages, including Taiwanese, Mandarin, English, Spanish, and German. They loved music and often sang and danced. During the Easter retreat, people of all ages came to join in the singing, which continued from dusk to dawn.

During my time in Costa Rica, the devotion of the church members greatly encouraged me in my walk. One sister spent two full years copying the Bible. She had entire chapters of the Bible written on a whiteboard, refrigerator and walls in her home. Other church members had a three and a half hour commute to get to church. So they recorded the sermons so that the next day, they could listen to it on their drive home.

I returned to California heavy-hearted, as I realized that this church was still without a consistent pastor. When I returned in 2006 to help out in the church's annual Easter retreat, I realized that one person would not be enough, and began to recruit volunteers. In 2007, a team of volunteers was assembled, and since then, we have led a team back to Costa Rica in each of the last three years. There have been new team members each year, and as part of the preparation, each team member has received prayers. Each year exciting things have happened both in the lives of our team members as well as in the church in Costa Rica.

As the years have gone by, our programs have expanded and enrollment in the Easter retreat has also grown. The retreat program has included drama, singing, dancing, wall bulletins, Bible memorization, radio-television advertising, clay molding, etc. Ultimately, the most important part of the retreat has been the introduction of our Lord and Savior, Jesus. Many parents have seen spiritual growth in their children following these retreats. Some of the teens who have been in Costa Rica for schooling and have said that their parents have supported their participation in church activities because it would keep them from going down the wrong path.

The most poignant night each year has been the last evening of the retreat. There is an altar call to invite each participant to come forward, as the Holy Spirit works amongst the audience. As each person approaches the podium, they often have tears streaming down their faces and thanksgiving in their hearts. Counselors then step forward to pray with them. Sometimes parents would come forward to embrace their children. Other times, children would come forward to embrace a weeping parent. These have been unforgettable moments. During the last session, we pass around yarns of different colors, using them to represent things we have learned during the retreat. As more people share, more colorful yarn would be woven together. By the end of the session, a colorful tapestry would be knit together, a reminder of our friendships and of God's love for all of us.

Whenever I think of my time in Costa Rica, I am deeply moved. Every year I eagerly look forward to Easter, and bringing a short-term missions team with me to Costa Rica, so that they too can be a part of this exciting ministry.

2007 作者翁蕭幸美於中美洲哥斯達黎加短宣(中舞者)
2007- Author Hsin-Mei Weng (center dancing) at Taiwan Mission in Costa Rica of Central America

美國台灣人社區的醫療傳道
Medical Mission in the Taiwanese Communities in America

楊士宏醫師
紐約長島台灣教會
台灣宣教基金會醫療傳道全球督導
Dr. Shug-Hong Young
Long Island Taiwanese Church
Global Coordinator, Medical Mission of Taiwan Mission Foundation

美國台灣人社區的醫療傳道

楊士宏醫師
紐約長島教會
台灣宣教基金會醫療傳道全球督導

台灣宣教基金會醫療傳道組自2007年成立後，即展開關懷癌患的事工。我們首先在長島台灣教會舉辦「癌患事工講習會」，繼於2008年5月3日及6月14日在紐約聖教會，2010年3月13日及5月23日在新澤西台語歸正教會，舉辦相同的講習會。

在這些講習會裡，通常先由陳信誠、黃正雅或趙坤山等醫師解說「什麼是癌症」，再由林瑞葉藥劑師介紹治癌的醫藥常識、謝吟雪護士講癌症療法及預防復發，然後由林順明牧師講述教會與會友如何藉建立信心、音樂治療、靈修治療、創意活動與運動治療等方式來協助癌症患者。

講習會後，台灣宣教基金會就贈送參與的教會一台乒乓桌，作為癌症患者復健運動之用。自從2009年，醫療傳道組更進一步踏出教會，進入社區進行醫療義診服務。我們於5月2日(2009)在長島台灣教會，對社區人士作免費的驗血糖、量血壓、測体重等服務，並由專業醫護人員提供個人保健的忠言。8月29日(2009)，我們在長島Patchogue社區義診，除了上述的服務外，又增加牙科與皮膚科的建言。9月26日(2009)，我們在白石鎮的以馬內利路德教會附屬小學進行義診，這回增加了眼科服務。爾後又於3月13日(2010)在新澤西台語歸正教會、5月9日(2010)在紐約聖教會舉行。

總計這五次的醫療義診服務，共有200多位社區人士接受診療，除了台灣鄉親，也包括了美國其他族群。熱心參與的醫療團隊義工包括十多位醫師：許登龍、楊冠傑、楊彰興、陳志山、吳嘉德、林彥哲、陳彰、郭惠美、鄭仁澤、施

淑娟和Janet Wu等，與護士潘惠敏、李桔、馮美蘭、黃連愛等，加上營養師黃瑞宏、復健治療師林妙瑛、醫學生Sophia Feng、急救生Curtis與Caroline Chen，以及義工蘇秋莉、羅純美、陳麗嬋、Julie Feng、Lauren Tetrocine、高王幸美傳道等多人，特予致謝。

台灣宣教基金會醫療傳道組，於5月2日(2009) 在長島台灣教會，社區進行醫療義診服務
TMF's medical mission ministry - health fairs at Long Island Taiwanese Church

後排左起: 作者楊士宏醫師, 吳嘉德夫人, 黃蓮愛護士, 李桔護士, 林妙瑛物理治療師; 前排左起醫師:施淑娟, 鄭仁澤, 許登龍, 陳彰, 吳嘉德, 郭惠美
9/26/09- TMF Medical Mission Team at White Stone Lutheran Church in New York.
Author Dr. Shug-Hong Young (2nd row 1st left)

Medical Mission in the Taiwanese Communities in America

Dr. Shug-Hong Young
Long Island Taiwanese Church
Global Coordinator, Medical Mission of Taiwan Mission Foundation

The Taiwan Mission Foundation (TMF) established an outreach ministry for cancer patients in 2007 via the TMF medical missions committee. The first set of ministry workshops for cancer patients were held at the Long Island Taiwanese Church (LITC).

The same workshops were later held at the Queens Taiwanese Evangelical Church (QTEC) (May 2 and June 14, 2008) and Fair Lawn Community Church (March 13 and May 23, 2010). The workshops were given by experienced cancer medical professionals. Dr. Timothy Chen, Jacob Chen-Ya Huang and Clifford Chao lectured on "What is cancer?" Then Sue Shui Yeh Wei, a pharmacist and Linda Hsieh, a nurse, educated participants on cancer medication, treatment and remission. After the workshops, each participating church received a ping pong table from TMF to support the church's ping pong ministry which served cancer patients going through rehabilitation.

Since 2009, TMF's medical mission ministry has participated in community-based health fairs in Williston Park (LITC, May 2, 2009), Patchouge (Lucero Foundation, August 29, 2009), Whitestone (Immanuel Lutheran Church, September 26), Fair Lawn Community Church (March 13, 2010) and Queens Taiwanese Evangelical Church (QTEC, May 9, 2010). The first health fair in Williston Park provided the community with a basic screening of blood sugar levels (diabetes), blood pressure (hypertension/hypotension), and body mass index (obesity). Dental and dermatological screenings were added for the health fair in Patchougue. Ophthalmic services were added for the health fair in Whitestone. Each additional screening was added as a result of participant recommendations.

A total of more than 200 people were served by these five health fairs. Volunteer medical mission team members have included more than 10 most active physicians such as Teng-Lung Hsu, James Yang, David Chang-Sing Yang, Chi-Shan Chen, Chia-Der Wu, Yen-Tse Lin, Patrick Chen, Amy Kuo, Jen-Tse Cheng, Shu-Chuan Shih, and Janet Wu. Nurses Emily Hui-Min Feng, Jyne Hsiau, Meilan Feng, Kathleen Lu and Wenly Chen have worked with nutritionist Jey-Hong Hwang and physical therapist Lydia Chen. Sophia Feng-a medical student, Curtis and Caroline Chen, Julie Young, Chun-Mei Wu, Li-Tsan Lin, Julie Feng, Lauren Tetrocine and Mi Mi Wang were also volunteers with the medical team. TMF would like to thank all those involved for donating their time and labor of love and making the health fairs a success.

2009護士潘惠敏(左一)與馮美蘭(左二)於長島為南美洲厄瓜多的新移民驗血糖
(台灣宣教惠的醫療事工會及其他族裔)
TMF Medical Mission at Lucero Foundation on Long Island, New York- Nurse Emily Hui-Min Feng (1st left) & Meilan Feng (2nd left) testing blood sugar levels

勝癌會
Triumph Over Cancers

林順明牧師
台灣宣教基金會醫療傳道與禮儀宣教牧師 - 紐約
Reverend Paul S. Lin
Medical and Ceremonial Missions Pastor of Taiwan Mission Foundation, New York

勝癌會

林順明牧師
台灣宣教基金會醫療傳道與禮儀宣教牧師-紐約

「勝癌會」於2005年10月6日在紐約市成立五年來,其活動分為下列五個部份:

一、建立信心
「勝癌會」每月選擇一個週六的下午,進行信仰造就,平均約三十名癌症患者參加。我們採取聖經中醫治與拯救的主題,參照普世的療傷復原之道,將之濃縮為「信心單元」,由指導者與癌症患者合力進行。結果第一年。即有四位非基督徒的癌患者接受洗禮,並且在康復後,繼續熱心服事教會。

二、音樂治療
「勝癌會」編寫二十餘首專供癌患者吟唱之治療音樂,並在所有「勝癌會」的活動中教唱,深受歡迎。我們希望藉著音樂,讓癌症患者有平安與喜樂的功效。

三、靈修治療
「勝癌會」每週三晚上七時進行癌患禱告會,為每位癌症患者的療程代禱。行動方便的癌患者常熱烈加入。我們引導癌患者建立心靈的力量,並教導他們釋放心靈的方法。

四、創意活動
「勝癌會」每兩個月舉行一次手工藝製作,如乾燥壓花等,每次出席皆超過四十人以上。我們運用各種手工藝活動的設計,開發癌患者的創意與生活的樂趣。

五、運動治療

「勝癌會」乒乓球隊每週三下午六時練球，平均約三十餘人參加。2006年4月，成軍四日的「勝癌會」女子乒乓球隊，參加大紐約區台灣教會聯誼會乒乓球團體賽，獲女子組亞軍，隔年勇奪冠軍。我們組癌患者乒乓球隊，提供義務教練，希望藉團體運動，重建癌症患者的社交生活。因此，乒乓隊員不限於癌患者本身，其家屬、義工、護士與醫師皆可參加。

此外，「勝癌會」亦與美國防癌協會及地方教會，合辦約二百到三百人參加的盛大癌患聖誕同樂會。

「勝癌會」的積極服務，曾名列美國亞太癌症支持團體的優良名單，並在台灣宣教基金會策劃下，在大紐約地區先後協助四個教會成立地區性的勝癌服務事工。海內外教會或團體皆可向台灣宣教基金會尋求「勝癌會」的協助，以建立更多地區性的勝癌宣教事工。

勝癌會女子乒乓球隊4/4/06成立- 作者林順明牧師/牧師娘(後右一二)，劉德來總教練(後左一)，楊宜宜傳道(後左五)，張音音教練(前排左四)
(TMF楊宜宜會長二女兒亦前美國青少年乒乓國手)
Women's ping-pong team of Triumph Over Cancer (TOC) was formed on 4/4/06. Author Paul Lin and wife (back 1st & 2nd right)

Triumph Over Cancers

Reverend Paul S. Lin
Medical and Ceremonial Missions Pastor
of Taiwan Mission Foundation, New York

"Triumph Over Cancers" is an organization established by Reverend Paul S. Lin in New York on October 6th, 2005. The five programs for cancer patients are described below:

I. Growing in Faith

One Saturday per month, the "Growing in Faith" class is held. The gospel of salvation and healing in the Christian Bible is the study theme. Units of faith that cover the universal healing process are studied. The average attendance is 30 people. In the first year, there were four non-Christian patients baptized through this program. After their recovery, they have continued to serve the church enthusiastically.

II. Music Therapy

We have successfully edited or written more than twenty therapeutic songs, and they have been embraced by the cancer patients, and are sung at all of our activities. Music therapy is calming, uplifting, and inspiring.

III. Spiritual Exercise

At 7:00 PM every Wednesday evening, we hold prayer meetings to intercede on behalf of all cancer patients. We guide patients through empowering Christian spiritual exercises and also teach them a method for releasing themselves from spiritual bondage.

IV. Creative Activities

We design bimonthly workshops of different crafts to encourage the development of talent and creativity. For instance, pressing flowers into art frames is a favorite. Average attendance in each session is more than 40 people. Craft workshops not only help develop creativity but also enhance the enjoyment of life.

V. Healing through Sports

A ping-pong team meets at 6:00 PM every Wednesday. About 30 people attend. In April 2006, our women's ping pong team came in second place in the Ping Pong Team Championship of the Fellowship of Taiwanese Christian Churches in Greater New York, even though the team was only established four days before the competition. The following year in 2007, the women's team came in first place.

Concluding Remarks

As a joint effort with the American Cancer Society and several local churches, Triumph Over Cancers hold a special Christmas event each year for cancer patients and their families. The attendance has always been close to 300 people.

Triumph Over Cancers has been acknowledged and recommended in the Asian American and Pacific Islander Cancer Survivors Capacity Building Project, which is funded by the Center for Disease Control and Prevention (CDC) of the United States Federal Government. Triumph Over Cancers is currently collaborating with the Taiwan Mission Foundation (TMF) to assist four church congregations in establishing local cancer ministries in the Greater New York area, and has become an instrumental part of the Medical Missions Ministry of TMF. Through TMF, Triumph Over Cancers will continue to provide assistance to local Taiwanese communities to build up their support for local cancer patients.

生命的見證
A Testimony of Life

林澄江
洛杉磯台福教會
Chen Chien Hsu
Evangelical Formosan Church of Los Angeles in California

生命的見證

林澄江
洛杉磯台福教會

人生總有苦難，我們即使不明白苦難為什麼會發生，仍然可以憑著信心倚靠神，知道在苦難中神必有美好的計劃。我是個很平凡的基督徒，沒什麼才能，只祈願一生為神所用。先生在台灣原是中學老師，我們育有一女一子。1976年我們移居巴西，1989年初與教會團體到以色列旅行，在旅途中我帶領五位慕道友決志，並在約但河受洗，這對我是非常有意義的領人歸主記。

1989年夏天我們自巴西移民美國，來到洛杉磯台福教會，夫婦倆隨即跟隨劉富理牧師學習個人談道。1990年教會開始「門徒之夜」，推動個人傳道和小組探訪，我們從未缺席，因這一直是我很有負擔的事工。1997年開始，我用五年的時間把神學課程讀完，高齡念書很辛苦，但很有收穫。

四面受敵，卻不被困住

這十幾年來，許多苦難和試煉接踵而至，幾乎要將我們擊倒。來美不久即投資失敗，多年積存的錢財瞬間都化為零。98年我們26歲的女兒得癌症，一年半後被主接回天家。04年我從梯子上摔下來，骨盤裂了。06年底我又得乳癌，經過一年半的開刀、化療和電療，得到痊癒。感謝主，經過這些試煉，我們與神更親近，信心更堅強，屬靈生命更茁壯。

因為女兒得淋巴癌而過世，弟兄姐妹常常把癌症病人介紹給我，要我去關心帶領。後來我自己得了乳癌，使我有機會接觸更多癌症病人，我也利用長途電話打到台灣及美國各地，去開導關心癌症病人。自07年開始，我們在禮拜五晚上開放家庭，(現在移至教會舉行)做些各式台灣美食，聚集一些癌友及其家屬，引導他們認識基要真理，並為他們禱告，幫助他們體會神的醫治大能。最多曾有15位來參加，08年有兩個家庭四個人受洗歸主。

08年我開始參與角聲防癌事工的姐妹會，每個月都有聚會，09年還帶一位年青的乳癌孕婦到洛福教會決志歸主。

聖靈做工，得人如得魚

06年我曾參與教會近鄰 Santa Anita 老人安養院的事奉。08年教會又開拓慈博安養院事工，我幫忙司琴和講道，在這裡一年帶領了13位長者受洗歸主，其中一位是盲人。最年長的是101歲的葉婆婆，受洗後一個禮拜，上帝就帶她回天家。

二、三十年來，神給我許多機會帶領各種背景的人信主，一年帶領十幾人，包括幾位後來獻身傳道。感謝主，讓我經歷苦難和病痛，才能體會當事人的心，才能用神所賜的安慰去安慰人。為了救人靈魂，我受點皮肉之苦又算什麼？這些都是聖靈的工作，我不過是平信徒傳道，神的器皿。願一切榮耀歸於主耶穌基督。

作者林澄江傳道(前起二)的癌患關懷事工
Author Minister Chen Chien (2nd bottom) Hsu with cancer patients support group

8/08 作者林澄江傳道(左一)探訪加州慈博護理中心跛者陳瑞鉅(坐輪椅)及盲者溫嬌(左二)，二者後來都信主
8/08- Minister Chen Chien Hsu (1st left) visited RC Chen (on wheelchair) & blind woman Wen Chiou (2nd left) and led them to Christ

A Testimony of Life

Chen Chien Hsu
Evangelical Formosan Church of Los Angeles in California

Suffering is unavoidable, but even though we might not understand why it happens, we can still rely on God because we know that He has good plans for us.

I am just an ordinary Christian with no special talents. My only wish has always been for God to use me to accomplish His will. In Taiwan, my husband was a junior high school teacher, and we had one daughter and one son. We immigrated to Brazil in 1976. In early 1989, we traveled to Israel with a tour group from a Taiwanese church, and on the way there, I led five seekers from that group to Christ. They were then baptized in the Jordan River. This was one of the most exciting and meaningful experiences I had ever had with evangelism.

In the summer of 1989, we immigrated to the US and joined EFCLA. We took a training course on evangelism taught by Rev. Felix Liu and joined the church's discipleship ministry to reach out to the Taiwanese community through visitations. We never missed any visitations since I was very passionate about evangelism. From 1997 to 2002, I attended a seminary to study theology. It was hard for an old lady like me to go back to school again, but it was very rewarding.

For more than ten years, we endured several afflictions and trials. First, after we moved to the US, we lost all our savings to bad investments. Then, our 26-year-old daughter was diagnosed with cancer, and God took her home in 1999. In 2004, I fell from a ladder and cracked my pelvis. I was then diagnosed with breast cancer in 2006 and went through surgery, chemotherapy, and radiation therapy. Going through all of these trials brought us closer to God, and as a result of this, our faith grew stronger.

After my daughter died of cancer, people started to refer their cancer-stricken friends to me. I had the opportunity to not only care for them but also to share the Gospel with them. When I myself had cancer, I then had many more chances to reach out to cancer patients. I could reach cancer patients anywhere in Taiwan or USA through long-distance phone calls.

Since 2007, we have opened our house every Friday night to cancer patients and their families. We make delicious Taiwanese food for them, teach them basic truths about the Christian faith, pray for them, and help them to experience God's healing power. We have had as many as fifteen people at our house, and in 2008 four people from two families were baptized. I have also participated in a sisters' group from the Herald Cancer Association that has been meeting monthly since 2008. I brought a pregnant cancer patient to EFCLA and she accepted Christ in 2009.

I joined EFC's ministry to convalescent homes in 2006. We started with the Santa Anita Convalescent Home in Temple City, and two years later expanded our ministry to include the Pacific Nursing Center in El Monte. I played the piano and preached. Thirteen people were baptized in one year, including a blind person. Mrs. Yeh, the oldest one at age 101, went to be with the Lord one week after she was baptized.

In the past twenty to thirty years, God has granted me many opportunities to lead people to Him (about 10 per year) including some who later went into full-time ministry. Because of the sickness and suffering I have experienced, I understood the pain people went through and, as a result, could comfort them with the comfort God gave me. My suffering was really only a small price to pay for the privilege of saving souls. I am just a lay minister, an instrument of Holy Spirit. To Christ, our Savior and Lord, be all the glory!

長島台灣教會暑期兒童營
Long Island Taiwanese Church Summer Camp
- Discover the Wonderful Love of God -

賴弘專博士與楊靜欣
維吉尼亞州
Dr. Hung-Chuan Lai & Daphne Yang
Virginia

長島台灣教會暑期兒童營

賴弘專與楊靜欣

維吉尼亞州

感謝上帝的帶領，讓我們有機會參與紐約長島台灣教會暑期兒童營的事工。由於教會裡年輕的一代並不多，同工們覺得唯有將觸角伸向社區，使社區的孩子們無論基督徒或非基督徒，都歡喜來教會，才能將信仰傳給下一代。因此，自2007年開始，咱教會勇敢接受挑戰，舉辦暑期兒童營。

由於咱教會會友的孩子們大都已成年，所以必須不斷地鼓勵非本教會的社區兒童前來參加。而咱教會所在的Williston Park又是個族群非常多元的社區，居民有白人、印度人、韓國人、中國人、廣東人、台灣人…等，因此營會與教學的方法都需要相當的設計，以迎合不同族裔兒童的需要。

暑期兒童營迄今已邁入第三年。回想起來，前兩年真是在摸索中度過。由於我們是來自台灣的移民，對美國文化十分陌生，因此要教育這些美國孩子們，剛開始真是困難重重，但隨後即發現主恩滿滿。

首先，報名的人數未如預期。我們原本預訂二十份教材，但報名的人數只有十位。由於美國教會設計的教材非常生動活潑，我們覺得如不能讓更多的小朋友受惠，實在可惜。因此在開營前一星期，我們打電話給已報名的家長們，請他們幫忙邀請其他小朋友參加。此外，我們還到教會附近的公園分發傳單。沒想到在兒童營開始前一天，不僅名額全滿，還超過一、兩位，讓大家士氣大增。

其次，在這次兒童營裡，有一位小朋友的情況比較特別，他的家長一開始就特別叮嚀，沒想到他第一天就適應得不錯。隔天早上，他的爺爺、奶奶和媽媽都來感謝老師。原來這位小朋友以前曾參加過一些營會，都有適應不良的問題，所以他的家人對他居然會喜歡參加這個營會，都感到訝異。

以後每一天，他都最早到，而且每天回家後，他都會告訴家人他今天所學到的聖經故事。更令人感動的是有一天，小組分班時，帶領的老師說了一個英文單字，被另外一個小朋友連續糾正兩次，正當這位老師感到不好意思時，這位小朋友居然對那位小朋友說：「It's all right（沒有關係）！」讓在一旁幫忙的我十分感動。還有一天下午，我們玩水球遊戲。這是許多小朋友非常喜愛的遊戲之一。可是一開始，這個孩子就被比較大的小朋友砸到水球，哭了起來。我把他拉到一旁，安慰他，他還是不斷地咒罵這個遊戲。但後來，他看見大家把水球丟來丟去，玩得不亦樂乎，居然笑了，又跑進去加入陣營，也玩得很開心。我們都很高興他在這個暑期營中成長不少。

營會結束後，有一位家長寫了一張卡片給我們，說她的女兒原本非常不喜歡到教會，但參加我們的兒童營後，竟不再排斥教會！這樣的卡片帶給我們許多的鼓勵，上帝在其中所動的工，確實超乎我們所求。

舉辦這種多族裔的兒童營，事工真是包羅萬象。然而我們的同工卻除了一對年輕夫婦外，其他人的平均年齡都超過六十歲。我們的阿嬤級同工每天輪流準備愛心午餐，阿公級教練則教小朋友打桌球，使歷年參加過營會的小朋友的球技都突飛猛進，頻頻向教練挑戰。

咱教會連續舉辦三年的暑期兒童營，收穫超出我們的預期。因為這個兒童營，使有些非基督徒家庭的孩子從而認識耶穌，當他們朗朗誦讀聖經的金句，帶給同工的喜悅真是無法言喻！尤有甚之的是過去三年，教會憑愛心舉辦營會，使教會的口碑在社區傳開，更使許多不同的族裔認識到台灣人與台灣教會。此外，教會同工也因舉辦兒童營，接觸到一些來自台灣的新移民家庭，得以與他們分享福音。

社區兒童事工的耕耘需要長久的付出，今年真是充滿感恩的一年。我們感受到過去的努力，一直在累積中。生命的成長猶如埋在地裡的種子，只要殷勤澆灌，終會萌芽、茁壯，相信在未來，會看到它開花、結果。

長島台灣教會暑期兒童營　319

Church Summer Camp

暑期兒童營的學生
Students of the summer camp

作者賴弘專傳道與夫人楊靜欣主持長島台灣教會暑期兒童營數年(攝於2007)
2007- Long Island Taiwanese Church Summer Children's Emotional Quotient (EQ) Camp led by Author Minister Hung-Chuan Lai & wife Daphne

2007長島台灣教會會友熱心協助暑期兒童營(左起: 謝克明, 蔡淑芳, 凌旭勢, 楊智惠, 李哖, 張子寬, 林士堂, 蕭桂榮, 陳介精)
2007- Volunteer staff members LITC EQ camp

Long Island Taiwanese Church Summer Camp
- Discover the Wonderful Love of God -

Hung-Chuan Lai & Daphne Yang
Virginia

We are so grateful to have had the opportunity to volunteer at the church summer camp for children at the Long Island Taiwanese Church.

Our church began its summer camp for children in 2007 in order to spread the gospel to our neighbors. Because our church was mainly composed of older adults, we found it was imperative that we reach out to our Christian and non-Christian community. Our goal was to help them get to know our church so the next generation could learn about the gospel.

However, there were many challenges. We had few young children in the church, making it difficult to attract children from the community to attend our summer camp. In addition, the diverse population surrounding the church -- Caucasian, Indian, Korean, Mandarin Chinese, Cantonese and Taiwanese families -- required more sensitivity in the children's program development.

We launched the summer camp program in 2009. The first two years were quite challenging. We felt like we were trying to find our way out of the dark. Taiwanese immigrants trying to teach American-born children at an American summer camp was quite difficult. However, we were blessed through our struggles.

Our first problem was the lack of children enrolled in our summer camp. We had ordered 20 sets of materials from the American Christian Society, however

Church Summer Camp

we only had 10 enrollees. We wanted to make sure that we utilized everything, so we invited families who had already signed up to encourage others to also join the camp. In addition, we went to a park near the church to distribute flyers. The day before camp began, our morale was boosted when we found out we had more than 20 children enrolled in the program.

The second issue was in regards to a little boy. Apparently, the little boy had attended other summer camp programs, but did not adapt well. The following day, his grandparents and mother came to thank us for our accommodations. To his family's surprise, they had found that the little boy greatly enjoyed our program.

From then on, that little boy was always the first to arrive. Then, he would go home and share the Bible story of the day with his family. One day, I was moved by this little boy. During a group activity, one of the students twice corrected an instructor for mispronunciation of a word. The instructor was quite embarrassed. The little boy comforted the instructor by saying "It's all right!"

One afternoon our group activity was a water balloon fight. It was a popular game, but one which could easily lead to conflicts. Just as the game was beginning, the same little boy was hit with a water balloon by an older boy. As he began to cry and complain about the game, I pulled him aside and comforted him. When he saw the other children enjoy the activity he began to laugh, and eventually rejoined the others. It was a pleasure to watch him mature during the summer program.

At the end of the program, we received a thank you card from one of the parents of a little girl. We found out that this girl originally disliked attending church, however, after our summer camp, she no longer refused to attend Sunday services. This card gave us a great deal of encouragement, reminding us that God provides beyond our prayers and expectations. A great deal of manpower was required to host a summer camp. We needed volunteers in all aspects of the camp. Aside from a young married couple, the average age of the camp staff member was 60 years old. We had grandmother volunteers taking turns, helping to make lunch for everyone. We had grandfather volunteers teaching the children table tennis. There have been some children who have come back every year for summer camp and they have gotten better at playing table tennis. These children now challenge their coaches in table tennis matches.

Our experiences in the past three years have surpassed our expectations. Some of the children who had attended our summer program came from non-Christian families, and we were able to introduce the gospel to them. We were speechless when we first heard these children recite Bible verses! Our church has become better known throughout our multicultural community because of our summer camps and because of the time and effort we put into getting to know our neighbors. Through our camps, our volunteers have also gotten to know some new immigrants from Taiwan and have been able to share the gospel with them as well.

Community volunteer programs are a long-term investment; they take time to develop and nurture. This past year was a year of thanksgiving where we were finally able to see some of the fruits of our labor. Our Christian walk and children summer programs are like a seed planted in the ground. We water it, nurture it and wait for it to sprout. Eventually, it blossoms and bears fruit.

讓愛走動
Passing on His Love

高如珊
紐約聖教會
Kimberly Kao
Queens Taiwanese Evangelical Church in New York

讓愛走動

高如珊
紐約聖教會

「高姐，如果沒有遇見你，我將會在哪裡？」在德國東部的一處禾場，一位初信主的年輕學子以這句話作為開場白，訴說她對神不盡的感恩。她說，若不是神藉著宣教士高姐及時地傳遞祂的愛，她幾乎就要放棄自己。若不是她明白自己在神眼中的珍貴，她幾乎要以黑暗墮落的人生來換取脫離貧窮的生活。

她的訴說將我的思緒帶回二十三年前的一個改變我人生的暑假。1987年七月的一個週末下午，一群喧鬧的高中生，擠滿了紐約聖教會高耀民牧師家的客廳。這二十多名青少年都是父母不在身邊的台灣小留學生，大家湊在一起，並不真正要尋找上帝，而是為了排解身處異鄉的寂寞。

那是我頭一次參加聚會，頭一次唱詩歌，頭一次聽人家禱告，頭一次知道有一群出於愛心的大哥哥、大姐姐們願意照顧我們。那天，紐約聖教會青年團契就在我的許多頭一次與一群年輕學生的喧嘩笑語聲中正式成立。

一大群小留學生們所面臨的問題，真是層出不窮。無論生活、學業或感情，都需要別人以愛心耐性地引導，尤其屬靈的成長，更需要漫長的時間。在這期間，感謝神為我們預備了許多愛主的輔導兄姐，在各方面給予我們平衡的教導與指正。

團契成立後兩年，大部份的孩子都成為神的兒女。雖然屬靈的年紀尚幼，但高牧師適時地讓我們參與服事，使我們在事奉中認識自己的恩賜。在往後這些年間，雖然我們曾經失落，也曾跌倒，但牧長與輔導的兄姐們卻不因此責備，反而迫切地為我們禱告，繼續肯定我們，重用我們。

我們也曾在彼此搭配服事中，歷經生命的破碎與被主重塑的感動。我們深知這是主那雙看不見卻又大有能力的手在當中掌權，同時也是高牧師與屬靈兄姐們對我們的愛與眷顧，才使這群孤寂與曾經受傷的心被神的愛挽回，得到醫治。

上帝的愛觸摸著我們，使我們因被主愛澆灌而深知愛是必須流出的。我們看到自己所居住的紐約裡，多少靈魂被捆綁，不得釋放。那種漂流在異鄉的孤寂、對未來的不確定與世俗眼光所帶來的壓力等等，都是我們這群小留學生所曾經歷也曾掙扎過的。因此在往後幾年，我們開始藉詩歌演唱、短劇與我們曾被主改變生命的見證，向鄰近社區的朋友或外州的鄉親們傳達神的愛。

在自編的許多短劇中，有的描述年輕人因被罪試探、積非成是，以致墮落。有的討論世態炎涼，人的愛何其有限，因此內心對永恆的愛具有無限的渴望。有的描述在不斷追求名利地位後，才意識到所求的都是短暫空虛，只可惜覺醒已晚，悔恨異常。我們每次排練，都有歡笑，也有眼淚。在用戲劇訴說人性的掙扎、也訴說自己的同時，我們一方面使自己得著建造，另方面也試圖喚醒觀眾的心靈，讓他們知道耶穌是唯一的盼望。

「如果沒有遇見你，我將會在哪裡？」這句話同樣訴說我對神的感恩。如果不是曾經藉紐約聖教會高牧師和一群屬靈兄姐們的引導，讓我得到主的愛，今天的我或許仍然迷茫、不知生命的意義，或自以為是、享受罪中之樂，甚至誤入歧途，到頭來空夢一場。

感謝神，二十三年後的今天，我們這群當年的小留學生都已長大成熟，被主分派到各處去傳播祂的愛，在各教會作美好的服事。回顧過去，到處都是恩典的痕跡。神的愛不止息，從昨天、今天，直到明天，乃至永遠。祂的愛要藉著我們，綿綿不絕地傳播出去，到世界的每一個角落。

紐約聖教會青年團契1995賓州佈道在高俐理家彩排
6/11/95- The youth of Queens Taiwanese Evangelical Church QTEC, rehearsing for a music crusade at Lily Kao's home in PA

Passing on His Love

Kimberly Kao
Queens Taiwanese Evangelical Church in New York

"Sister Kao, if I had not met you, where would I be?" With these words, in East Germany, a young student, a new believer, expressed her gratitude to God. If God did not show His love through missionaries, she could have given up on herself; if she had not understood how valuable she was in God's eyes, she could have fallen from virtue and chosen a life of darkness in order to escape from poverty.

Her story reminded me of the summer when my life was completely transformed. One weekend in July of 1987, a group of boisterous high school students were crowded into the living room of Pastor Kao of Queens Taiwanese Evangelical Church. There were over twenty Taiwanese teenagers who had come to the United States to study, without the company of their parents. They were together not because they wanted to seek God, but rather to ward away the loneliness of being away from home.

As for me, it was the first time I sang hymns at a meeting, and the first time I knew there was a group of young adults who were willing to take care of us, be with us, and love us without reason. On that day, accompanied by many of my "first-times" and lots of ignorant clamors, the Youth Group of QTEC was officially founded.

There were endless issues dealing with a group of young international students; being with us required a great deal of kindness and patience. Even more time was needed to guide us in our spiritual growth. During those times, the Lord prepared many God loving counselors for us. They put their kindness into action, offering us honest teachings and criticisms.

Two years after the Youth Group was established, most of the youth became God's children. In the mean time, Pastor Kao, who never looked down upon us for our young age, allowed us to participate and use our gifts to serve the Lord, and allowed us to learn more about ourselves through serving. We did go astray, we did fall, but the pastor and the counselors never condemned us. Instead, they prayed for us in earnest, continued to encourage us, gave us chances and trusted us with great responsibilities.

In collaborating with each other and in serving, our lives were broken and rebuilt by the Lord. Deep in our hearts we knew it was God's mercy. It was Pastor's Kao's burden to care of the souls of Taiwanese expatriates. It was the brothers and sisters in Christ who offered their youth and energy, and it was God's invisible but powerful hands that have healed those of us who were once desolate and heartbroken, and redeemed us through God's love.

God's love touched us. Showered and filled with God's love, we knew love was something that needed to be passed on. Looking at New York City, where we lived, we saw the souls that were in bondage to the world's values. The feelings of being in a foreign land, the uncertainty towards the future, and the pressures of worldly values were our struggles and what we were going through. In later years, through singing, through skits that we wrote, and testimonies of how the Lord had changed us, we began telling our friends in the community and our fellow countryman in other states about God's love.

In many of our skits, we depicted scenes of how young people were tempted by sins, how lies and wrongs were being passed around for a long time and were taken as truths, and causing young people to fall from virtue. We contemplated the fickleness of human relationships, the limitation of human love, and the infinite desire for eternity. We talked about the futile efforts of pursuing fame and fortune and the regrets after one realized it was too late to mend our mistakes. There was always laughter and tears during each rehearsal. As we described human struggles and told our own stories through drama, not only were we being built up in character, we were also attempting to wake up the souls of our audience, to let them know that Jesus is our only hope.

"What if I hadn't met you (Pastor Kao and each and every one of the counselors in QTEC), where would I be?" This thought also represents my gratitude to the Lord. If I had not met God through QTEC, I might still be lost, not knowing the meaning of my life. I might even have become self-righteous, enjoying the happiness of sin, taking the wrong path, but still feeling empty.

Today, however, we, the group of young teenagers from twenty-three years ago, have all grown and matured and are in different parts of the world spreading His love and doing good works in different churches. Looking back, I see the path filled with God's grace. God's love never ceases. It was in the past, it is here today, and it will be there tomorrow. His love will be passed on endlessly through us to every corner of the world.

1994紐約聖教會十週年感恩禮拜
10th anniversary Thanksgiving Service

1994紐約聖教會十週年詩歌佈道
1994- Music crusade held at QTEC 10th anniversary in NY

兩個海外台灣留學生團契
Two Overseas Taiwan Student Fellowships

李昱平牧師
安雅堡台灣長老教會 - 密西根州
Pastor Fred Lee
Ann Arbor Taiwanese Presbyterian Church in Michigan

兩個海外台灣留學生團契

李昱平牧師
安雅堡台灣長老教會-密西根州

成立於1970年代的安雅堡台灣長老教會，一直致力於建立一個福音廣傳的台灣人社區。透過耶穌的愛，我們要愛人與見證人生命的轉變。不論是誰，來自怎樣的宗教背景，我們都誠心邀請他(她)加入我們的福音事工。因著主的愛，我們在這美麗的大學城相聚，也期盼將上帝的恩典帶入在這城市裡擁有相同文化背景的台灣人社區。

以下是我們這些年來福音事工的簡介：

一、芥菜種查經團契-
「芥菜種查經班」是一個由在密西根安雅堡的台灣留學生所組成的信仰團契。在主的愛中，來自不同背景的我們一起分享留學生的生活點滴，與經由信仰見證滋生的友情，共同體驗生命的成長。

芥菜種查經班係依馬可福音第四章「芥菜種」的比喻而命名的：「我們要把神的國比作甚麼呢？我們可以用甚麼比喻來形容它呢？ 它好像一粒芥菜種，剛種下去的時候，比地上的一切種子都小。種下以後，生長起來，卻比一切蔬菜都大，長出大枝子，甚至天空的飛鳥都可以在它的蔭下搭窩。」

查經班每週五晚上固定聚會。大家經由詩歌與查經來認識上帝的愛和恩典。此外，每年還有多樣豐富的活動，如迎新與送舊茶會，讓大家在主愛中成為一家人。介於迎新與送舊之間的，還有秋初的北密州賞楓之旅、十月由團契弟兄所掌廚的男士烹飪大賽及電影欣賞會，皆樂趣無窮。

每年歲末，由安雅堡台灣教會所主辦的「福爾摩沙之聲」音樂會，更是當地台灣人社區的一樁盛事。來自台灣的優秀音樂家，包括在密西根大學音樂研究所

就讀的台灣學生們，不僅以美妙的音符傳遞福爾摩沙之聲，亦使大家藉此機會歡聚一堂。此外，我們也透過歌頌恩典的「讚美之夜」，唱出對主恩的感謝。夏天的密西根分外美麗，我們每年七月都舉辦「沙山露營」，在雪白的沙丘與翠綠的湖畔紮營，享受自然美景，也迎接新生，同時分享彼此的信仰見證。

我們相信芥菜種查經班將帶給異鄉遊子許多真誠的友誼與溫暖的關懷，也相信在學生團契中傳福音，就像在撒芥菜籽，雖不知道會不會結果？何時結果？但撒種的工作不能停。我們的信心或許如芥菜種般地小，上帝卻會透過這個團契讓我們不斷地成長，直到有一天，曾經受過鼓勵的要去鼓勵人、曾經接受幫助的要去幫助人、曾經在這個團體中感受到被愛的，也要去愛人。

二、迦拿團契

「迦拿團契」是一個以年輕家庭為主的團契。由於安雅堡是個大學城，我們主要的福音事工固然以學生為主，然隨著教會中已婚青年的增加，我們於是在2009年元月成立一個讓年輕家庭共聚一堂的「迦拿團契」。

我們基於一個共同的異象，就是大家一起分享對聖經與信仰的認識，也關懷每個家庭的喜與憂，同時讓孩子們一起學習、成長，共同過著充滿愛的團契生活。

因此，「迦拿團契」在每個月的第二個週末下午聚會。當團契的妻子們把豐盛的菜餚端上桌時，大家便圍在一起禱告，共同獻上感恩。我們過去一年的討論主題包括夫妻相處、婚姻生活、兩性溝通、育兒、工作、旅遊、投資、宗教與婚姻、家庭與服事等等。藉著團契生活，我們一起在婚姻的課題中成長，從彼此身上看見上帝的榮耀與恩典，更會在彼此有需要時，互相幫助。

我們深知我們皆非完美，因此，希望透過教會的服事與團契的生活，來共同仰望上帝。如果你有機會到密西根的安雅堡，歡迎你加入我們這個溫暖的大家庭！

Two Overseas Taiwan Student Fellowships

Pastor Fred Lee
Ann Arbor Taiwanese Presbyterian Church in Michigan

The Ann Arbor Taiwanese Presbyterian Church (AATPC), which was established in the 1970's, is committed to spreading the Gospel to the Taiwanese community. Its aim is to transform lives using the love of Jesus. Everyone is invited to join this community, no matter his or her religious background. We embrace God's love and grace in this college town and look forward to sharing it with the Taiwanese people in this community.

The following are descriptions of the major ministries of the Ann Arbor Taiwanese Presbyterian Church:

Mustard Seed Fellowship

The Mustard Seed Bible Study Fellowship is mainly composed of Taiwanese international students at colleges and universities in the Ann Arbor, Michigan area. Through God's love, the fellowship witnesses to others from different backgrounds through shared experiences. As members of the fellowship mature in their walk with God, individuals learn to care for each other as God's people and learn to follow His commands.

Mustard Seed Fellowship is named after Mark 4:30-32 - And he said, "With what can we compare the kingdom of God, or what parable shall we use for it? It is like a grain of mustard seed, which, when sown on the ground, is the smallest of all the seeds on earth, yet when it is sown it grows up and becomes larger than all the garden plants and puts out large branches, so that the birds of the air can make nests in its shade."

This fellowship offers Taiwanese students a Christian perspective on the world through sharing, worship, and weekly Bible studies. Bible studies are held every Friday night

at the home of Mr. and Mrs. Liao. Mustard Seed Fellowship also invests in students'
lives. We involve ourselves in a variety of annual outreach events and witness each person being formed in Christ-like character, being loved as part of the Christian family. From every orientation to every farewell party as each year passes, we praise the Lord for nurturing us in His love, changing our lives, and working with us to call more and more people into relationship with Jesus.

Taking the geographic advantage of being Michiganites, we kick off a whole year of new friendships and blessings with an autumn leaf peeping trip to northern Michigan. We indulge ourselves in nature and praise the great creation of God along the way. This event is followed by Men's Top Chef, an annual contest for gentlemen to present cooking not only in theory but in practice. Contestants are judged by a special jury formed by ladies as the Top Chef is awarded to the one who wins the majority of votes. This is without a doubt a night full of laughter and joy.

Through an uncompromising commitment to Performance, Worship, and the Taiwanese heritage, Ann Arbor Taiwanese Presbyterian Church, along with the Mustard Seed Fellowship, serve Michigan audiences by bringing to our community an annual concert every October –The Sound of Formosa—featuring talented Taiwanese artists, who represent excellence, commitment and the contribution of Taiwan to today's vigorous and exciting live performing arts world. Concert performers are mainly music majors and alumni at the University of Michigan.

In mid-semester, a praise team led by students presents A Night of Praise, which brings people from all over Ann Arbor and beyond together to worship God in a new and exciting way. In between school quizzes, tests and exams, we host movie nights for students to talk, relax, and to learn about God, who He is, what He has done and what He is going to do. We also spend a weekend in July sand dune camping by the Lake of Michigan, for the true beauty of Michigan lies in its summers.

We believe that God calls us to help form the character of the next generation of Christian leaders. The university is a marketplace of ideas. Students are challenged to understand competing worldviews. Although our faith is as small as a mustard seed, we believe that God will develop us as a group until one day, those who had been given a hand will reach out, and those who felt loved through the ministry will share God's love with others too.

We also believe that you will be embraced by friendship, care and love at Mustard Seed. In addition, you will experience the joy and peace you can have in life. If you have a chance to stop by, or are on your way to Ann Arbor for school or work, the door to the big family of Mustard Seeders is open for you 24/7! How convenient is that?

Cana Family Fellowship

Cana is a family integrated fellowship. Since Ann Arbor is known as a college town, the student-oriented Mustard Seed Fellowship has been the major ministry of Ann Arbor Taiwanese Presbyterian Church. However, as the number of married young adults in the church has increased, a family-oriented fellowship was started in 2009 at the Ann Arbor Taiwanese Presbyterian Church.

Our vision is, in turn, to warmly welcome people from all religious backgrounds. We are also committed to articulating faith in the context of marriage. We are committed to sharing our lives and God's Word with each other.

We meet once a month on the second Saturday evening. We say grace before dinner, giving thanks to God. We discuss all topics related to marital relationships, communication, childrearing, jobs, travel, investments, religion, and ministries. Through this fellowship, we have all grown closer together and have seen God's glories and blessings in each other's lives. We also provide help and support when needed.

Ann Arbor Taiwanese Presbyterian Church is made up of ordinary people from all walks of life who understand that they need to continually rely on God. We hope to bring you closer to Him through all works we are committed to do. If you ever have the opportunity to come, please join us here.

密西根大學音樂系博士班學生與來自紐約的女高音鄭怡君(右二)
共同呈獻『福爾摩沙之聲』音樂會。
Graduate students, with PHD in Music, from Michigan University performed in "Sound of Formosa" concert together with professional soprano Sharon I-Chun Cheng (second from right).

辛城台灣長老教會的留學生事工
Overseas Taiwan Student Ministry

郭正義
辛城台灣長老教會 - 俄亥俄州
Cheng-Yih Kuo
Cincinnati Taiwanese Presbyterian Church, Ohio

辛城台灣長老教會的留學生事工

郭正義
辛城台灣長老教會 - 俄亥俄州

俄亥俄州辛辛那提的「辛城台灣長老教會」自2000年3月5日成立以來，在十年中，雖僅三年多有駐堂牧師，卻有二十五位成人及幼兒接受洗禮，所擬的事工也都能按部就班地進行。感謝上帝數不盡的恩典、多位牧者不辭辛勞地證道與主內兄姐同心協力地同工，使這個新而弱小的教會得以逐步地成長。

教會成立之初，我們即本着以台語禮拜、領人歸主為宗旨，同時特別關懷辛城的台灣留學生事工。

辛城是俄亥俄州西南端的一個大城，城中有頗具規模的辛辛那提大學(University of Cincinnati)和Xavier 大學，隔著俄亥俄河，南岸即是肯塔基州，有北肯塔基大學。此地的台灣留學生約有五十名，大部分集中在辛大，攻讀醫學、藥學、理工、建築、設計及音樂⋯等科系。為關懷台灣留學生，我們特別成立「辛大學生團契」，提供台灣留學生們生活的協助與文化適應的輔導，並引領他們認識基督信仰。

「辛大學生團契」每週五晚間聚會，內容有詩歌分享、聖經查考、專題講座、彼此代禱⋯等。每逢單數的週五晚間，我們以未信主的留學生為對象，請大家分享生活經驗、促進情感交流，並且贈送聖經給學生們，引領他們認識主耶穌。每逢雙數的週五晚間，則由基督徒學生帶領，對經文作深入的探討，以培育靈命。此外，我們有時也在週末舉辦賞楓、郊遊等聯誼活動。

教會兄姐們對照顧台灣留學生，可說無微不至。除了準備團契餐點、過年過節的愛餐外，還參加畢業典禮、幫忙籌辦婚禮，亦舉辦求職與生涯規劃、汽車維修常識等講座，讓身處異鄉的台灣遊子能因鄉親們的關懷，稍解思鄉與適應新環境之苦。

「辛大學生團契」裡有許多位會友就讀辛辛那提大學音樂學院，經常以他們主修的鋼琴、聲樂、管風琴、絃樂、管樂⋯等恩賜來服事主。他們在教會司琴、奉獻優美的歌聲，如逢節日，更以舉辦音樂會來引領未信主的鄉親們踏進教會之門。同樣地，熱心的兄姐們也都參加他們的音樂演奏會，並為之準備會後餐點，使演奏會盡善盡美，並藉此分享主的愛。

感謝上帝的恩典，讓咱教會能不斷地在年輕人身上播撒福音的種子。願他們畢業後，無論到何處，都能蒙神賜福，繼續發揮所長，成為教會的基石。阿們！

辛城台灣長老教會2009復活節四位接受洗禮者
郭正義長老與夫人陳恩惠(前右一、二)
Easter 2009- Four newly-baptized believers with Cincinnati church leaders. Author Cheng-Yih Kuo and wife (Front 1st & 2nd right)

辛辛那提大學台灣留學生團契週五查經一景
2009- University of Cincinnati Taiwanese Student Fellowship/Friday Night Bible Study

2009辛辛那提大學台灣留學生秋季賞楓之旅
2009- University of Cincinnati Taiwanese Student Fellowship/Fall Colors Hiking

Overseas Taiwan Student Ministry

Cheng-Yih Kuo
Cincinnati Taiwanese Presbyterian Church, Ohio

The Cincinnati Taiwanese Presbyterian Church was established on March 5, 2000. Through the testimonies and care from ministers, evangelists and brothers and sisters working together, the church has grown. A total of 25 adults and children have been baptized in the past ten years, despite only having a pastor for three of those years. Thank God for His grace and His provision of selfless individuals who have participated in the growth of this church.

The church was established to worship God in the Taiwanese language and to bring others to Christ, especially Taiwanese graduate students attending universities within the Cincinnati area. Cincinnati is a big city located in the southwest of Ohio, north of the Ohio River. Across the Ohio River is the State of Kentucky and Indiana State is on the west side. The more famous universities include University of Cincinnati (UC) and Xavier University. Across the river is the Northern Kentucky University. There are about 50 graduate students from Taiwan. Most of them attend UC and major in medicine, pharmacy, engineering, architecture, design, music, and other fields. In order to best serve these graduate students, the church began the "University of Cincinnati Christian Fellowship." The fellowship provides the students a safe place to ask about how to best adapt to their new environment, as well as a place to better understand the Christian faith.

Currently, UC fellowship meets on Friday nights. The fellowship includes hymns, bible study, special topic discussions and prayers. On every odd Friday night, the fellowship's focus is to reach out to non-Christian graduate students. We have fellowship, discussions about everyday events, and Bible study led by Christian students. On the even Fridays, the students study the Bible in depth in order to nurture their spiritual life. In addition, the fellowship also organize special activities, such as leaf peeping in the fall.

The brothers and sisters of the church do their best to take care of these students. They wholeheartedly prepare meals for fellowship meetings, coordinate wedding ceremonies, attend graduation ceremonies, help with job hunting and career planning, and assist with vehicle maintenance. The love and care they receive from the church family helps relieve home sickness, and helps the students adjust to the American culture and society.

Many students in the UC fellowship attend the College Conservatory of Music (CCM) and major in piano, voice, organ, string instruments, wind instruments, etc. They often serve as piano accompanists or sing praise songs in church. On special holidays, CCM students share their musical talents in order to bring more people from the Taiwanese community into the church. Church members often attend their concerts and prepare food for their music receptions. This is to share God's love and make all events more memorable. God has been gracious, allowing the Cincinnati Taiwanese Presbyterian Church to help spread the seeds of the gospel in the hearts and minds of these graduate students. The hope is that no matter where they go, they will continue to serve God and become witnesses for Him and glorify His name. Amen.

UC學生楊心新(Harmony Yang左三)和陳麗安(LI-An Chen 右二)畢業典禮後與專程從New York來祝賀的台灣宣教基金會楊宜宜會長(右三)及張富雄董事長(右一)，郭正義長老與夫人陳恩惠(左一、二)合影

Author Cheng-Yih Kuo and wife (1st & 2nd left), TMF board member Morgan Chang and President Eileen YiYi Chang attended the Cincinnati Taiwanese Student Li-An Chen's and Harmony Yang graduation ceremony.

溫馨的橋水查經班
The Bridgewater Bible Study Class

楊遠薰
華府台灣基督長老教會
Carole Yang
Taiwanese Presbyterian Church of Washington, D.C.

溫馨的橋水查經班

楊遠薰
華府台灣基督長老教會

1987年，我家從愛荷華搬到紐澤西，聽到鄰鎮有一所台語學校，便很高興地為一對剛屆學齡的孩子註冊，以後每星期日都送孩子去上課。

台語學校座落在「紐澤西台美團契長老教會(TAFPC)」裡，教會的人常很熱心地邀請家長們進教堂作禮拜。當時完全不認識主的我僅是基於禮貌，偶爾上上教堂。兩年後，同住在橋水鎮的台語學校校長梁耕三說，他內心有一種渴求，想探討聖經，建議我們兩家每隔兩週的星期五晚上在一起查經。我答應了，同時邀請鄰居一對電腦族夫妻英才與慧芬參加。

於是不久，六個非教徒便聚在一起查經。剛開始，真的是讀得出字，卻讀不懂經文的意義。譬如有一次，我們查「三個僕人的比喻」(馬太25：14-30)，一個說：「為什麼主人給五千，得還一萬？猶太人真會賺錢哦。」
另一個道：「是啊，借一千，還一千，有什麼不對？結果不但挨罵，還被趕出去，這主人真苛薄！」

「這個道理太難了，留給上帝回答吧！」主持查經的耕三兄在找不到適當答案時，便如此笑瞇瞇地說。

「好吧，這節就跳過去」有人提議。

於是跳過這，跳過那，我們的查經像在讀片斷的故事。查完經後，大家聚一起享用香噴噴的米粉湯等宵夜，倒也樂融融。

過一陣子，這個小小的查經班竟得到鎮上TAFPC兄姐們的青睞，紛紛加入。結果往後定期參加的都有八至十對夫妻，加上一群生蹦活跳的孩子們，十分熱鬧。有了基督徒加入，查經班比較上軌道。建信兄會領我們唱聖詩，愛信姐會幫我們禱告。查經時，在大家頻發謬論之際，已受洗的兄姐會引我們「回歸正途」。然因慕道友比基督徒多，我們在討論問題時，難免口無遮攔。

溫馨的橋水查經班

不久，TAFPC的謝敏川牧師開始派當時在鄰近大學進修的幾位年輕台灣牧師，輪流來帶領我們查經。鎮上則有幾位鄉親聽說我們的查經「發言很自由」而自願加入，所以我們的人數一度增至二十多人，必須藉每家的地下室舉行。查經時，我們常就創造、復活、得救、永生、罪、死…等問題，辯得唇槍舌劍。查完經後，又快樂地聚在一起吃主人備辦的豐盛宵夜，十分開心。

「你們怎會有那麼多問題？妳知道嗎？那些問題，我以前想都沒想過。」有幾次吃宵夜時，坐我旁邊的申怡這麼對我說。

「因為妳來自基督教家庭，自小相信所有的教義。我們來自迥然不同的思維環境，讀起聖經來，總覺得怎麼會這樣，怎麼會那樣。」我振振有詞地回答。

自1994年起，其時在杜魯（Drew University）大學攻讀宗教心理學博士的洪健隸牧師開始固定帶領我們查經。他初來時，聽到我們的發言，常有「秀才遇到兵，有理說不清」的感覺。後來，他一條條地記下我們的發問，等下回再來時，便翻著一本貼著許多小紙條的聖經，努力地解釋經文給我們聽。我們不見得聽明白，但見他如此認真的樣子，便覺得也該「鳴金收兵」。

就這樣，我們繼續查經，也繼續辯論，雖然好幾位都也沒受洗，卻也都在星期日上教堂，而教會的兄姐們也都以平常心，對待這些冥頑不靈的子民。

九十年代，黑名單突破，海外興起返鄉熱。我們橋水查經班的「班頭」耕三兄是個傑出的物理學家，亦決定回台服務同步幅射研究所。他過去十分沉迷「羊可複製，人亦可複製」的想法，常對創造論持懷疑的態度，然在回台之前，卻棄甲繳械，帶領全家，完全歸順於主。

一年後，電腦族的英才與惠芬相繼受洗，學加的信仰亦趨堅定，查經班已從慕道友多逐漸變成信徒與慕道友各半的情勢。這時，又有幾對夫婦加入橋水查經班，有的太太信主，有的先生信主，另一半都還徘徊在門外。查經時，很自然地分成兩邊，各提出看法，然而質疑的氣氛已較前緩和許多。

不記得從何時開始，我已不像從前那麼愛發問。1999年，因為學加工作的緣

故，我們決定搬到馬里蘭州去。 在回顧住在紐澤西這十二年的歲月，我赫然發現神是多麼地眷顧我！祂差遣如此多的牧長與兄姐來引導我認識祂、領受祂的恩典，讓我們的生活天天充滿平安與喜樂，我是何其地有福氣！剎那間，我忽然覺得疲倦，想歸順於主，從此仰望祂，倚賴祂，讓祂的愛如我腳前的燈，引我前進。於是，我在那年(1999)的感恩節在TAFPC受洗，然後在主的保守下，於2000年搬到馬里蘭州，隸屬華府台灣基督長老教會。

奇妙的是在我離開紐澤西的半年內，橋水查經班一些久久不受洗的弟兄們如清一、文義、景山、崇仁等竟一個個地相繼受洗。很難想像這麼多年來，這些任憑主內兄姐千呼萬喚就是不肯就範的迷羊，如今一個個低著頭，鑽進主愛的國度裡，哈利路亞！

「沒有一條漏網之魚！」如今每當老友重逢，提起橋水查經班的種種，便不禁如此開懷地說。如今，儘管有人搬進搬出，橋水查經班依舊溫馨地繼續進行，當年一起查經的弟兄姐妹，無論留在紐澤西、或搬到外州、或回台灣的，都在主內服事。至於曾經帶領我們查經五年半的洪健隸牧師，如今則是華府台灣基督長老教會的駐堂牧師。

感謝主的慈愛與寬容，使我們得以進入祂的殿堂，領受祂的愛與教導，一切榮耀歸主名！

作者楊遠薰
Author Carole Yang Shu

The Bridgewater Bible Study Class

Carole Yang
Taiwanese Presbyterian Church of Washington, D.C.

In 1987, my family moved from Iowa to New Jersey. We soon sent our children to learn our mother tongue at a Taiwanese school, where we were also invited to attend the Taiwanese American Presbyterian Church. To be honest, at the time, we accepted the invitation more out of courtesy than a desire to be moved by God. Nevertheless, it provided an opportunity to interact with the church.

Two years later, in order to minimize commuting to and from work, we moved from Hillsborough to Bridgewater. Not long after moving, our friend Liang Keng San, who also was the principal at the Taiwanese School, suggested that we organize a biweekly Bible Study to gain a better understanding on what this world renowned book was all about. Later, we even invited our neighbors, Ying Chai and Teresa, a young couple who worked in the IT industry, to join us.

At the beginning, because our group was made up of non-Christians, we had a difficult time understanding many of the verses even though we had the desire to learn. We would often jump from verse to verse, turning our Bible study into more of a history lesson. And at times, even the history was too difficult to comprehend. Once, when studying the Parable of the Talents (Matthew 25:14-30), we were really at loss on the meaning of the parable. Out of frustration, following comments started to surface:

"Why did the servant who was given five thousand talents have to return ten thousand talents? These Jewish people really know how to make money."

"Right, what's wrong with taking a thousand and returning a thousand. Not only was the servant chastised, he was fired. This master is so stringent!"

The Bridgewater Bible Study Class

Whenever there were questions that we couldn't answer, our leader Keng San, would often suggest: "It's too hard, we'll leave it to God to answer!" And, I would often follow with, "Okay then, let's go relax and have some rice noodle soup."

Maybe it was because we always had good refreshments, but in a relatively short time, our group began to grow as more and more members from the TAF-PC church began to attend. At the time, our regular attendees were eight to ten couples plus some children. It was a lively group. With so many Christians in the group, we were more on track. Jian Shin would lead the praise time and Ai Shin would lead the prayer, but because there were more non-believers in the group than believers, it was not unusual for there to be heated discussions.

Concerned that these discussions would lead to the misinterpretation and misunderstanding of the Bible, Pastor Hsieh Min Chuan asked a young local pastor who was still in seminary to come lead us. Our group had once grown to more than 20 people since the free atmosphere of discussion attracted many to join us. We had to take turns using different members' basements for meetings. We often had heated discussion on different topics such as creation, resurrection, salvation, eternal life, sin, death, etc., but after Bible study, we always had a great time having refreshments prepared by the host.

Once while having our refreshments, my good friend Shen Yi turned to me and asked, "How did you guys get so many questions? You know, I've never thought of any of these issues before." I replied, "Because you grew up in the church, all of these things seem normal. But to us, these things are very different from what we were taught in school and in our upbringing, so many things seem contradictory and hard to understand." Starting in the 1990's, the era of martial law in Taiwan ended, leaving it possible for many oversea Taiwanese to return. Among those returning was one of our members, Keng San. During his time with us, he had struggled with the idea of God's ultimate creationism, especially following man's genetic cloning of a lamb. But right before he returned to Taiwan, he and his wife both accepted Christ.

One year later, our neighbors Ying Chai and Hui Fen were also baptized. Soon afterwards, Pastor Hong Jian Dih, who was studying social psychology at Drew University, came to lead our bible study group and stayed for six years. With his guidance, we grew spiritually and our discussions became more deeply rooted in biblically sound theology. There were still times, though, when we would have discussions on the differing views of world religions and Christianity.

I don't remember exactly when things started to change, but my questions became fewer and the doubts less frequent. In 1999, Hsueh Chia's work relocated him to Maryland, so our family had to move. Reflecting over the past twelve years in New Jersey, I found that God had been more than gracious to me. He sent so many brothers, sisters, and pastors to lead me to know Him, and gave me peace and happiness in my life. I was so moved that I decided that I wanted to become a member of this big family before leaving New Jersey. I was willing to let God be the lamp to my feet and the light to my path and lead me forward. I became a Christian on the eve of Thanksgiving 1999.

Amazingly, within half a year after I left New Jersey, the nonbelievers in Bridgewater Bible Study group: Ching Yi, Wen Yi, Jing San, and Chong Ren, one by one also came to accept Jesus as their Lord and Savior. The Lord sure acted in its own magical way. "Not a single one escaped the net," we joked amongst ourselves when old friends met and reminisced on the good old times in Bridgewater. The Bible Study Group continues to meet, with people moving in and out. The early members of the group are now all dispersed. But, regardless of whether they remained in New Jersey, moved to other states, or returned to Taiwan, they are all serving the Load in different capacities. Reverend Hong who led us for five and half years in Bible study, is currently the Minister of Taiwanese Presbyterian Church in Washington DC.

Thanks to God for his everlasting love and patience in bringing us to join his family. All praises belong to him.

十字架的道路
The Way of the Cross

陳義達
Carruthers Creek 社區教會 - 加拿大
Daniel Gi-Tat Tan
Carruthers Creek Community Church in Canada

十字架的道路

陳義達
Carruthers Creek 社區教會 - 加拿大

「十字架的道路雖難走，但仰望主耶穌，跟從祂永不退後。以愛以信以光明的盼望，將上帝的國，建立在地上⋯ 使上帝和平公義，刻在人心中。」

這首由我所寫、由爵士音樂家李奎然教授譜曲的詩歌，道盡我人生的經歷。上帝奇妙的恩典祝福我，畢生得以參加各項的宣道事工。

1952年，我高中畢業，參加花堯奇博士的「天幕佈道團」。 這會幕是可容一千至一千兩百名會眾的大帳棚。主賜我宏亮的歌喉，可免用麥克風，歌聲即可傳達全場。佈道期間，天天有許多人悔改接受主，情境十分感人。

大學期間，主藉美國宣教師威爾遜博士傳講的信息，打動我剛硬的心。 雖然我曾參加天幕佈道團半年，看別人悔改，但自己的生命還是沒有改變。威爾遜牧師說：「我不問你何時去教會、何時受洗，但我要問你何時能重生？」

聖靈大大地動工。因為我有難改的抽煙惡習，口袋裡這時正有兩包煙。隱藏的陰暗及難改的惡習受光照，一生頭一次流淚，在宣教師、朋友及家人面前悔改，真正接受主耶穌做個人的救主，並將兩包煙丟入茅廁，從此一生跟從主。我隨後服事校園團契和教會，並和幾位弟兄利用暑假環島佈道旅行。我看見愛喝酒抽煙的原住民流淚悔改接受主。當我們搭車離開台東原住民村落時，他們緊緊跟在車後跑，大聲用日語喊：「大學生朋友，請你們再來吧！」 那種愛慕飢渴主道理的心，實在令我們終生難忘。

1961年，我在金門服兵役期間，發生另一件更令我終生難忘的事。有個星期天，我從教會回到營地的途中，同連的幾個士兵神色倉皇地朝我奔來，告知班長和士官長都喝醉酒，正大聲地吵架，兩人都拿著槍，準備互相射殺。作為一個基督徒，我立刻在主面前默禱，求主賜我勇氣與智慧，化解危難與衝突。然後在很短的片刻，我站在兩位怒氣沖沖又持著槍枝的士官中間，雙手抓住兩支

槍，大聲說：「在前線悍衛國家的你們，任務未完成以前，假如你們有彼此難以容忍的怨恨，非互相殘殺不可，那麼當排長的我寧可讓你們殺！」

兩個充滿火氣的士官被我突如其來的行動訝住，忿怒的情緒慢慢平靜下來，然後收了槍枝，向我致敬和道歉。感謝主，使我能免除生命的危險，並及時制止可能流血的衝突。

後來在另一次大演習中，一顆未爆的炸彈落在全連當中，五秒之內即會爆炸。在這千鈞一髮之際，那位前些時醉酒衝突的班長突然奔向炸彈，從口袋取下一枚安全指針，扣住炸彈引信，及時止住爆炸。感謝主！這位班長救了全連官兵的生命！

退役後，我回台灣，遇到一位從前一起環島佈道的朋友，才知道有一天聖靈感動他，要他為在金門前線服役的陳哥哥和士兵們禱告，而那天正是我們大演習、炸彈落下全連當中之日，怎能不令人讚美神的奇妙？其後，主引導我在馬偕醫院服務三年多。作為一位平信徒的福音使者，我常在檢查室忙碌後，與宗教部的委員逐一拜訪每個病房，為病人禱告，也為主差遣。當我回顧往昔，只有讚歎！

移民北美洲後，主差我擔任早期的「北美洲台灣基督教協會」的執行總幹事。2004年，我罹患難以治療的擴散性淋巴癌。由於癌細胞已擴散全身，我被斷定只能活三個月。主施恩憐憫，竟使我化療後，得以康復。從事醫學研究的我深深明白除非神蹟顯示，我的病不可能醫好。為此，我在上帝面前跪下，深深為自我的驕傲徹底悔改，並獻上感謝。

2005年，我和內人淑貞一起回台灣，在嘉義縣太保市的嘉南台福教會作八天的短宣。這間教會的開拓者是放棄美國高薪、來自加州的南灣台福教會的游象輝與吳智慧夫婦。此處的宣教大門大開，我們得以到隔鄰的安東國小，教小學生公民德育課程，並開辦英語夏季營。下課後，我們在教會繼續開課外輔導班。我也在週日的培靈會裡，以「完美的人生」見證上帝的奇妙醫治，即刻有人流淚接受耶穌為救主。感謝主，願我們恩上加恩，力上加力，繼續做上帝愛的器皿。

The Way of the Cross

Daniel Gi-Tat Tan
Carruthers Creek Community Church in Canada

"The way of the cross is fraught with obstacles; yet trusting in God we will not fret from following Jesus. With love, faith, and hope, we bring the Kingdom of God on earth.… May God's peace and justice etch deeply in human hearts…" The song, for which I wrote the lyrics and jazz musician Professor Kenneth Lee wrote the music, captures God's amazing grace in my life. By His grace I have been richly blessed with the privilege of participating in many missions projects.

After graduating from high school in 1952, I joined Dr. George Hudson's Evangelical Tent Crusade. Each meeting took place in a huge tent that could hold 1000 to 1200 people. God gifted me with a voice that could fill the whole tent without a microphone. Each day of the crusade, many people repented and received the Lord. It was a very moving experience.

When I was in college, God touched my heart through the messages of the American missionary Dr. Wilson. However, even though I had participated in the Evangelical Tent Crusade for half a year and had seen other people repent, I myself had not changed. Dr. Wilson once said, "I won't ask when you go to church or when you were baptized, but I do want to know when you will be born again." I was deeply moved by the Holy Spirit. I had been in bondage to smoking. At that moment, I had two packs of cigarettes in my shirt pocket. A deep dark secret came to light, and for the first time in my life I broke down in tears. In front of the missionary, friends, and family, I repented and threw away the cigarettes. From that moment forward, I truly followed Jesus.

Soon afterwards, I served in a campus fellowship and in a church. During summer vacations, a few brothers and I would travel around Taiwan sharing the Gospel. When we went to an aboriginal village in Taitung, I saw people who struggled with alcoholism and smoking addictions come to the Lord. When we were leaving, they ran after our car and shouted in Japanese, "Our college friends, please come again!" Their hunger and desire to know God was something we would never forget.

An even more unforgettable thing happened in 1961 when I was serving in the military and stationed at Kinmen. One Sunday after church, as I headed back to the military base, a few soldiers were panicking as they ran towards me to tell me that two soldiers had gotten drunk and were in a heated argument. They were both armed and ready to shoot each other. Being a Christian, I immediately prayed for courage and wisdom to resolve this conflict. Then I stepped between the two angry armed soldiers, grabbed their guns, and shouted, "We are on the front line protecting our nation and we haven't yet completed our mission. If you hate each other so much that you're ready to kill each other, then I your sergeant would prefer that you kill me!"

These two enraged soldiers were shocked at my response and they gradually calmed down. Then they put down their guns, apologized, and saluted me. Thank God for using me at just the right time to prevent a potentially deadly incident!

Sometime later, during a military training exercise, a grenade fell near my unit and would have exploded in five seconds, but one of the two soldiers in the previous incident suddenly rushed over, pulled the safety pin, pinched the fuse, and stopped the bomb from exploding just in time. Thank God! That soldier saved all of our lives. After I retired from the military and returned to Taiwan, I happened to bump into a friend from college who went on a summer mission trip with me. Only then did I realize that the Holy Spirit moved him to pray for me and for my unit on the front line in Kinmen the very day of this incident. Then, God led me to serve at a Mackay Hospital for three and half years. I often went with ministers to visit patients and pray with them. I cannot help but praise God when I look back on those days.

Afterwards, I immigrated to Canada. From 1983 to 1985, I was honored to serve as the executive director of the Taiwanese Christian Church Council of North America (TCCCNA). In 2004, I was diagnosed with metastatic lymphoma and given three months to live, but God was gracious to me, and against all odds I recovered after nine months of chemotherapy. As a medical researcher, I knew that this was nothing short of a miracle. I grieved because of my arrogance and asked God to forgive me. My wife Lily and I often gave thanks to God together.

In 2005, we went back to Taiwan. We were at the Canaan EFC Church in Taipao (in Chiayi County) for an eight day missions trip. That church was founded by Mr. Shiang Hui Yu and his wife, Chu-Huie Wu, formerly of EFC South Bay. They gave up well-paying jobs in the US. We taught civics and hosted an English summer camp at the An-Tung Elementary School. After classes were over, the church held after-school programs. We also held a revival meeting during which we shared testimonies about God's healing power. Several people wept and received Jesus as their Lord and Savior.

May God continue to strengthen and empower us to become the instrument of His love in the world!

2005 嘉義短宣-左起:作者陳義達與妻子淑貞；蘇啟宏& 林達明
2005-Mission in Chiayi- From left: Author Daniel Chen & wife Lily; Edward Su & Benjamin Lin

人生漫談
台灣學堂
今夜，阮有一個夢
天涯若比鄰
疼你的厝邊
好厝邊
台福民謠見証團
今夜，阮有一條歌
牽阮的手
黃昏的故鄉
海外基督徒聯合通訊

我的生命獻給祢
I Offer My Life to You

陳隆
洛杉磯台福教會
Long Chen
Evangelical Formosan Church of Los Angeles in California

我的生命獻給祢

陳隆
洛杉磯台福教會

每當我靜下來回顧，過去四、五十年的宣教情景總會重回腦海，歷歷如在眼前。在台北的少小時期，深受史懷哲博士非洲濟世的宣教事蹟感動，高中時也受陳溪圳牧師、郭馬西牧師的影響，常隨牧長們去探訪孤兒院、醫院與痲瘋病院，大學時代又投入原住民服務與監獄佈道。

1972年赴美深造時，我受到父母與大哥的鼓勵，加上接觸許多來美移民的鄉親，覺得要實踐信仰，必須走出教會圍牆，深入人群，尋找拯救貧苦無助的同胞與失喪的靈魂。

劉富理牧師受聘為台福教會主任牧師後，三十多年來，成了影響我最深的良師益友。爾後，我們更被上帝巧妙地安排為親家。因著他的鼓勵，我與摯友楊建民於1975年在南加州開始輔導最早期的小留學生，成立小留學生的少年團契。如今回首，當年受過輔導的少年，如今幾乎個個都成為教會的重要人才。

上帝接著帶領我到北加州，交給我全新的職場，那就是與美國聯合衛理公會有關的社區服務。在敬重的 Bruce McSpadden牧師、戴俊男牧師與楊文得牧師的輔導下，我擔任「舊金山灣區台灣人社區發展中心」主任長達七年。在這七年中，Bruce McSpadden牧師鼓勵我參加許多集會，並接觸舊金山地區的難民與流浪者，予我甚多的造就。

上帝藉此開展我的心懷與視野，使我服務的對象不只限於台灣來的鄉親，更包含中國、香港與東南亞各地的新舊移民。我為長輩們成立了長輩會，關懷他們，並與南加州的台灣長輩會締結為姐妹會。

1984年底，上帝安排我回洛杉磯。在劉富理與吳德聖牧師等人的鼓勵下，我與黃寶儀、劉富佐、潘世安等人成立了一個「台福民謠見証團」。自1984年至1993年期間，我們在美國、加拿大與日本，舉辦了數十場的民謠見証晚會，撫慰了許多異鄉的心靈，也感召了許多人信主。

為了實踐走出教會圍牆的理念，劉富理牧師於1989年成立了「愛加倍社區服務中心」，我立刻加入，在南加州亞洲電視台製作主持一個每星期一集的電視福音節目：「天涯若比鄰」，台語名稱是「好厝邊」。這是海外首創的台語電視節目，一時頗為轟動，播出後廣受好評。劉牧師與蔡麟牧師乃決定大量拷貝，讓全世界各地鄉親都能有機會觀賞。

不久，上帝又賜我機會回台灣服務。1994年，在好友許丕龍力邀之下，我回台展開為期三年的電視廣播工作。除了在電視台擔任協理外，自己也擔任新聞主播，並主持一個叫「今夜，阮有一條歌」的現場音樂節目，同時在每個主日下午製作現場直播福音節目：「疼你的厝邊」。此外，我還在電台製作「人生漫談」、「牽阮的手」及「台灣學堂」等三個談話性的節目。我很自然地將主耶穌的愛與救贖的福音融入節目裡，十分受到歡迎。那三年可說是我人生最多產、最美好的一段時光。

後來因為母親的年邁與對兒女的職責，我於1997年申請調回南加州。爾後在好友與台灣人社團的資助下，我租了一個電台，繼續製作與主持談話性的節目：「黃昏的故鄉」及「今夜，阮有一個夢」。

同時，我經常在基督教論壇報寫詩與散文，並常為台灣教會公報、民眾日報與自由時報寫稿，也曾經主編過「海外基督徒聯合通訊」。

通過平面媒體、電台與電視的事工，我充分感受到「五餅二魚」的喜悅。只要虔誠的獻上你的五餅二魚（詩、散文、小說、話劇或廣播電台、電視節目），經上帝的淨化與祝福，必能成為上帝所喜用、餵養眾人的靈糧。

我每日吟唱一首台語聖詩叫「我的生命獻給祢，做祢路用到一世」。如今雖然逐漸步入晚年，我仍然以此詩歌對主耶穌說：「我的生命獻給祢，願祢使用我到一生一世。」阿們！

我的生命獻給祢　　**357**

1996人間對話 全民衛視
People Dialogue CBT TV

1989 台福民謠見証團
EFC Gospel and Folk Song Group

2003 夏威夷台灣基督長老教會民謠見証晚會
Performing Gospel and folks songs at Taiwanese Presbyterian church in Hawaii

1995 全民話題 /全民衛視
People' Talk / CBT TV

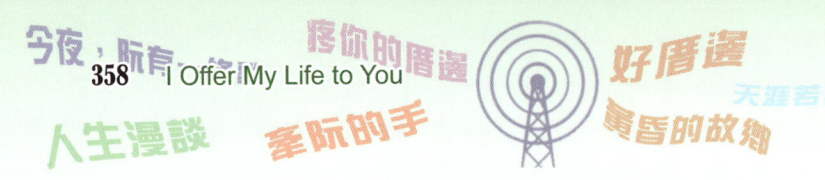

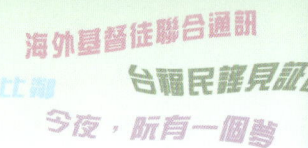

I Offer My Life to You

Long Chen
Evangelical Formosan Church of Los Angeles in California

As I look back on my past fifty years as a missionary, the memories come back to me as clearly as if I were living them out again. When I was growing up in Taiwan, I was so inspired by the missionary work of the famous theologian Albert Schweitzer in Africa that when I was in high school, I was always tagging along with Pastors Chen Xi Chuan and Guo Ma Xi visiting orphanages, hospitals, and mental institutions. Then, in college I became involved in ministries that served aborigines and prison inmates.

In 1972 with the encouragement of my family, I moved to the United States to pursue my studies, and as I came into contact with other Taiwanese immigrants, I felt that in order to put my faith into practice, I had to leave the comfort zone of church to seek out and serve the poor, the helpless and the lost.

Pastor Felix Liu, who has been the Senior Pastor of the Evangelical Formosan Church of Los Angeles for over 30 years, has been a cherished teacher and friend of mine. In 1975, with his encouragement, my friend Yang Jian Ming and I began a ministry to serve elementary and junior high students sent by their families in Taiwan to study here in the US. Today, almost all of those we have served in that ministry have grown up to become active church members.

After serving in that ministry for some time, God led me to serve in San Francisco doing community service within the United Methodist Church. Under the diligent guidance and encouragement of Reverend Bruce McSpadden, Pastor Dai Jun Nan and Pastor Yang Wen De, I became the director of the San Francisco Taiwanese Community Center and served there for seven years. During those seven years, Rev. McSpadden also encouraged me to attend meetings and trainings that would equip me to reach out to many refugees and immigrant workers in the area. Over time, through my work in the community, God began to open my heart to all people, not just Taiwanese but also people from China, Hong Kong, and Southeast Asia, and I founded a senior citizen community group.

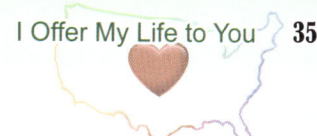

In 1984, God once again led me back to Los Angeles. With the encouragement of Pastor Felix Liu, Wu De-Sheng, and some others, I founded "台福民謠見証團," an EFC music group that communicated the Gospel through folk songs. The group included Huang Bao Yi, Liu Fu Zhe, Pan Shi An and several others. From 1984-1993, we performed over 20 concerts in the US, Canada and Japan, and led many to Christ.

In 1989, in order to serve the community, Pastor Felix Liu established the Ai Jia Bei Community Center. When I heard about this ministry, I immediately joined it, hoping to use the gifts and experiences God had given me to support their mass media ventures. While in this ministry, I hosted the weekly Christian show "天涯若比鄰" (Tian Ya Ruo Bi Ling) on the Southern California Asia Television Channel (In Taiwanese, the meaning of the show title is "Good Neighbor"). It was the first overseas-produced show in Taiwanese, therefore it had a relatively good following. With its success, Pastor Felix Liu and Pastor Tsai Lin soon decided to let the show be distributed worldwide.

In 1994, God yet again called me to a new ministry in Taiwan. With my friend Hsu Pi Long, I worked for three years in television as an anchor and host. One of the programs included a live music show called "今夜，阮有一條歌" ("Tonight, We Have a Song") which ran for over a hundred episodes. On Sunday afternoons, we broadcasted a live show called "疼你的厝邊" ("Love your Neighbor"). Other programs produced and broadcasted over the radio included "人生漫談" ("Life Chat"), "牽阮的手" ("Hold My Hand") and "台灣學堂" ("Taiwan School"). Those three years were possibly the most productive and fulfilling in my life as I was able to openly share the good news with many of those who watched or listened to our programs.

In 1997, due to responsibilities to my children and my mother, I requested a transfer back to Southern California. Once I returned, I rented a radio station with financial assistance from good friends and a Taiwanese organization, and hosted the programs, "黃昏的故鄉" ("Hometown of the Sunset") and "今夜，阮有一個夢" ("Tonight, We Have a Dream"). I also wrote many poems and articles for Taiwanese church publications and for Taiwanese newspapers.

As I reflect upon the way God was able to use me, his humble servant, in both print media and radio/TV ministries, I feel as though God was able to bless the multitudes in the same way he did when he fed a crowd of 5000 with five loaves of bread and two fish.

As I advance in age, I do not want to forget to continually offer myself to God, so as part of my devotion each day I sing a hymn in Taiwanese called "I Offer My Life to You" that reminds me that I must do so regularly.

1994 每個主日下午製作現場直播福音節目：「疼你的厝邊」
On Sunday afternoons, we broadcasted a live show called "Love your Neighbor"

1999 西羅亞女聲三重唱在洛杉磯
Siloam Female Trio in Los Angeles

「台灣宣教基金會」緣起

楊宜宜牧師/會長　2-17-2008
台灣宣教基金會 - 紐約

世界名著<<雙城記>>描述女主角的愛心，好似「一條金線」將她的家族及身邊的人穿在一起。同樣，我感到好似也有條無形的「金線」貫串我的一生，直牽引到「台灣宣教基金會」的設立。

關於台灣，外公是台灣第二個律師，也是早年鄭姓宗親會的領袖。他常帶著我及兄弟三人旅遊台灣各地，並介紹鄭成功軍兵屯墾的「王田」，使我們幼小心靈即摯愛台灣這塊美麗的土地。可惜近日讀到1661年鄭成功來台逐出所有荷蘭軍兵及宣教士，嚴禁基督教並殺死五千名排灣族基督徒(載於宣教日引1-10-08)，頗令我錯愕難過。

至於宣教，英籍宣教士戴德生的曾孫戴紹曾宣教士，1960年代當高雄聖光書院院長期間，即由高雄鹽埕教會長老暨好友的先父楊天和醫師教授台語會話。我1970來美之前也數度到戴院長家學英文會話；念台大外文系期間，並自友誼之家(Friendship Corner) 美國宣教士Miss Margaret Sells得到英文名字Eileen沿用至今。

留美期間，先生和我在1973-76創辦海外第一份全球性的「海外台灣基督徒聯合通訊」。1977-82進一步道成肉身跨出教會藩籬創立「台灣之音」，以電話廣播服事當代全球台灣社區，提供海外台灣遊子一份屬靈及精神的食糧。

1998是我人生轉折之年。以色列春旅震醒了我懵懂之心，也催我嚴肅反思自己信仰及身為選民的真義。當體悟到以色列選民兩千年不忠於上帝的託付--"把福音傳給萬民，致令上帝揀選「新選民」基督徒來取代他們，我遂多次呼籲基督徒趕緊宣教，否則恐落相似下場，因為第二個兩千年又要到。同年秋天蒙上帝呼召，又得早年高雄鹽埕長老教會主日學老師(亦前台福神學院即今正道神學院) 副院長蘇文隆牧師的引介修讀神學。在學期間發生台灣921大地震，次春即隨紐約一支短宣隊去重災區埔里，踏出個人畢生首次的宣教步履。98年底又在三年一次的中國差傳年會深受感動。宣教的種子及熱情迅速在心中滋長，並在大紐約幾間台灣教會熱切傳遞宣教異象。

「台灣宣教基金會」緣起

近十年「中國宣教」蓬勃發展，偶而會自問「台灣宣教」在何處？但因畢業隨即從事神學教育，而把那份宣教之念懸置到2005神學教育告一段落。該年底即進入美國伯特利神學院美東分院修讀教牧博士科。次年(2006)5月1日突接加州愛恩教會張玉明主任牧師(我前神學院教授)一通電話，告知第二代青年回台教國小國中生美語一星期，75%的孩子會信主。張玉明牧師非常期盼我在美東推動「台灣宣教」。一方面訝異於聽到「台灣宣教」，二方面訝異於公認硬土難傳的台灣，會有75%的信主率，我感到上帝正在大開台灣宣教之門，所以一口答應：「我會去。」當然也想親睹實況再說。我一連參加2006夏、冬及2007夏三季台灣短宣，看遍沿海四周、中央山地及勞工區，內心感動久久不去。尤其眼看台灣一百五十年來基督徒比例一直偏低，總未能突破3%；而台灣四周國家近來基督徒增長頗速，南韓35%，中國10%，回教國的印尼、阿富汗或伊拉克都有4%，更感愧疚與沉重。

2006九月首次在紐約長島豐盛生命教會，以「美麗孤島的宣教」講題分享「台灣宣教」，也把講章分送加州林華山醫師及紐約法拉盛第一浸信會關榮根牧師(伯特利美東分院宣教學教授亦我屬靈父親mentor)。關牧師2007年1月24日遇到我就說：「妳何不設立一個組織去推動『台灣宣教』呢？你的律師女兒張音音可以幫妳去登記！我可以當妳的顧問。」這時上帝突然大大開路，許多台灣教會及團契紛紛邀我去分享「台灣宣教」。不少牧師問我：「妳代表什麼組織這麼熱心呢？」一月底加州愛恩教會的張玉明牧師、莊澤豐牧師及林華山醫師討論的結果是：「妳應該在美東自己設立一個組織去推動，因為我們是一個教會。我們會繼續當妳的夥伴。」2月28日賓州來的伯特利神學院美東分院院長Dr. Douglas W. Fombelle 聽完我的分享說：「如果妳設立『台灣宣教』的組織，把我列入妳的顧問團。」我心想：「沒有『台灣宣教』的組織，大家卻都要當顧問夥伴，太好笑了！」

三月三日紐約大雪紛飛，先生出差亞洲，我首次安靜認真地回想這短短一個半月，為什麼三地五人會說同樣話「妳設立『台灣宣教』的組織」呢？但組織怎麼設呢？如果我不理它，萬一這是上帝透過他們要向我說話，那就糟了。怎麼辦呢？拿起電話找好朋友紐約聖教會的林妙瑛姐妹談談。我把最近的故事奇事道與她並說：「宣教怎麼推動呢？尤其『台灣宣教』氣氛不濃的美東。」這時

我突然想到那些必須修讀宣教課及實習的神學生。何不在神學院設「台灣宣教」獎學金「一千元贊助一位神學生組短宣隊去台灣實習」呢？教會方面也鼓勵牧師或召集人組台灣短宣隊，照樣贊助一千元。這樣千元就能支持一隊，那是「One Thousand One Team」！「One Thousand One Team」也是不錯的口號啊！太好了！太好了！興奮地掛上電話才想到「錢從那裡來呀？」隔天起，天天尋求主，也不斷和主爭論：「主啊！就算我願意，如果沒有人沒有錢，那可別怪我啊！不過我承諾一定不會懶惰。」想到一切資源在主手中也就釋然。但要募多少款呢？一百萬嗎？想到富豪企業家輕易就以一百萬設立一個私人基金，難道我們這一大群基督徒合起來才募集一百萬嗎？真會給人笑話我們的　神太小了。「主啊，那麼一千萬好了」。設個千萬元的「台灣宣教基金會」，用千萬宣教基金，拯救千萬靈魂。如果向30人各募30萬，用一千萬當永久基金，年孳息5%可得五十萬。另外向30人年募一萬可得30萬，再向200人年募一千可得20萬。這樣每年就有一百萬，可不斷送短宣隊去台灣，並支持長期宣教士，來達到十年台灣基督徒達百分之十的異象(得自林華山醫師)。不過凡事得從自己做起。隨即和先生商量把在紐約Forest Hills 區最好地段一個公寓捐出來，市值30-40萬。又近年先生每年聖誕節送我一張一萬元支票，也捐出來。我告訴 上帝說，若有五人年捐一萬我就去登記。有了具體募款及支持宣教的方案，我開始逢人就談。

四月初參加合唱團，趁空檔照樣向左邊的廖萃美姐妹分享。她說：「我的阿姨有筆錢要奉獻還沒決定對象。」我請她「立刻」幫我約阿姨，唯恐隨時會「飛掉」。四天後的四月九日晚八點，我在萃美的阿姨鄭清妍姐府上向她家族五人分享。分享完，清妍姐說：「我出一萬」。萃美自己的母親清愛姐也說：「我也出一萬」。清妍姐又說：「我再給妳30萬。」我整個人傻在那裡不會說話，不知那是不是真的。清妍姐幽默的說：「妳明天可以開始工作了」，並歡欣地合照一張相片留念。4月15日先生說他的公司高盛Goldman Sachs 替副總裁投資，他還得繳稅，所以願再拿出一萬。哇！四個「一萬」了！奇妙的是次晨長島的許登龍醫師夫人瑞鳳姐電話說：「登龍本要給妳五千，但覺這事工實在太重要，決定增為一萬。」哇！五個了，五個「一萬」了，立刻去電女兒Karen律師。當律師樓Perlman & Perlman老板發現是Karen的媽媽要登記，就說：「免費」！哇！多大的恩典！女兒這律師樓是專門代理非營利機構的，只一週在4月24日就登記完成。而我的生日是4月25日。我立刻知道這是上帝賞賜我的生日禮

物。我更謙卑的承認，上帝自己開始的事，祂必親自成就！旋即，一位年輕幹練的彭榮仁牧師續加入董事會，上帝的恩典確實超過所求所想！

2007年4月25日正式設立「台灣宣教基金會」，不到半年的10月10日收到美國政府捐款免稅許可，認捐者紛紛捐出。11月17日我們立刻舉辦一場感恩會感謝上帝的恩典及弟兄姐妹的支持。2007年底，基金會已經撥款兩萬元支持兩隊短宣隊、設立神學院的「台灣宣教」獎學金，並支持鄉福、基福、工福、客宣、生命線、福音傳播、癌患、傷患，並購置墓地供貧困患難的人使用等等宣教及慈善的事工。留學生事工及宣教訓練學校也在規劃中。我們堅信以愛心慷慨撥出，上帝必再豐富賞賜。畢竟，一切資源都屬於上帝自己。甚願福音早日遍傳台灣！阿們！

「任何一個福音工場，最重要的就是要有上帝的呼召，以及受過聖經訓練被聖靈充滿而膏抹過的本國籍人。」~引自戴永冕(戴德生孫)「今日乃明日之父」

3/18/10楊宜宜會長夫婦(左二三)變賣紐約森林小丘公寓支持台灣宣教，手續完成支票交財務鄭清妍長老(左一)
The closing date of a Co-Op apartment donated by President Eileen Chang's family"

11/17/07 TMF第一次宣教大會主講,並促成本會成立的張玉明牧師(右)及本會會長楊宜宜和同工林朝瑩(左)
First TMF convention keynote speaker and TMF mentor Rev. Joseph Chang(right), President Eileen Chang and Co-worker Jack Lin(left)

1/26/2012本會法律顧問台裔第二代律師張音音獲得由紐約州律師公會評選的2012傑出年輕律師榮譽
Karen I. Wu (Taiwanese 2nd generation), TMF legal advisor, has been named the recipient of the New York State Bar Association's Outstanding Young Lawyer Award for 2012

Origin of the Taiwan Mission Foundation(TMF)

President Eileen Yi-Yi Yang Chang
translated by Sandi Liu
2-17-2008

The world-famous novel, A Tale of Two Cities, describes the female protagonist's love as the "golden thread" that held her family and the individuals around her together. In the same way, feel that the Taiwan Mission Foundation is much like the "golden thread" that has pervaded my life, culminating in its founding in 2007.

With regards to Taiwan, my maternal grandfather was the country's second lawyer, and the leader of the Cheng Family. He often brought me and my two brothers along on his travels throughout Taiwan, and he introduced us to the "Wang-Tian" (meaning King's Lands) farmed by Koxinga's (Cheng Cheng-Gong's) army. These trips caused our young and impressionable hearts to fall deeply in love with the beautiful island. Unfortunately, I recently read that in 1661, upon Koxinga's (Cheng Cheng-Gong's) arrival on the island, he deported all the existing Dutch armies and missionaries, banned Christianity, and killed five thousand aboriginal Pai-Wan tribe members of the Christian faith (recorded in the daily devotion of Crossroads Publications 1-10-2008 in Chinese, translated from Global Prayer Digest). This shocked and saddened me greatly.

As for missionary work, Rev. James Hudson Taylor, III, great-grandson of English missionary James Hudson Taylor, was the Kaoshiung Holy Light Bible College President in the 1960s, where he was receiving lessons in conversational Taiwanese from Kaohiung Yan-Chern Presbyterian Church elder and good friend Dr. Yang Tien-Ho, my father. Before my arrival in the United States in 1970, I also learned conversational English from President Taylor's family at his home. While doing a foreign language degree at National Taiwan University, I was given the English name "Eileen" by the American missionary at Friendship Corner, Miss Margaret Sells, and I have continued to use the name to-date.

After moving to the United States, my husband and I started the first global Taiwanese Christian monthly chronicle, Overseas Taiwanese Christians United Press, which we published from 1973-76. Later, we stepped out of the confines of just serving in the church, and in true 'Word was made flesh' spirit, founded and operated the Voice of Taiwan from 1977-82 to serve the global Taiwanese community through telephone news broadcasts and provide nourishment for their spirit and soul.

1998 was a turning point in my life. A spring trip to Israel awoke me from my innocence and urged me to solemnly reflect on my faith and the true meaning of being God's chosen people. When I realized that God elected the "New Chosen People" – Christians – to replace the Israelites due to the Israelites' failure for two thousand years to bring God's blessings to all the nations on earth, I began urging fellow Christians to pick up the pace on spreading the Gospel, or we might end up like the Israelites at the turn of the second two thousand years. In the fall of that year, upon God's calling and upon the suggestion of Pastor Wilfred Su, who was previously my Kaohsiung Yan-Chern Presbyterian Church Sunday school teacher and former vice president of the Logos Evangelical Seminary, I decided to do graduate studies in theology. In the middle of my studies, Taiwan suffered the massive 921 earthquake, and the following spring, I started out on my first missionary steps and headed towards the heavily affected area of Puli with a New York group for a short-term missions project. At the end of 1998, I was once again moved after attending the Chinese Mission Conference, which is held once every three years. The seed and passion of missions work blossomed inside me and moved me to promote mission by giving testimonies of other churches to Taiwanese churches in the greater New York area.

With the rapid development of "China Mission" in the last ten years, I have sometimes asked myself where is the development of "Taiwan Mission?" I placed my thoughts about missionary work on hold until after 2005, after I had wrapped up the theological education ministry that had occupied me since graduation. At the end of that same year, I entered a Doctor of Ministry program at the Bethel Seminary of the East. On May 1 of the following year (2006), I suddenly received a telephone call from Joseph Chang, senior pastor of Evangelical Formosan Church of Irvine in California, who was also my former seminary professor. He told me that his church had a 75% success rate of bringing Taiwanese children to Christ as part of their missions program, which engaged second generation youth from the United States in teaching English to elementary and middle school students in Taiwan for a week. Pastor Chang very much looked forward to having me jump start this program on the east coast. I was, on the one hand, surprised to hear about the idea of a "Taiwan Mission," and, on the other hand, shocked at the 75% success rate in Taiwan, which was known for its difficulty with missionaries. However, upon hearing this news, I felt God was opening the great door to Taiwan missions in general. Without hesitation I said, "I will go." I wanted to see it myself first-hand. I ended up participating in three consecutive short-term missions trips: summer and winter of 2006, and summer of 2007. I saw much saddened and filled of Taiwan's coast, plus mountainous inland aboriginal and industrial areas, and the emotions they stirred up stayed with me for a very long time. It particularly saddens and fills me with guilt to see the number of Christians in Taiwan never surpassing 3% and even continuing to decline, while neighboring countries have been experiencing rapid growth in their numbers: Korea 35%, China 10%, even in the Muslim countries of Indonesia, Afghanistan, and Iraq, 4%.

In September 2006, I shared for the first time my thoughts on "Taiwan missions" via a sermon entitled "The Mission of an Isolated Beautiful Island." I also gave a copy of the sermon to Dr. Howshan Lin in California and Pastor Henry Kwan of the New York First Baptist Church of Flushing (also professor of Missions at the Bethel Seminary of the East and my mentor). When Pastor Kwan saw me on January 24, 2007, he said, "Why don't you start an organization to promote 'Taiwan mission'? Your lawyer daughter Karen I. Wu can help you incorporate it! And I can be your advisor." This was the moment that God opened the road ahead of me. And opened it wide He did. From then on, many Taiwanese churches and fellowships began extending invitations to me to share about "Taiwan mission" with them. Many pastors asked, "Why are you so passionate and which organization do you represent?" At the end of January, the conclusion from a discussion between Pastor Joseph Chang, Pastor Tse Feng Chuang, and Dr. Howshan Lin of the California EFC Irvine Church was: "You should set up your own organization on the east coast, because we are only a local church. We will definitely continue to be your partner on this project." On February 28th, Dr. Douglas W. Fombelle, the Dean of Bethel Seminary of the East, who is from Pennsylvania, said after my sharing, "If you form a 'Taiwan Mission' organization, put me on your advisory board." I thought to myself, "There is no 'Taiwan Mission' organization, yet everyone wants to advise for it! This is too funny!"

March 3rd saw heavy snowfall in New York, and my husband was in Asia for a business trip. For the first time, I deeply and quietly reflected on the past month and a half, and thought about why five different people physically located in three separate places would ask me to set up a "Taiwan Mission" organization. But how do I go about it? If I ignored all this and it happened to be God speaking to me through all these people, it would be terrible. What should I do? I had to speak to someone further about this. So I picked up the phone and called my good friend, sister Lydia Lin Chen from the Queens Taiwanese Evangelical Church. I told her all the amazing things that had happened to me in the past year and a half, especially in the past month and a half. I said, "How do you promote missions, especially in the northeast, where people are generally not excited about Taiwan Mission?" It was during this time that I suddenly thought about those seminary students who were required to take missions classes and participate in mission field internships.

Why not establish a one thousand dollar "Taiwan Mission" scholarship that would assist a seminary student with putting together a short-term mission team to Taiwan as their internship? And we will encourage pastors and organizers from churches by also providing this opportunity to them if they are interested in forming short-term mission teams. In this way, one thousand dollars may support a team, and it will be "One Thousand One Team"! What a nice slogan this forms! This is great! This is wonderful! Only after excitedly hanging up the phone did I think about, "Where would the money come from?"

Starting the very next day, I began to plead with God daily, and constantly debated with Him: "God! Even though I wish for this to happen, if I don't get the money or the volunteers, please don't blame me! But I promise I will not be lazy." Knowing that all the resources are in God's hand actually relieved me. But how much should I raise? One million dollars? When I thought about how easily rich entrepreneurs could set up a private foundation of one million dollars, I wondered if we could not do better pooling all these Christians together? That would make people laugh at the power of our God. "God, then how about ten million dollars?" Form a ten million dollar "Taiwan Mission Foundation", and use the ten million dollars to save ten million souls. If we raise three hundred thousand dollars from thirty people, we can set aside the ten million dollars as a permanent endowment fund, and generate five hundred thousand dollars on 5% interest each year. Separately, we can annually raise another three hundred thousand dollars from another thirty people (ten thousand dollars each), and one thousand dollars each from two hundred people, totaling another two hundred thousand dollars. In this way, we will have one million dollars every year to continually send short and long term missionaries to Taiwan, and support an on-going campaign to reach the goal of 10% Christians in Taiwan in 10 years (this vision was first articulated by Dr. Howshan Lin).

However, everything must start with us taking action ourselves. After discussing it with my husband, we decided to donate a two-bedroom apartment we owned in the best location of New York's Forest Hills, worth three hundred to four hundred thousand dollars. I also decided to donate the ten thousand dollar checks that my husband had been giving me these past few years for Christmas. I told God that if five people volunteered to donate ten thousand dollars annually, then I would establish the foundation. With a formulated fundraising and missions-support plan, I started telling everyone I saw about it. I joined a choir at the beginning of April, and during our break, I shared my vision with my sister friend sitting to the left of me, Tsui-Mei Liao. She said, "My aunt has a sum of money that she wants to donate but she has not yet determined where it should go." I asked her to immediately contact her aunt to set up an appointment, in fear that the money might "fly away" any minute.

Four days later, on April 9th, I arrived at sister Ching-Yen Cheng's (Tsui-Mei's aunt's) house at 8pm to share my vision with her and four other members of her family. When I finished, sister Ching-Yen said, "I'll give you ten thousand." Tsui-Mei's mother, sister Ching-Ai, also said, "I will give you ten thousand, too." Sister Ching-Yen then continued, "I'll give you another ten thousand." I sat there shocked, unable to speak for a while, wondering if it was all real. Sister Ching-Yen then joked, "You can show up for work tomorrow," and joyfully we took a formal picture to commemorate it all.

On April 15th, my husband told me that when his company, Goldman Sachs, invested money on behalf of its vice presidents, he still needed to pay taxes on it, so he was willing to give me another ten thousand. Wow! Four "ten thousands"! Miraculously, the next morning, Dr. Teng-Lung Hsu's wife Jui-Feng talked to me on the phone, "Teng-Lung was going to give you five thousand, but felt that this project was too important, so he has decided to give you ten thousand." Wow! That's five! Five "ten thousands"! I immediately called up my lawyer daughter Karen. When the boss at her firm, Perlman & Perlman, found out that it was Karen's mother who wanted to set up a nonprofit organization, he offered to provide the legal services for free. Wow! What a grand blessing! Especially since my daughter's firm specializes in assisting non-profit organizations, the incorporation was completed within one week, on April 24th. And my birthday was on April 25th. I knew right away that this was God's birthday present to me. I must humbly admit, what God starts, He will fulfill Himself! Immediately after this, a young and competent pastor, David Peng, also joined TMF Board. God's grace indeed is immeasurably more than all we could ask or imagine.

The "Taiwan Mission Foundation (TMF)" was formally founded on April 25,

Origin of the Taiwan Mission Foundation(TMF)

2007. Less than half a year later, on October 10, the United States government granted it tax-exempt status, and donations started pouring in. On November 17, Taiwan Mission Foundation held its first Thanksgiving Meeting to give thanks to God and fellow Christians for their support. By the end of 2007, the Foundation already used twenty thousand dollars to support the following missions and charitable activities: support two short-term missions teams; establish two "Taiwan Mission" scholarships at seminaries; support various missions organizations, including Gospel Village Mission, Taiwan Grass-Roots Mission, Industrial Evangelical Mission, Hakka Mission, Lifeline, Gospel Communication; support cancer patients and accident victims; and help the poor with cemetery plot purchases. An Overseas Student ministry and a Mission Training School are also in the works. We firmly believe that when we generously give with love, God will provide abundantly. After all, all resources belong to God himself. May the Gospel reach every corner of Taiwan with speed! Amen!

"In any mission field, the most important thing is to have God's calling, and to have native countrymen who have been trained by the Bible, filled with and anointed by the Holy Spirit."- From Rev. James Hudson Taylor, II (grandson of English missionary James Hudson Taylor), "Today is Tomorrow's Father"

2/2/13 農曆新年感恩同工午餐會
2013 Lunar New Year Co-Workers Appreciation Luncheon

Appendix 附錄

11/17/07-成立半年即舉開首次宣教感恩年會以感謝上帝的奇異恩典(於紐約聖教會)
11/17/07- TMF First Annual Convention (Conference) at Queens Taiwanese Evangelical Church

10/1/07-首次禱告會於紐約皇后區法拉盛鄭清妍副會長府上舉行
10/1/07- First TMF Prayer Meeting at Elder Ching-Yen Cheng's house in Flushing, Queens, NY

11/1/08-台灣宣教基金會第二屆感恩宣教大會九十餘位出席(於紐澤西第一長老教會)
11/1/08- TMF 2nd Annual Convention at NJ First TPC with 90+ attending

9/13/08-同工為宣教感恩大會開籌備會(於紐澤西第一長老教會)
Coworkers met at First Presbyterian Church NJ to plan for the 2008 Annual Convention.

8/21/09-楊會長(右三)訪台灣同工支持者於斗六: 左一總幹事薛端端; 左二七蘇慶章醫師夫婦; 左四五董龍佳醫師夫婦;右二周清芬
8/21/09- President Eileen (mid) visiting Taiwan coworkers/ supporters in Touliou, TMF General Secretary in Taiwan, Grace Tuan-Tuan Hsueh (1st left)

附錄 Appendix 373

6/14/09-癌患關懷講座主講謝吟雪(左三）和林瑞葉（左五）在紐約聖教會舉行. 本會提供四個講座並贊助一張乒乓桌給參與教會
6/14 /09- TMF Cancer Seminar speakers Linda Hsieh (3rd left) & Sue Lin (5th left) at Queens Taiwanese Evangelical Church. With this program TMF provided 4 seminars and 1 ping pong table for the participating churches

6/25/09-楊宜宜會長受邀擔任美國路德會全國講座主講介紹台灣宣教基金會事工（於紐約上州路德會Concordia學院舉行）
6/25/09- President Eileen presenting TMF at National Lutheran Seminar for World Religions and Evangelism of Church at the Concordia College in New York State

6/25/09路德會全國講座的台灣宣教節目中由紐約台灣基督徒提供山地舞蹈
6/25/09- Minister Mi Mi Wang (2nd left) led Taiwanese Folk Dance at Lutheran Seminar

6/20/09-宣教訓練學校蕭淵明校長(左三)及同工義工
6/20/09- Mission Training School Dean Samuel Siau (3rd left) with coworkers and volunteers

8/17/09-莫拉克颱風88世紀大水災後TMF組美台六人救難隊, 李方素、王真如、林恩衍、楊宜宜、周清芬（攝影: 杜秀全）
8/17/09- TMF organized a rescue team in Taiwan at disaster site in Lin Pian Village caused by Morkot Typhoon. Sue Fan-Su Li, Katie Wang, Ian Lin, Eileen YiYi Chang, Ching-fen Chou(photo by: Shio-Chuan Tu)

6/20/09-宣教訓練學校邀請台灣神學院副院長鄭仰恩教授首開『台灣宣教史』課,吸引136位學生參加,盛況空前 (於紐約聖教會)
6/20/09- First Class of Mission Training School taught by Dr. Yang-En Cheng "Taiwan Mission History" (Queens Taiwanese Evangelical Church) with 136 students

本會雙語聖經事工同工謝克明長老(左)和林義堅長老(右) 2008年6月開始以幫助贈送雙語聖經支持留學生事工至2013已送出300本至多國多州 (紀念林義堅長老於2013年12月蒙主恩召,本會感念他的忠心服事。)
TMF bilingual Bible coworkers Koming Shieh (left) and Franz Lin helping distribute 300+ Bilingual Bibles that had been sent for Overseas Taiwan Student Mission to US, Taiwan, Costa Rica & Canada (In memory of Franz Lin who rested in peace in December of 2013. His faithful service is forever remembered.)

3/13/10本會醫療宣教的義診與癌患事工講習會於新澤西台語歸正教會舉行"
3/13/10- TMF Medical Mission (Health Fair & Cancer Seminar) held at Fair Lawn Community Church in New Jersey

11/7/09-本會第三屆宣教大會於紐約白石鎮路德會學校體育館舉行
TMF 2009 Annual Convention at Immanuel Lutheran School Gym at Whitestone, New York

附錄 Appendix 375

11/6/10-宣教大會提供"救難訓練"課程，特邀Paul Mikov博士/牧師亦世界展望會聯合國代表(右)來主持訓練，葉介庭（左）任翻譯（由宣教訓練學校籌辦）
TMF Convention keynote speaker Dr. Rev Paul Mikoff (right) and World Vision Delegate to United Nations for Rescue Methods & interpretor, Ting-Yeh (left)

11/6/10-第四屆宣教感恩大會逾百多人參加.(中)二位著西裝的為主講員郭恩信牧師及溫宗義傳道
Annual Convention two speakers in suits, Pastor En-Hsin Kuo & Minister Chung Yi Wen (front center)

5/13/10退休宣教師關懷事工-本會同工尋訪韋瑪俐宣教師(中)帶去感謝與關心.
5/13/10- TMF coworkers visiting retired missionary Marie Wilson (middle)

5/30/10楊會長因受邀主持"台灣巡禮"的雙語音樂佈道而成立台灣宣教基金會樂團(本會首度在紐約公園以主題"歸家"開佈道會）
5/30/10- First Evangelical Event "Come Home," TMF Ensemble performing on stage (Passoport to Taiwan at Union Square in New York City)

11/5/2011台灣加利利宣教中心陳坤生牧師（前左一）和本會楊宜宜會長（前右一）共同簽署締結姐妹會盟約，見證人蕭清芬牧師（前中）和TMF董事們
Pastor Kun Sheng Chen (front left) of Galilee Mission Center of Taiwan and TMF President Eileen YiYi Chang(front right) were signing the Covenant, with Pastor Ching-fen Hsiao(middle) and TMF board members as witness.

3/30/11 楊宜宜會長夫婦拜訪台灣血液(血庫)之母林媽利醫師並誠邀其為本會顧問(於台北馬偕紀念醫院)
President Eileen and husband visiting Dr. Marie Lin, Mother of Taiwanese Immunohematology (blood banking) at Mackay Memorial Hospital in Taipei, inviting her to be TMF advisor.

3/31/10-為出版本書<<台灣宣教展翅飛>>，主編楊遠薰及副執行編輯黃文秀請教於賓州使者書房蘇文哲總經理
3/31/10- Publishing <<Taiwan Mission Taking Off>> with Carol- Chief Editor & Wenly- Vice-Executive Editor seeking advice from Ambassador for Manager Timothy Su

3/14/11遺產規劃首次會議於紐約皇后區舉行(左前起:鄭清妍副會長，楊會長，二顧問B. Mellon博士和 蕭清芬牧師，右前起:美國伯特利神學院美東分院院長 Fombelle 博士，財務同工陳禹辛，廖萃美)
3/14/11- First meeting of Estate Planning Committee in Queens, New York, Advisors Dr. Brad Mellon & Dr. Ching-Fen Hsiao (2nd & 3rd left), Dean of Bethel Seminary of the East in Pennsylvania Dr. Fombelle (1st right), Financial coworkers Sueman Chen & Tsui-Mei Liao (2nd & 3rd right)

5/5/2012 TMF五周年感恩慶典紐約長輩會賀詩
TMF 5th Anniversary Celebration: Senior Citizen Assn. of Taiwanese Christians in Greater NY choir singing

附錄 Appendix 377

2011- TMF 所差第一位長期醫療宣教師李穎明醫師到恆春基督教醫院
2011- TMF First sent long term medical missionary Dr. William Lee to Heng-Chun Christian Hospital

4/25/11 喜樂的巧合：台灣宣教基金會月禱會及四周年慶. 舉起小鳳梨(旺來)祝福台灣宣教/福音興旺
A Joyful Coincidence: Prayer Meeting & TMF 4th Anniversary. Blessing TMF with small pineapples (meaning prosperity in Taiwanese)

6/18/2011本會董事會熱情歡迎陳彰醫師(左一)加入執行董事行列。這是本會成立四年以來首次擴大執行董事會陣容。陳彰醫師和夫人郭惠美醫師均為台灣醫療宣教尖兵。
6/18/2011 TMF warmly welcomed a new member, Dr. Patrick Chen (first left), to join the board. Dr. Chen is a pioneer of medical mission, as his wife, Dr. Amy Kuo.

5/21-22/2011 本會醫療傳道組自紐約前往亞特蘭大長老教會帶去義診及癌患社區服務。
5/21-22/2011 TMF Medical Mission team went from New York to Atlanta Taiwanese Presbyterian Church to hold the community Health Fair and Cancer Patient Caring Seminar.

9/18/2011台灣宣教基金會和新澤西台語歸正教會合辦救難訓練。由美國Iris 救濟組織的Yi-Han Cheng(亦台灣第二代)(前右三)根據她救援日本地震海嘯核災難民的經驗

TMF & Fair Lawn Community Church in New Jersey cosponsored a Rescue Training Seminar by Yi-Han Cheng (Taiwanese 2nd generation) of Iris Relief based on her rescue experience from Japan's nuclear disaster in 2011

10/14-16/2011　翁蕭幸美連繫本會醫療團隊等在中美洲哥斯大黎加的San Jose市與當地醫療人員配搭從事醫療短宣義診癌症事工。當地四間教會聯合響應這個活動。

TMF medical mission team serviced along side with local doctors at Health Fair and Cancer Patient Seminar in San Jose in Costa Rico of Central America Four local churches responded to this activity, coordinated by Minister Hsin-Mei H. Weng

6/02/2012　本會醫療團隊在紐澤西Lawrenceville聖恩教會舉行義診，另有紐澤西台美團契長老教會及費城台灣感恩教會等共同協辦

TMF medical team held a health fair at Grace Taiwanese Presbyterian Church in Lawrenceville, New Jersey. Joined by the Taiwanese American Fellowship Presbyterian Church and the Taiwan Grace Church of Christ in Philadelphia

12/01/12本會從2009年至2012 以聖誕禮金安慰受莫拉克颱風之災無家可歸的81個那瑪夏鄉布農族孩子

12/01/12- TMF supported the 81 homeless children of Namasia-Burun Tribe affected by the Markot Typhoon using Christmas moncy gifts

台灣宣教基金會

Taiwan Mission Foundation

TMF

Sh

Savin